# OUR CITY

# OUR CITY

*Migrants and the Making of Modern Birmingham*

Jon Bloomfield

**Unbound**

This edition first published in 2019

Unbound
6th Floor Mutual House, 70 Conduit Street, London W1S 2GF
www.unbound.com
All rights reserved

While every effort has been made to trace the owners of copyright material
reproduced herein, the publisher would like to apologise for any omissions
and will be pleased to incorporate missing acknowledgements in any further
editions.

Text Design by Ellipsis, Glasgow
A CIP record for this book is available from the British Library

ISBN 978-1-78352-716-8 (trade hbk)
ISBN 978-1-78352-718-2 (ebook)
ISBN 978-1-78352-717-5 (limited edition)

Printed in Great Britain by CPI Group (UK)

1 3 5 7 9 8 6 4 2

In memory of my mum and dad,
for whom self-improvement and social justice went
hand in hand.

# Contents

# *Foreword*

Jon Bloomfield has written a timely and significant reflection on the impact of migration in Birmingham – England's 'second city' – and my home. Having been raised and educated in Birmingham, involved in a range of campaigns affecting Birmingham residents, and having the privilege of being elected to represent an inner-city ward as a local councillor, I am fiercely proud of my city. There are many issues that still need addressing, but I strongly believe that there is a lot that many places nationally and around the world can learn from Brummies. The city's self-effacing vibe conceals strengths that should not be underestimated.

The issue of immigration is rarely out of the news. Indeed, since Enoch Powell's speech denouncing immigration fifty years ago, it has become a cliché of British political life that speaking out against immigration is breaking a taboo. From Margaret Thatcher's invocation of British people being 'swamped by people with a different culture' in the 1970s, to David Cameron referring to refugees in 2015 as a dehumanised 'swarm', to UKIP's use of billboards proclaiming in large letters that the UK was at 'Breaking Point', fearful and alarmist tropes have very much characterised the mainstream discourse on immigration.

What has largely been missing from the so-called debate are the voices of immigrants themselves, and an examination of their practical experiences in light of various policy approaches. Jon Bloomfield addresses this gap in an engaging and accessible manner. As a daughter of immigrants myself, I could relate to so many of the experiences he has captured through his interviews of first-, second- and third-generation residents. It was refreshing to see the nuances reflected, as well as humbling to be reminded of the difficult journeys of belonging and contribution of so many in our city.

However, this is not simply a book celebrating the contribution of immigrants. It examines some of the challenges around integration and the merits and failures of various approaches. Importantly, it emphasises the need to address economic, not just 'cultural' policies in ensuring that Birmingham builds on its strengths and fosters a climate where everyone has a true sense of belonging. In doing so it offers readers not just rare and enjoyable insights into individuals' lives, but an analysis that should form an important contribution to the future direction of both my city and others in the UK and across Europe.

Salma Yaqoob

# *Introduction*

A few years ago my sister went on a holiday in Eastern Europe to trace the towns and villages from which our grandparents had fled a century before. She went to Łowicz, a textile town one hour from Warsaw where my mum's father grew up. Then she travelled to Osiek, a small village in the south-east of Poland close to the border with Slovakia where our mum's mother lived; then on into present-day Ukraine to find Bolechów (present-day Bolekhiv) south of Lviv where our dad's mother was born; and, finally, to Bucecea in neighbouring Romania where our paternal grandfather was born. A century before, Łowicz was part of the Russian Empire while Osiek and Bolechów had formed part of Galicia, a province of the Austro-Hungarian Empire. In some of the places little had changed and in two of them she found overgrown, neglected Jewish cemeteries. Our grandparents were among the waves of Jewish peasants, labourers, artisans and traders subjected to ethnic pogroms in Eastern Europe and Tsarist Russia at the end of the nineteenth and start of the twentieth century who had fled west to Frankfurt, Antwerp, London and New York. My grandparents remade their lives in the East End of London. They and their children survived the existential battle against fascism, both on the streets and underground shelters of Stepney and in the British Army. They contributed to the post-war settlement and welfare state, of which my sisters and I were major beneficiaries: decent schools and houses; cod liver oil and orange juice; free university education; and little overt anti-Semitism.

In her nineties, my mum spent her last years as the resident of a north London nursing home. In one of those ironies that history often throws up, more than half the staff working there came from Romania and Poland. They have followed in the footsteps of my grandparents, but driven by the hope of economic improvement rather than by fear of persecution. Like my grandparents, they have to cope with the venom and vitriol of large chunks of the tabloid press.

People have always moved. They have gravitated to cities such as Birmingham, which forms the centrepiece of this book. During the nineteenth century, America was the magnet. Sixty million Europeans crossed the Atlantic in the hundred years from 1820 to 1920. They are the ancestors of the Italian, Polish, Irish, German, Jewish and French diaspora found across the United States and Canada today. But since the Second World War, the pace of population movement across the globe has accelerated – with Europe becoming a magnet rather than a source. This has been prompted by three main factors. Firstly, there is the long-term trend of people migrating from rural to urban settings as indus-trialisation and the spread of manufacturing has intensified. Across the world more than 50 per cent of people now live in cities. This sucking in of labour has been occurring in the UK since the Enclosure Acts of the eighteenth century. When labour was needed after the Second World War the countryside was largely exhausted as a source of prospective workers. Instead, Britain looked to its former and existing colonies, firstly the Irish, but then people from the Caribbean and those from India and Pakistan. The Netherlands and France looked to their colonies, too, notably the East Indies and the North African Maghreb, while the German economic miracle was powered by labour from southern Italy, the former Yugoslavia and Turkey. In the 1950s and 1960s in Spain, rural labourers flocked to the main cities and then on into France, while many Italians from the *Mezzogiorno* went to the northern cities of Milan and Turin or on to Switzerland and Germany. The picture was broadly similar in the United States as people left the countryside for the cities and migrants entered from both Europe and increasingly from Central and Latin America. China reflects this picture but on a grander scale: in the two decades from 1990 more than 120 million peasants and farm labourers – equivalent to the total population of Britain and France – moved from the country to the city.

Secondly, the impact of globalisation has exacerbated these migratory trends. One key element has been the development of extensive, cheaper air travel. The onset of mass tourism makes getting to the developed world much easier. With the diffusion of the internet and new technologies, the images and attractions of other places through television and mobile phone are now much more accessible to the majority of people. And once diasporas get established in cities, then other villagers have contacts there, relatives or friends with whom they can make their initial base before striking out into the unknown. Such examples litter the pages of this book as newcomers start off their stay lodging with family and friends.

Thirdly, political changes have prised open the world. The closed systems of the former Communist bloc have collapsed. Their opening up to trade and commerce has been accompanied by new opportunities for some of their citizens, too, through education and travel. This has been most evident in Europe with the accession of former Communist bloc, East European countries to the European Union suddenly making the richer West accessible to the poorer East. At the same time previously frozen conflicts burst asunder. During the 1990s as an immediate consequence of the ending of the Cold War there was a sharp rise in the number of asylum seekers and refugees fleeing conflicts and civil wars in places such as Yugoslavia, Afghanistan and Somalia. A relative lull in numbers in the first decade of the twenty-first century has been followed by a sharp rise again following the ongoing crises in the Middle East and the upheavals of the Arab Spring. This had a dramatic political impact on Europe during 2015 but the numbers of people seeking asylum remain a fraction of those refugees being accommodated in countries directly neighbouring these conflicts such as Lebanon, Jordan, Pakistan and Turkey.

Over half a century these processes have completely transformed Europe's cities. Today in Birmingham, around 44 per cent of the population have a migrant background, of whom half were born abroad. In Birmingham's sister city of Frankfurt, Germany, 37 per cent of the population have a migrant background with people coming from over 170 countries.[1] In its Italian sister city of Milan the foreign-born resident population is estimated at 20 per cent[2] while, in its French sister city of Lyon, 13 per cent of the population were born abroad.[3] The figures for the latter two cities do not include second- or third-generation migrants and thus seriously understate the proportion of people with a migrant background. These figures are examples of trends that are common to all the major cities of Western Europe. Their demographic character has dramatically altered. As the migrants have generally been young and the women gone on to have families, these demographic shifts will continue. Newcomers have settled in Europe's cities from all corners of the globe. They, their children and now in many cases their grandchildren are making their lives here. There is no going back.[4]

Race and migration are the most volatile and dangerous issues in European politics today. Across Europe, they are hurting the established parties severely, with the Left hardest hit of all. When combined with the economic insecurity arising from globalisation and the financial crisis, it is causing a significant haemorrhaging of political support from working-class and low-income households and giving impetus to the populist and neo-fascist right. Some senior centre-right politicians are following in their wake, while in Eastern Europe there are now governments which echo the far right and court support with explicitly anti-migrant and xenophobic policies. In response, most Christian Democrat and centre-left parties have remained uncertain and equivocal.

There are several distinct elements to this issue: migration from within and from outside the EU; the separate if related issue of asylum seekers and refugees; how these issues are dealt with and managed politically; and finally, what the most effective approach is to ensure that all newcomers settle into the receiving country. The fast pace of change in a rapidly globalising world has disrupted economies, communities and traditional institutions. Together, they have undermined long-established political parties and ideologies. Many have struggled to make sense of what has been happening. This book attempts to do that. It shows how crucial migrants have been to the city's economic survival and daily functioning; the social and cultural impact they have made; and how the tensions that have arisen have gradually been addressed. In the process Birmingham has been transformed.

Once Europe turned from being an exporter to an importer of labour, difficult issues were bound to arise. The American model of the melting pot, with its guarantees of liberty under a common Constitution and all migrants getting ahead, was a 'non-starter' in Europe. It was feasible in largely 'settler' countries where it could brutalise existing indigenous communities such as Native Americans or Aborigines. In Europe, newcomers had to relate to large, established communities and settled institutions. Individual countries followed different approaches. The Germans offered their southern European workers temporary, guest-worker status in the initial expectation that they would only remain for a short while and then return home. France, drawing on its republican tradition, adopted an assimilationist approach, declaring that all migrants were equal and that the key task was to integrate newcomers into the host society. Any differences were minor compared to a common adherence to republican ideals and virtues. They forbade any counting of migrants or identification of migrants' background in the official statistics.

With only Magna Carta rather than a Constitution as a reference point, a more pragmatic approach occurred within the UK. Earlier generations of Irish and Jews had clustered together in ports and big cities when they first arrived in the UK – Liverpool,

Glasgow, London, Leeds – and organised around synagogues and Catholic churches. West Indians, Kashmiris, Bangladeshis, Indians, Chinese, Somalis and Kurds followed in this tradition, organising in workers' associations and community bodies as well as on a religious basis. This acknowledgement of difference and acceptance of the self-organisation of migrants and refugees were two key elements which helped to tackle the racism and discrimination that migrants confronted in the 1960s and 1970s. They gave a basis from which to organise. In alliance with liberals, socialists and trade unionists – as in the Grunwick dispute on trade union recognition, 1976–8 – this helped the development of a multicultural approach which aimed to tackle the discrimination, structural obstacles and institutional barriers blocking the advancement of migrants within British society.

None of these models has offered an easy route to integration. In the United States, extensive, repeated racism continues to blot the country's educational, police and criminal landscape. In Germany, the *Gastarbeiter* programme collapsed as most Turks stayed and their children and grandchildren eventually had to be offered citizenship. In France, the rhetoric of equality contrasts with the reality of life in the *banlieues* (desolate, tower block suburbs), while in 2016 the then Prime Minister, Manuel Valls, proclaimed republican values while calling for a ban on women wearing headscarves in French universities.[5]

In the UK, the public racism of half a century ago had largely disappeared prior to Brexit and the doomsday diatribes of Enoch Powell have not come to pass. In the daily lives of our cities there is still an air of peaceful coexistence, although this has been disturbed by the anti-migrant rhetoric of the Brexit campaign and its aftermath. More than a quarter of players at the football clubs we support are black.[6] Powell whipped up fears over the nasty smells of curries. Today chicken tikka masala and rogan josh are the nation's favourite dishes, while one Asian woman wins the vote for the TV *Great British Bake Off* and another hosts the BBC's showpiece *Today* programme. Those migrants interviewed for this book give a largely positive account of their experiences of Britain and display a strong commitment to the opportunities it offers. Sadiq Khan, elected Mayor of London in May 2016, expresses the change in a very direct way: 'When he [my dad] and my mum first came to this country there were signs up where they lived: "No blacks, no Irish, no dogs." He saw his children being racially abused and getting into fights. His twenty-five grandchildren have never experienced that. That's why I'm an optimist.'[7]

Yet despite these real achievements in the emergence of a multi-cultural Britain there has been an insular and increasingly divisive debate in the UK about how best to cope with today's ever-growing cultural diversity. For many years some right-wing tabloid commentators have launched unceasing tirades against 'the perni-cious policy of multi-culturalism'.[8] They have been joined by the former head of the Equalities and Human Rights Commission, Trevor Phillips, who calls for replacing 'the failed policy of multi-culturalism',[9] while an influential political commentator, David Goodhart, has argued that migrants and refugees must assimilate to 'British' values. He insists that integration cannot be a 'two-way street' as immigrants 'must carry the burden of any adaptation that is necessary'.[10] This assimilationist trend increas-ingly expressed as English nationalist, identity politics has been growing stronger and more vocal post-Brexit. The assimilationists' case is mirrored by multicultural communitarians who increasingly emphasise collective apartness. Tariq Modood argues for a distinct public role for religion being recognised within the society and wants Muslims, Sikhs and Hindus recognised as legitimate groups in their own right, not as Asian Britons. Muslims need a public identity and to be able, along with other minorities, to pursue it.[11] In contrast to this binary divide the Indian-born, Nobel prize-winning economist Amartya Sen offers an alternative way forward. He characterises the multicultural approach as lapsing too often into plural mono-culturalism where some wish to retain a separate, 'fenced off' identity, with different ethnic communities living side by side but with little, if any, interaction. This then leads to the real prospect of ghettos and separate development. Both sides in this argument draw on bloc mentalities and assume frozen communal identities rather than acknowledge that society gives individual citizens the right to choose, that people have multiple identities and that values change over time. This challenges both assimilationist and communitarian ways of thinking. As Sen puts it, 'the early success of multiculturalism in Britain has been linked with its attempt to integrate, not separate. The current focus on separatism is not a contribution to multi-cultural freedom but just the opposite.'[12]

These are not new issues.[13] More than a century ago, the 'Austro-Marxists' Otto Bauer and Karl Renner, wrestling with the challenge of how to generate solidarity among workers of different nationalities in Vienna, arrived at their individualistic 'personality principle', which recognised the basic idea that individuals should be able to choose their ethnic or national affiliations.[14] It was an idea well ahead of its time. Instead the Nazis determined that Jews would be collectively dehumanised and communally slaughtered. The post-war United Nations and European commitment to universal values was designed to reinstate the individual as democratic citizen, enjoying human rights and the rule of law.

With the reappearance across Europe of parties of the extreme and racist right, it is even more important to stress these values against nationalistic particularism. To indulge populists with insidious slogans such as 'British jobs for British workers' as Prime Minister Gordon Brown did in 2009 just feeds narrow nationalism. The alternative is not the ill-defined British idea of 'community cohesion',[15] and still less the government's stigmatising 'Prevent' programme. This is supposedly designed to prevent the slide of youth to fundamentalist radicalisation but has been seen as the indiscriminate targeting of Muslim communities and has had particularly negative responses in Birmingham. Rather, it is the wider notion of inter-culturalism developed by the Council of Europe and fleshed out in its *White Paper on Intercultural Dialogue* of 2008 that offers a new way forward.[16] With a firm foundation in universal norms, this argues that tolerance and respect for others can best be fostered by governments that provide for equality of individual citizenship, reciprocal recognition of our common humanity and impartial treatment by public authorities. These issues percolate through the book and are explored in the later chapters on education and religion.

These values are increasingly vital in an ever more interdependent world where cities are microcosms of the wider planet. To adapt to these changing circumstances cities need to adjust to the global diversity within their midst and a number have begun to follow the Council of Europe's lead.[17] It sees integration and social change as a two-way process dependent on the host society itself recognising difference and acknowledging that the process of integration means that it changes, too. But it also requires the newcomers to want to integrate. In other words, there is change on both sides: it's a two-way street.[18]

It is these models and the interculturalist potential that this book explores through the experience of the city of Birmingham. Cities are the test beds of integration. They are where migrants and refugees congregate and where the capacity for an interactive process of integration is tested. The experiences in this book reflect both a specific and also a wider national and European story.

From the start of the Industrial Revolution in the late eighteenth century till the end of the nineteenth, the population of Birmingham grew from less than 100,000 to more than three-quarters of a million. It continued to grow and reached a post-war peak of 1,179,000 in 1961. The city's initial population growth came from people migrating off the land. Later they travelled from Wales and Scotland. After the Second World War, flows of migrants came in significant numbers from Ireland, the Caribbean and then the Indian subcontinent.

From 1961, the city's overall population declined steadily, in common with almost all other UK and major West European cities. It had dipped below one million by the turn of the century. The influx of newcomers did not offset the numbers leaving the city, often moving to the leafier suburbs surrounding Birmingham. This was the age of the car, motorway development and long-distance commuting. However, as with other major cities in Britain and Europe, there has been a reversal over the last two decades. Birmingham has experienced a significant upturn, so that by 2011 the city's population had reached over a million, approaching its 1971 levels. The mid-2016 figures indicate that this growth trend is continuing at 1,124,000 and that the city will soon surpass its 1961 peak.

Of this number, more than a fifth were born overseas, of whom nearly half had been resident in the UK for less than ten years. The largest totals come from the former British colonies but now there are significant numbers from Europe – both East and West – as well as growing numbers from Africa, China and South East Asia. The figures indicate the diverse range of newcomers who are making their lives in the city and the impact of globalisation in all its guises. Together they make Birmingham one of the most mixed, multi-ethnic cities in Europe and thus particularly appropriate to tell both a specific and a wider story on migration.

The scene looked very ominous in the 1960s. Then it seemed as if Birmingham and the West Midlands conurbation could become a cauldron of racial bigotry and violence. In the 1964 General Election, while Labour won nationally, the Conservative Peter Griffith won the Smethwick constituency, neighbouring Birmingham, on a 7 per cent swing by campaigning on the immigration issue, using the slogan 'if you want a nigger for a neighbour, vote Labour'. Four years later to a Conservative gathering in Birmingham, the senior Conservative figure Enoch Powell delivered his infamous speech on immigration with its various warnings '. . . of an alien element introduced into a country . . . like watching a nation busily engaged in heaping up its own funeral pyre . . . Throwing a match onto gunpowder . . .' and concluding with the claim that 'As I look ahead, I am filled with foreboding: like the Roman, I seem to see "the River Tiber foaming with much blood."'[19] Similar sentiments were evident among the members of Birmingham City Council. Following in-depth interviews with half of all councillors undertaken in 1971, the author Kenneth Newton records that they 'speak volumes about the depth of ignorance, fear and hatred which exists among some members of the city's political elite'.[20]

Today, there exists a very different picture. This book illustrates the journey that Birmingham has made. It is based on forty-six formal interviews and many other conversations which took place during autumn 2015 and through to summer 2016. The interviewees were not selected as a scientific sample but, rather, cover the main waves of migrants who have moved to the city and the main areas where they have found work. Twenty-eight of them were men; eighteen were women. Half were first-generation migrants, the remainder second- or third-generation. They or their family came from thirteen countries, most from Pakistan or India followed by Poland, the West Indies, Ireland, Somalia and Bulgaria. By age they ranged from those in their twenties to those in their eighties.

In contrast to other studies, this book focuses firstly on work since, contrary to oft-repeated myths, the basic reason that people have come here has been in order to get a job. The interviewees were chosen to reflect and span a broad range of employment. This enables the book to look at the economic contribution that newcomers have made to various sectors of the local economy: heavy manufacturing; health; the burgeoning service sector; entrepreneurship; higher education; and the casualised, low-paid sector of the economy. This explains how the interviewees were identi-fied. Where requested, their names have been disguised. The result is that these chapters are organised around the main economic sectors where migrants have been employed and give a flavour of their working experiences.

The second half of the book goes on to address some of the key cross-cutting issues that shape migrant reality and relate to their wider experiences of integrating within a new city. These chapters tackle the issues of racism, education, religion, relationships and politics. They explore the journey of migrants from the margins into the mainstream; the achievements of a multicultural approach; its limitations; and how a broader, more interactive model could now be developed. Many interviewees appear in several chapters. Some are more prominent than others. Their number is designed to convey the variety of the migrant experi-ence and to let their voices be heard. The book would have been impossible without their generosity and good humour. A complete list of interviewees is included at the end of the book.

With regard to terminology, generally the book follows the terms and phrases used by the interviewees themselves. These are the words that migrants use in everyday life. For a book designed to appeal to the general reader, these are the terms that make the book accessible and readable. They are often a shorthand. For example, the common use of the term 'Asian' covers a spectrum of people either born or from a background within the Indian subcontinent covering those whose origins can lie in Bangladesh, India, Pakistan or Kashmir. It does not coincide with all those born on the Asian land mass. On specific occasions I refer to national heritage but often it is the more generic term that is used. When relating to bodies such as the NHS or universities, the chapters adopt the more formal categories used by those organisations.

The casual, public racism and violence common in the 1960s and 1970s has been minimised. To give two small examples from that time, I recall an arson attack on a mixed-race band playing at the Star Social Club and a National Front volley of bricks and stones at a socialist feminist meeting on the same premises. Substantial moves towards a more accepting multicultural community have been secured. Yet the country remains a place where many are not at ease with the issues of migration and integration. In reaction to the inadequacies of assimilationism, there has been too easy an acceptance of a model of multiculturalism which has often overemphasised 'difference' and lapsed into a conservative, plural monoculturalism with overtones of separate development. The political ability to chart an interculturalist course that opens up our cities to the talents of all remains elusive.

The reality is that successive waves of migration have changed the character of all the major European cities for ever. Living with difference is one of the greatest challenges for European politics in the twenty-first century. Newcomers have made a profound contribution to the economic, social and cultural life of Birmingham since the Second World War, just as they have in London, Paris, Barcelona and Berlin. They continue to do so, yet plenty of difficulties remain.

This book addresses that challenge. It offers insights for readers who recognise that all Europe's large cities are now ethnically diverse and are interested in their future development and success.

I have lived and worked in Birmingham for forty years, twenty of them at the City Council as an officer in Social Services and then as head of its European unit. The book is written from the perspective of someone with a lifelong attachment to the principles of liberty, equality and solidarity. Using those principles as a guide and drawing on the observations of the interviewees, the book offers new thinking on how to develop our multicultural cities so that they are fit for the twenty-first century. It refutes both the nasty nationalism of UKIP and much of the tabloid press, but also the 'soft' nativist nationalism of 'Blue Labour' and David Goodhart. To adapt a phrase, it proposes a 'Third Way' between their assimilationism and the cul-de-sacs of conservative, plural monoculturalism. A new politics is emerging, especially among the younger generations, where genuinely mixed, open cities can develop. In the coming decades this is the path that Europe's cities consciously need to follow.

# 1

## *At the Heart of Britain*

Birmingham has always been a city of inward migration. It grew hugely during the first Industrial Revolution when the inventiveness and enterprise of industrialists such as Matthew Boulton and James Watt and the ingenuity of Thomas Telford and James Brindley led to the creation of a canal system which enabled the city without a river to become a world centre of manufacturing. From the late eighteenth century until the end of the nineteenth, the city's population grew from less than 100,000 to more than three-quarters of a million. By 1900, 75 per cent of the workforce was employed in manufacturing. Its population continued to grow as Birmingham became synonymous with the major growth industry of the first half of the twentieth century – the motor car.

In 1951, nearly two-thirds of the workforce was engaged in manufacture – almost 400,000 people, with most employed in vehicles, engineering, electrical goods and metal trades. At this time, industry was buoyant. There was a shortage of labour and earnings were high, particularly for male manual workers whose wages were often boosted by long hours of overtime. Most years, the unemployment rate was under 1 per cent. Between 1948 and 1966 unemployment only ever rose over 2 per cent in one year, 1962. It was a similar picture across the Midlands – from Wolverhampton to Derby. With such a high demand for labour and nearby reserves of labour exhausted – many Scots had come south before the war and the Irish immediately after it – companies and the government began to advertise for workers from across the British Empire, firstly in the West Indies and then in Pakistan and India.

Mashood was part of that wave. Now in his mid-seventies, he calmly describes how he arrived in Birmingham from Karachi on 12 December 1963. Born in Bihar, India, in 1941, he had endured a fraught childhood caught up in the horrors of the British-imposed partition of the country as the price of independence. During partition the family had to move to Calcutta, where they thought they had a safe house, but with the widespread ethnic cleansing of Muslims they fled in the middle of the night and made the forty-eight-hour journey to Karachi via Amritsar. Crammed into one corner of a carriage with his mother, six brothers and three sisters, for Mashood the journey evokes very painful memories. As they approached Srinagar, he knew there was trouble as they were stopping trains and taking away Muslims.

'Luckily, our driver refused to stop even though they were trying to block the train. We got to Lahore where there was a little bit of peace and then we went to Karachi. We were very lucky that we had somewhere to stop, not like what is happening at the moment with Syrians . . . The Pakistani government built a kind of quarter and we then rebuilt our life.'

Mashood went to school and technical college and learned engineering and design skills. Then he went to work in the Karachi shipyards. He was working on turbines when he saw that the UK government was advertising in Pakistani newspapers for labour. The advertisements said that if you have qualifications you could apply for a work permit. They were looking for anybody with any kind of skills but they very much preferred technical qualifications. Mashood answered the advert. It took him just a fortnight to get a permit.

It wasn't a wrench leaving home. He was a young man looking to his future and Pakistan was very poor then. He didn't know where he wanted to go. He could have gone to America but the opportunity that arose was the UK and he came to Birmingham as his brother was already here. He didn't get the work he wanted straightaway. The only job they offered him at the Labour Exchange was selling cosmetics. He didn't want to sit around and get a handout so he took that job. After six weeks he found an engineering job in Camp Hill repairing motors and armatures. Later, he applied for a job at Lucas. At the time this was one of the country's premier engineering companies responsible for the electronics, lights and fittings for major chunks of the British car industry. Mashood got a job as a quality surveyor at its Shaftmoor Lane plant. He worked there for the next twelve years before leaving to set up an engineering company with his brother.

This story of newcomers from the Commonwealth looking for a better life and coming to work in Midlands factories and foundries, on buses and building sites is repeated whenever the sons and daughters of first-generation immigrants recall the lives of their parents. Sam's parents came from the small town of Huntspen in Clarendon, Jamaica. Both parents were involved in small-scale farming and related income-generating activities such as charcoal. Like Mashood, Sam's dad got his job through an advert in the local newspaper. He went for car manufacturing, whereas others were attracted by the nursing, bus and train-driving jobs. He came to Birmingham in 1961 and worked at the huge Longbridge car plant, which then employed more than 24,000 people. Sam recalls that he wore a work-issue donkey jacket with the letters BMC, British Motor Corporation, on the back. He started off in general maintenance and then later moved onto the assembly line. He spent the rest of his working life there, staying until the mid-1990s.

Mo tells a similar story. His mum and dad came from Barbados and Jamaica. They came to Birmingham as they had family connections here and people from the islands had written back to their relatives telling them about the city. As Mo explains: 'Across the Caribbean, the British government embarked on a marketing programme to bring people to the motherland in order to work in industries that needed labour, one of those being nursing and the other being engineering and the railways, which is where my parents both worked. Dad worked on British Rail. Mum as a nurse within the NHS. They came in late 1950s, got married in 1961. They came here to work. Their motivation was to find work; to make an income; to make a go of it.'

Mandeep's dad came with her granddad from the Indian Punjab. Her granddad worked at Fords and her dad worked in a foundry in Birmingham.

'Both were really hard workers. Dad got a job easily. He travelled every day on the train into Birmingham. He got up at five in the morning. He worked at a steel works. He was employed for nearly fifty years at that foundry and got a long-service award from the company.'

Salma's parents were from the Pakistani Punjab and her dad first came over in the late 1950s. He was a welder working in different Lucas factories in Hockley and Hay Mills. Her mum only worked when the children were teenagers, in a factory making rivets and mirrors, which she sorted and packaged for delivery. Her dad did a lot of night work and unsocial hours. It was very hard, physical labour with low basic wages. The family never went hungry but it was a tough upbringing.

Rehman's family comes from Mirpur in Azad Kashmir. They were part of the major exodus from the area in the 1960s when the huge Mangla Dam was built to create storage capacity from the monsoon rains and thereby enable the Indus Plain to be effectively irrigated in the main growing seasons. More than 280 villages and the towns of Mirpur and Dadyal were submerged and over 100,000 people were displaced from the area as a result of the dam being built. The UK government was one of the international guarantors for the irrigation project and the displaced were awarded work permits to come to the UK as part of the compensation package. As a result, in Birmingham and elsewhere in the UK the majority of the Pakistani community originate from the Dadyal–Mirpur area of Azad Kashmir.[1] Rehman senior came over in the early 1960s with lots of other people from his village. He went to work in a foundry in the Black Country. As Rehman observes, 'It was very easy to get a job in them days, not like today.' Fatima's dad also came from Mirpur. He came with his uncle in 1965, when he was just fifteen. He worked in a factory that produced steel parts. He would check the parts to ensure they were all made to the required standards. Similarly, Ashraf's father left Mirpur in the 1960s and was employed as a steelworker before moving to the Dunlop tyre plant.

Others came to manufacturing and construction jobs elsewhere across the Midlands. Hasan's parents were from Gujarat in India. His dad came from a farming background and didn't go to school after the age of eight. He had the perception of England as a very positive place. He saw the chance for a better life for him and his wife and the opportunity for a good education for their children. His dad came in the early 1960s, followed eight months later by his mum. He found work without any problem at the Vauxhall car plant in Luton as a manual labourer. He worked there for more than a decade. Then the family moved to Nuneaton and his mum got a job in the textile industry and worked on sewing machines for twenty years. Raj's parents were born in the Punjab, India. His dad was a skilled carpenter working from an early age, learning from his own father. In the 1960s there was a call from England for skilled people to come to the UK. Raj recalls that his dad and a few of his friends thought it was a great idea. 'You go to England, you'll make a better living and have a better life for your family and your children. Obviously leaving the family was difficult but coming with his mates made it a lot easier. They helped each other out.' He arrived in Wolverhampton and found a job within a week. He proved himself very quickly with the foreman of a large construction company and worked for them for the next twenty years, on major projects across the West Midlands such as shopping centres, hospitals and swimming pools. He then worked with other contractors for the rest of his life, developing a range of his skills as a bricklayer and plasterer.

After the Second World War this pattern of economic development became the norm across Europe and North America with the big cities and industrial conurbations sucking in labour from abroad, often drawing people off the land from former rural communities. It was to be a pattern repeated on a larger scale by China from the 1980s onwards and is to be found today across the globe. All the evidence points to a continuation and acceleration of this global trend. More than half the world's population now live in cities and by 2050 this is expected to have risen to 70 per cent. As ever, the dream that drives the migrant to leave home – whether to travel from the countryside to the nearby town or thousands of miles to a strange land – is the hope of a better life with more opportunities for them and their children. But, as ever, reality turns out to be harsher.

For the post-war migrants to the UK, life in Birmingham, as elsewhere, was hard. Jobs were easy to find but they were often physically demanding with long hours in challenging environments. For many, over a period, the harsh working life took its toll. Salma's dad suffered from depression as he found the work too difficult and had to stop, obliging her mum to work. Hasan's dad had a serious industrial accident at the car plant which stopped him doing any further manual work. Fatima's dad suffered a heart attack that required a heart transplant. Following it, he was forced to go onto incapacity benefit, as was Rehman's father, who was badly burned in an accident at his foundry. Mandeep recalls the impact foundry work had on her father: 'It was really hard work and very, very hot. I remember at home how he would spit out little bits of steel and black stuff, cough it up. He would never moan about it but he did become a heavy drinker at the weekends.'

It was not just the work that was tough. Finding a place to live was not easy either. Birmingham had very old, dilapidated housing stock with lots of houses with no indoor toilets or bathrooms. The city undertook a huge slum clearance and tower block development programme from the late 1950s until the early 1970s, in both the central areas and along the eastern and southern edges of the city with 464 tower blocks being built, around 7 per cent of the UK total. Yet at that time the city had a housing allocation policy that required a five-year waiting period before you could qualify for council accommodation. This clearly discriminated against newcomers. So, just as the Irish had done a decade earlier, immigrants gravitated to the districts with lots of large Victorian and Edwardian terraced houses or to the small pre-First World War terraces in the eastern and south-eastern inner-city ring. Peggy, a nurse from Co. Mayo, recalls how in the 1950s, 'You saw lots of houses with a card in the window saying "rooms to let, no Irish need apply".'

When Irish people owned a house, then there was nothing on the card, and whoever came got the room. The Irish lived by getting their own houses and letting out the rooms to other Irish people. And that's the pattern that many West Indians and Asians followed a decade later, which then created its own problems of multiple occupation and overcrowding. Peggy recalls, 'the only relief we got was when the coloured people came. Then the signs went up, "no blacks, no niggers". In the early 1960s, it was terrible in Birmingham, in them times. If you weren't from here, you just weren't accepted.'

There was some solidarity and empathy between the Irish and the next waves of newcomers. Sam's family grew up in Balsall Heath in private accommodation rented from Irish landlords. It was only later that they were able to move into a council house in Ladywood. Mo's family followed the same route. Salma's family started in a shared house. Then her mum and dad borrowed money from others from their village who had migrated, too, and had a little bit of spare cash. They lent this to the family at no interest, thereby enabling them to purchase a small house.

Mashood lived in a flat in Balsall Heath with his brother. When they had to leave they went to Edgbaston to look for a bedsit.

'We went up and down the roads and you'd see a sign for this, a sign for that, "no dogs, no blacks", "no this no that". It was quite explicit stuff. I avoided anything like that. I just left it and moved on. Wherever we saw any sign in the window, we'd just leave. We only asked where there was no sign. That's how we got a room.'

Then there was the wider discrimination to deal with, given its most powerful expression through the speeches of the senior Conservative MP for Wolverhampton, Enoch Powell, but echoed in many ways by councillors on Birmingham City Council and in the local press. There were many factors that led to the dire scenarios of Enoch Powell being refuted and that minimised the casual, public racism of the 1960s, not least the passage of the race relations legislation introduced by Roy Jenkins, the MP for Stechford in East Birmingham and Home Secretary in the two Wilson governments of the mid-1960s and mid-1970s. But another factor at play, more especially in the larger workplaces, was the active countering of racism by both trade unions and management. There weren't many black or Asian workers among the 3,000 workers in the Lucas factory when Mashood joined the Amalgamated Union of Engineering Workers. But he was elected a shop steward and eventually became the overall convenor on the site, winning 75 per cent of the vote.

'There was lots of racism individually but they still elected me as a shop steward and then as their convenor, as I fought for them and could put their case to management. Outside, people could say whatever they liked but not in the factory. They couldn't say anything in the factory because if they did they knew they would be sacked. Management was quite strong on this. They knew that we will all come out if they didn't act. I found that management was quite good. If I raised a case with them they understood. The union was very good on that issue in 1970s. It was much better inside the factory than outside.'

No one found Nirvana in Birmingham. The first wave had plenty of trials and tribulations. But they earned a living and made new lives for themselves and their children. Yet none of the children quoted above took up heavy industry, engineering or construction jobs. They pursued different careers in the growing white-collar sector or sought entrepreneurial opportunities.

David, however, decided to follow in his father's footsteps. Tall and slim with three teenage kids, today he lives in a semi-detached house in a south Birmingham suburb. In a tidy front room over a cup of tea, he tells me his story. His dad, from St Kitts in the Caribbean, moved to the UK in 1959, followed two years later by his mum. It was a difficult decision, but he was looking for the opportunities that were here in the 'Mother country' as he called it. He knew he was coming to Birmingham before he left St Kitts. He arrived at Southampton and then came up to the Midlands.

Already trained as a welder, he found fabrication work easily in the construction industry. As a welder and as a contractor he worked all week and at factories over the weekends. David's mother was a cleaner and later a cleaning supervisor at the central sorting office at the Mailbox. She did the cleaning and mopping up in the corridors, offices and toilets. David recalls how he would go into town on a Saturday with his brothers and meet her at one o'clock and get the shopping.

'My parents would be up and out before we went to school, both of them. That is what I remember very strongly growing up. I very rarely saw them even at weekends because my mum worked six days a week and my dad worked seven days a week. I only saw them in the evenings. My dad got home at eight o'clock. I had to do the basics and learn to feed myself.'

They lived in Nechells in a small two-bedroom, old-fashioned place with a shared outside toilet and a tin bath hung up in the alleyway – a classic back-to-back – before they moved to a council house in Bordesley Green where they had a front and back garden. David went to a secondary school in Nechells, the same one as his elder brothers, and then in 1979, aged sixteen, he applied for and got offered two apprenticeship places, one with British Steel, the other with British Leyland. These were proper four-year craft apprenticeships in the traditional sense. David chose British Leyland: 'I reckoned even at that stage that the automotive industry had better prospects than the steel industry.'

In fact, the prospects for both – and indeed the entire manufacturing sector – were grim. The post-war decades where the West Midlands had prospered as the manufacturing heartland of the United Kingdom with low unemployment, relatively high wages and plenty of semi-skilled and skilled manual factory jobs came to a dramatic end at the start of the 1980s. When Margaret Thatcher was elected in May 1979 the unemployment rate in Birmingham stood at 6.9 per cent. A year later it was 8.6 per cent. In May 1981 it had doubled to 16.2 per cent. By May 1982 it was 19.4 per cent and by October 1982 it reached 21.5 per cent.[2] Recession hit the region hard – and deep. Deindustrialisation proved no temporary phenomenon. Many industrial plants, factories and companies closed for good. In this period Birmingham lost more manufacturing jobs than Scotland. Coventry became known as 'ghost town'. Average male unemployment levels exceeded 20 per cent and in some wards reached 50 per cent.

This was the world of work that the teenage David was entering. Yet in 1979 the Longbridge plant still employed over 20,000 people – automated robots were still in the future – and the company took on ninety apprentices each year. David was an electrical apprentice who moved around the factory and learned all the basic craft skills – milling, turning, metal bashing, fabrication, electrical stuff – and went on day release to college for one day a week; he received a weekly pay packet. It gave him a good grounding. He worked with craftsmen in all the disciplines and with different age groups. It set him up for a career in the car industry but being qualified as an electrician meant he could move into other industries or set up on his own. When he finished the apprenticeship they did not have enough jobs at Longbridge so he went down to the brand new robotic workshop at Cowley, Oxford, for two years. They were commissioning new robots that did all the welding and there were German engineers down in the plant. David found it fascinating.

'There was this one particular robot; it was supposed to be stationary but you could see its welding fingers were moving very, very slowly through the air. The commissioning engineer looked at it and he went over to this control hub, which was the size of a big fridge freezer. He opened it up. It was full of racks and racks of printed circuit boards, with wires going everywhere. He pulled out a board; connected an oscilloscope to it that had a lovely little wave on it that was slowly moving along; put a screwdriver onto this printed circuit board, tweaked a little resister and the robot stopped. And I thought. "Wow. I wish I had the knowledge and skill to do that. I want that sort of knowledge. How am I going to get that sort of knowledge? I need to get more educated." It was a combination of that and sitting on the nightshift with the maintenance engineer who was sixty-two and I was twenty-one. I thought to myself, I am a maintenance electrician at twenty-one. Am I still going to be doing the same job at the age of sixty-two? I hope not.'

Together, it made him realise that he needed a higher level of education, so he did a year studying for a Higher National Diploma, received a distinction and, encouraged by his supervisor, went on to study for a full degree. After that he found his way back into the car industry, which was not so easy. The stabilisation and slow recovery during the mid- and late 1980s ended with a further recession in the early 1990s. If the first earthquake in the early 1980s devastated the motor and engineering industries this subsequent quake confirmed that the age of mass manufacturing was drawing to a close. The tremors and after-shocks continued at intervals for the next fifteen years, with the closures of the Rover, Jaguar and Peugeot plants at Longbridge, Browns Lane and

Ryton signalling the demise of mass-volume car manufacture in the West Midlands. Following a series of hefty cutbacks, the full closure of the once mighty Longbridge plant in 2005 drew the final curtain.

This did not mean that all manufacturing activity ceased, but it no longer held centre stage. Automation, computer processes and robots replaced men – and a few women. In July 2016 the UK government re-established a department which has Industrial Strategy in its title. For four decades, this phrase had been deemed irrelevant. The 'making of things' was cast as yesterday's world; financial engineering replaced mechanical engineering as the economic priority and aspirational gold standard. The financial services sector trumped all else. During this period the UK's share of world exports of goods halved, so that by 2017 it was just 2.5 per cent.[3] Industrial activity did not stop in Birmingham and the West Midlands, but it shrank dramatically. Today, advanced engineering still employs around 115,000 people in 1,500 businesses around the region, but it offers fewer opportunities for unskilled and semi-skilled labour.

For a while David couldn't get a job. His bank manager said he was overdrawn and they wouldn't give him any more loans, but then a job vacancy came along with Automotive Supplier, a Japanese company which had just set up in the UK, based in Redditch. From there he went to Jaguar Land Rover as a product engineer starting at Lode Lane, Solihull, where they make the vehicles, and then moving on to the research centres, first at Whitley and now at Gaydon. Neither Jaguar nor Land Rover had ever been mass-volume manufacturers. They were always focused on the top end of the market. After a merger and takeover, they survived the turmoil by modernising their production models and reaching into new markets among the emerging upper classes in China and elsewhere. David had the skills and knowledge they needed as they revolutionised their production processes. In the company's matrix management system he is the skilled engineer developing all the driver information displays on the speedometer and gauges combined with the managerial role to make sure that projects keep on track and are delivered on time. He has good pay and conditions; as he puts it, 'in terms of pay we sit towards the top end of the scale'. However, the pride and pleasure comes from the knowledge and skill that he has acquired. The years of hard graft have paid off: 'I feel having knowledge is part of the reward. It's a bit strange really but the fact that I know about lots of things makes me feel better about myself.'

He has broken through a glass ceiling. Among the ninety apprentices at Longbridge only one was black and one was Asian. However, over the last ten years things have changed noticeably, particularly at Gaydon. Part of this is due to the link to the parent company, Tata. But among the skilled engineers there are not just Indian staff but more black UK staff as well as guys from Nigeria, the Caribbean and elsewhere. Globalisation has reached into the heart of British manufacturing. 'We have become very international.'

# 2

## *From the Cradle to the Grave*

Peggy is in her eighties and moves slowly. She sits in her tidy sheltered housing flat in north Birmingham. Having served me up with an ample portion of Irish broth, she recalls her early life and how she came to England. She was born on 17 March 1935 in Co. Cavan, one of thirteen children – four boys and nine girls. There were too many to stay in the one house opposite the village shop. Her mother and father couldn't stop having kids. In those days the priest decided these things. If you didn't have a child every year he'd be coming to the house to ask why.

Peggy had an enjoyable childhood, but when she was fourteen she applied for a job in a boys' care home in Dublin. She wanted to be a nurse. She eventually managed to get hold of the £50 entry fee when she was seventeen, so she secured her training place and went to a hospital where she did 'plenty of study' while also meeting the man who became her boyfriend.

The training and the work went well. After about a year and a half a letter came from the government in England. There had been an outbreak of the Asian flu so they were making a request for nurses to go to England. The letter asked for eighteen nurses to be sent from every hospital. There didn't seem to be much choice. 'We all got inoculated. We were in bed three days due to the inoculation. Then we went over on the *Princess Maude* from Dun Laoghaire to Holyhead.'

Peggy was allocated to St Thomas' Hospital in Bromley-by-Bow, in the East End of London. It was difficult work and some of the doctors and nurses died during the epidemic. The experience opened her horizons. She became best friends with a Jamaican nurse; she had never met a black person before. Her boyfriend had gone to Birmingham, not to London as he didn't want the family to think he was following her over. He came down and asked her to marry him, but he wanted them to go back to Birmingham as it was quieter. She got married in a big church in Hammersmith where her aunt lived. They went to Birmingham where they rented a room on the top floor of a large old house in Aston owned by a Jewish opera singer. Her husband Michael worked in different factories, as a stacker truck driver and then a machine tool operator. But, astonishingly for modern readers, Peggy was no longer allowed to be a nurse.

'Once you were married in them days, you were barred from nursing.'

So she got a job soldering at GEC Witton and then went to Dunlops, the large tyre plant in north Birmingham. At the gate was a sign reading, 'no Irish need apply'. She demanded to see the manager and told him that it was an Irishman who had started this factory. The manager didn't believe her but checked it out and said she was right, so he let her in. She didn't get a job on the factory floor but in the social club, first as a cleaner and then behind the bar. The trained nurse ended up working for the same pub manager for the next twenty years in different pubs around the city.

Anne's background was similar. Born in Co. Mayo, one of eleven children, she trained as a nurse in Castlebar and then in Dublin. For many qualified people there wasn't a lot of work and, with the establishment of the NHS, she saw an opportunity in the UK. She came to West Bromwich hospital in the early 1950s where she worked for the rest of the decade, eventually becoming a radiographer while also giving support and advice to the footballers from the local club, West Bromwich Albion. After she got married in 1959 and had children, she stopped working.

Her husband, James, was born in Dublin and trained as a doctor. He emigrated after the war and worked for a while in Hereford, undertook further training in Ireland and then came back to practise in Bordesley Green, in inner-city Birmingham. From there he moved to a surgery on the Stratford Road in the suburb of Shirley. He worked as a GP in Shirley until his retirement at the age of seventy in 1992. His son Chris remembers him as absolutely dedicated to his work, well regarded by his patients and having a successful professional career. Chris recalls that there was a huge Irish professional – as well as labouring – population in the UK in those days, loads of medics, dentists and nurses. His parents were part of this vibrant social community across Greater Birmingham, especially in the Harborne/Edgbaston area near to the main hospitals based around Birmingham University.

The National Health Service was created in 1948. For many health professionals from Ireland it acted like a beacon, a new model of health care delivered free to all citizens when they needed it. Since the 1930s, UK governments had resolved staffing crises in hospitals by recruiting workers from overseas. The creation of a truly national and innovative health service funded through general taxation made this an attractive proposition to those starting out in their careers abroad. The Irish came to the Midlands in large numbers. They were soon followed by waves from the West Indies and then from other parts of the emerging Commonwealth.

It has been like that ever since. People from all parts of the world – from Fiji to the Philippines, and in more recent times from Poland to Portugal – have come to Birmingham and the rest of the UK to work in the NHS. At the same time, it has offered fulfilling jobs and employment opportunities to the daughters and sons of first-generation migrants already in the city. Across Birmingham today they form a significant proportion of NHS staff working in hospitals, doctors' surgeries, health centres and outpatients' clinics. Many remain on the basic grades but some manage to break through the glass ceiling.

Salma is a softly spoken, middle-aged woman, a single parent bringing up her teenage children. One of six children from a working-class family from Pakistan, she went to school in south Birmingham, took a couple of A levels and then followed the example of her best friend in applying for nursing. She was offered a state-enrolled nurse post but her friend advised her not to accept it as she had also applied for a state-registered nurse (SRN) position. She was accepted for the SRN course, which was higher grade and gave a proper career opportunity.

'This was quite a common experience for black and ethnic minority nurses . . . many were not offered SRN courses.'

Salma did her three-year course, followed by two years on the wards at Selly Oak hospital, and then became a midwife, first at Solihull hospital, followed by two years at City Hospital. She then moved on to health visiting and worked in the Black Country for two and a half years. With this varied portfolio she was well equipped to move into management, working mainly with GPs and in primary care within various health authorities and trusts. In 2012 she became the Chief Executive of the Walsall Clinical Commissioning Group (CCG), working with fifty-nine GP practices in the town to propose hospital, community and mental health services for the local population.

After twelve years at the grass roots, followed by eighteen years in various managerial roles, Salma has some measured observations on how the NHS has adjusted to the growing diversity and multicultural reality of the UK. As an Asian woman starting off in a basic grade job, she has been able to progress through its ranks.

'I haven't been held back by my colour. That is my experience. It has been easier to progress because I came up the nursing route. It would have been harder if I had come up the general manager route. Not many come up that way.'

However, after a period of expansion, when cutbacks occur and middle and senior management posts are merged, then black and Asian staff lose out. Across the country there were ten black Directors of Nursing when Salma was in post but with all the reorganisations they gradually 'got whittled out' and now there are only two.

'Black people don't survive structural change in the NHS. They don't have the networks and the profile, along with an element of discrimination. The diversity agenda loses its way.'

Concerning the wishes of a diverse workforce, her experience has been that hospitals and primary care services pay due regard to the Race Equality Act and follow workforce policies that are permissive enough to take into account people's cultural preferences. For example, women are not now required to wear a skirt and can cover up their legs and arms.

'But they don't allow you to cover up your face. Staff need that interaction with the patient. So hospitals will allow nurses to wear a headscarf but not allow staff to cover up their whole face. Staff have to be able to communicate with the patient and there must be no barriers. So there are certain degrees of what is allowed and what is not.'

These developments have not been straightforward. When it was first created, the NHS was a white-dominated service, serving an almost exclusively white population. Almost seven decades later, the NHS employs around 30 per cent of its nurses and doctors from black and minority ethnic groups with approximately 30 per cent of its doctors and 40 per cent of its nurses having been born outside the UK.[1] These trends are broadly reflected in the staff breakdown for two of the largest hospital trusts in Birmingham. At both the prestigious Queen Elizabeth Hospital, with over 8,800 staff, and at the Heartlands Hospital, covering all of east Birmingham, just over three-fifths of the staff are white British, while the Queen Elizabeth records that 28 per cent of its staff are drawn from black and minority ethnic communities. Interestingly, both show a growing number of white, non-British staff – 6 per cent at the Queen Elizabeth and 8 per cent at Heartlands – reflecting the attraction of the NHS to citizens from across the European Union.

When I attend the outpatients' department at the orthopaedic hospital I am seen by Iosif, a trained registrar from Greece. When I go for my follow-up appointment Jakub sees me. In his mid-thirties, he is an orthopaedic and trauma registrar at Birmingham's Royal Orthopaedic Hospital with over 1,300 staff. He came to the UK after completing his medical school studies in Gdansk in 2007. Originally from the city of Torún, Jakub came to Oxford and worked as a health and social care assistant before getting a job in the NHS. He decided to specialise in orthopaedics and has been working his way through the practices and qualifications necessary to become a consultant. It's a ten-year cycle which took him to Liverpool, Milton Keynes and Watford before he settled in Birmingham. Reflecting the diversity of the NHS, he works in a mixed team with a Greek colleague and an Indian manager. He speaks excellent English. He tells me that one of the attractions of coming here is the fact that English is the international language of medicine; the research journals and key academic papers are all written in English.

He has been in Birmingham seven years now; finds little racism; lives in Bromsgrove on the outskirts of the city. His Polish wife is a skilled engineer who works as a quality assurance manager at Jaguar Land Rover in Solihull. They have a one-year-old child and have no plans to return to Poland. They like it here and are thinking of applying for British citizenship. Since Brexit 'you can feel a bit more tension', but so far he has faced nothing serious.

As I leave the hospital, I am grateful for his expertise and careful explanations but cannot avoid dwelling on the moral question that his presence raises. Poland has spent a lot of time and effort on training Jakub. After six years of higher education he then clears off to the UK and brings his skills to our NHS, while the Polish health service gets nothing back. If he was a footballer, at least they would have received a transfer fee.

Compared with the time of its inception, the NHS now also serves a much more diverse, multicultural population, especially in the major conurbations, for many of whom English is not the first language and where different backgrounds and lifestyles have led to a higher incidence of particular diseases and conditions. How to address the needs of these communities has become an issue of sharp debate, one which reflects discussions in the wider society about how far a national service should both encompass differences and run distinct services to address them. When considering services to be provided to black and minority ethnic communities, there has been tension within the NHS between its universal ethos and the fact that not everyone is the same, which is why you need positive action. Access is a key issue, with language being of particular importance for the elder generations from the Indian subcontinent. Then there are some areas of ill health such as kidney disease and diabetes, coronary heart disease and mental health whose rate of incidence is higher among ethnic minorities and therefore requires particular attention.

Salma recalls that in the late 1990s and early 2000s there was a lot of additional money and you could invest in new programmes. In that period parts of the NHS ran distinct parallel services for black and minority ethnic communities. Although it made a difference at the time, this 'probably wasn't the best use of investment'. In hindsight, this running of segmented services 'stopped us from doing other things'. She believes that in some ways it stopped services being mainstreamed. The NHS missed the opportunity to train up staff and to make general services more accessible to all. She has no problem organising services to address language or cultural needs, but she sees the priority as recasting the mainstream services so that they are accessible and meet the needs of a diverse population. She does not think you can tailor the NHS to the wishes of everybody, but, rather, you need to focus on ensuring that all citizens have the maximum access to it. She is dismissive, for instance, of those arguing for faith healing to be part of the NHS.

Sam came into NHS management by a different route. A burly man in his early fifties, with wavy hair, large eyes and a touch of grey appearing in his goatee beard, Sam is a classic working-class boy made good. With a strict disciplinarian upbringing, Sam was one of nine children brought up and educated in Birmingham by a Jamaican migrant family, whose father worked at the Longbridge car plant. Sam went to Staffordshire Polytechnic where he studied computing science and French and took a job with ICL, where he worked for eight years. He was then head-hunted by Andersen Consulting, where he stayed for ten years. After eighteen years as a high-flyer with two global brands he moved into health care, as Director of Transformation in the Birmingham East & North Primary Care Trust. He worked there for seven years, responsible for using data to improve the NHS's commissioning of services; to strengthen the NHS's knowledge management systems; and improve staff training programmes.

A key part of his remit was to make NHS services more accessible to the local population. Until then, the organisation had a one-size-fits-all approach to its work such as with their quarterly newspaper that was circulated to all people in the area. The language was overly professional; it was complicated and inaccessible to non-professionals; and the organisation didn't know how to use social media. Sam looked at the different segments within the local population, analysing by class, gender, ethnicity, age, etc., and assessed how to engage with different types of people and across the age range. He looked at 'fellowship' in new ways, at where people actually operated, where they concentrated their social interactions, the point of contact, which he renamed the 'point of care'.

This was exploring in a more detailed fashion the same issues that Salma had been trying to address. To assess the needs of black and Asian people in the north and east of Birmingham, Sam and his colleagues explored Lozells, Nechells, Perry Barr and elsewhere looking for the key points of contact for the different communities such as black West Indian, where a key focus was the barber's shop. For the elderly from the various Asian communities it was around the mosque or gurdwara (Sikh temple); while other Asian men, both Sikh and Muslim, were to be found in pubs and drinking venues. For the younger generation not so culturally constrained, Sam and his colleagues went to youth clubs and nightclubs.

Out of this fieldwork they encouraged primary care teams to undertake preventative work through these venues, for example running anti-obesity campaigns in cooperation with and at mosques.

'We didn't pitch up in an evangelical way, wagging our finger, but rather understood how the different communities are waxing and waning on a daily basis. You have to engage with them on that perspective. That leads to much more productive conversations and activity.'

The objective was to strategically redesign public services to achieve better outcomes for target beneficiaries. That meant having an active outreach programme rather than just assuming that all citizens would just turn up at the hospital or GP surgery.

This is a topic that a number of the clinical commissioning groups are starting to explore, prompted by their new responsibilities under the Public Sector Equality Duty (PSED) and Equality Act 2010. This duty aims to make sure public authorities think about things like discrimination and the needs of people who are disadvantaged or suffer inequality, when they make decisions about how they provide their services and implement policies. Thus the Birmingham CCG has developed a community engagement strategy, a diversity implementation group and in October 2015 launched its People's Health Panel. This is designed to enable people from across Birmingham to tell the CCG their views and to shape health services to improve people's health. Within a month the Panel had nearly 1,500 members with a balance proportionate to the ethnic demography of the city, with a 42 per cent Black Minority Ethnic (BME) profile.[2]

These are signs that parts of the health service are both responding to the varied needs of Birmingham's diverse population and adopting more participative approaches. Sam and his team recognised that these changes are crucial to the wider agenda facing the NHS, namely how in the twenty-first century can people stay fit, healthy and well in an ageing society. The answer to those questions often lies outside the hospital and frequently outside the responsibilities of the health service. Their work found that big problems often arose when people were discharged – they dubbed it Point of Care Zero. These people's ongoing health depends on the links and engagement that they have within their local community.

'Public service provision has lost that sense of connectedness, how to connect in the twenty-first century. We should use data sets so that we can personalise messages to citizens. This requires the adoption of a holistic approach to a whole range of issues, which go beyond professional silos. That means looking for a coalition of organisations to achieve wellbeing outcomes for communities outside of the hospital or the doctor's surgery.'

Sam has now left his comfortable, well-paid job within the NHS to set up a new social enterprise to pursue these ideas. He senses that the health care of the future will have to change and adapt to these changing times. Will the NHS have the agility to be able to respond, especially given the mounting pressures it is facing? The population is living longer and coping with conditions that were previously terminal. Even in Birmingham, with one of the youngest population profiles in Europe, the eighty-five-plus population is predicted to increase by 75 per cent by 2035, while its pensioner population will increase by a third. This inevitably means additional pressures on hospital, community health and social care services, all heavily reliant on migrant labour. The initial post-Brexit signs are worrying. There was a sharp rise in the number of EU doctors leaving the NHS in the immediate after-math of the Referendum vote and an even more pronounced fall in the number of EU nationals registering as nurses.[3] Ever since its inception the NHS has relied on a foreign workforce, as has the burgeoning residential and social care sector. In the short to medium term this situation is not going to change. To paraphrase the words of a famous general, our country needs you.

# 3

## *Moving On Up*

Raj loves numbers. Neat, bespectacled and smoothly dressed, he combines a dry sense of humour with the qualities of the consummate professional. He grew up on a 1920s owner-occupied housing estate in south Wolverhampton where his parents had come in the sixties after leaving the Indian Punjab. He could have done better at school, but he was never that motivated. His parents pushed him, but the laid-back teenager was more interested in drinking and going out. He did GCSEs and A levels and then went to Loughborough University where he studied maths and economics. But it was only six months after getting his degree that he finally got his head screwed on and decided he wanted a professional qualification. The calm, measured tones of the dispassionate accountant are dissipated on a surge of enthusiasm as he recalls this period: 'That was the only time I was really motivated. I passed most of my exams first time . . . It took me three and a half years with twelve exams and lots of week-end study.'

From then on, he never looked back. He worked as a management accountant for three large private companies and is now at a Birmingham technology and property company which supports young innovation businesses and also runs new programmes for start-up companies. These are grant-funded, which for Raj, as the head of finance, brings additional complications. Raj loves the job and is pleased that there are lots of ethnic minorities in accountancy and other professions.

'There are loads of them. Because when you grow up as an Indian, the objective is to be a lawyer or a doctor, an accountant or a dentist. Those are the occupations that your parents drill into your head from an early age. Those are the professions that your parents think will give you a good status and do them proud. It is common to Hindus and Sikhs and similar to Pakistanis. My uncle, even now, he loves saying, "Raj is a chartered accountant".'

Many others have followed Raj's path: the second-generation migrant avoiding the fate of their fathers working in heavy manufacturing industry, metal bashing and construction. Instead they have opted for the growing white-collar and office sector, some with a professional status but many in the administrative and support services category.

In 1951 just over a third of the working population was employed in the entire services sector in Birmingham. Of these only 10,534 were engaged in insurance, banking and finance, a mere 1.7 per cent of the workforce. Today, services dominate, with manufacturing occupying a severely diminished role. These developments reflect long-term trends, but they did not occur simply by chance. They were spurred on by a conscious strategy of economic intervention pursued by the Labour council leadership when it regained power in Birmingham in 1984.[1] Dick Knowles, the leader of the council from 1984 until 1993, was a brusque trade union official, both recognised and popular among traditional Labour voters in the city. His main younger ally, Albert Bore, the chair of the Economic Development Committee, had a strong grasp of economic strategy. In contrast to other Labour councils who at that time were embroiled in head-on confrontation with the government over illegal budgets, Knowles and Bore pursued a more pragmatic approach, recognising that without investment from business the local authority could not deal with the effects of the economic crisis.

In the mid-1980s Birmingham was facing economic meltdown due to the collapse of employment in traditional sectors related to the automotive industry. The early 1980s exposed the fundamental lack of competitiveness of Birmingham's engineering and automotive industries. The new leadership, drawing on the mantle of Joseph Chamberlain's 'municipal socialism' from a century earlier, believed this had to be addressed by government leadership and that Thatcherite laissez-faire economics was not enough. Albert Bore outlined the initial thinking when he launched the priorities for economic development in Birmingham in June 1984 which laid the foundations for the city's approach for the next two decades. Knowles then convened a broader policy conference, symbolically at Highbury, Chamberlain's former residence in Moseley, to agree principles that would guide the strategy. These were 1) that the council had to lead and take responsibility for the city's economic survival, 2) that public investment should be used to leverage, rather than substitute for, private investment with a particular emphasis on the role of European Union funds, and 3) that the focus should be on city centre enhancement as a means of attracting investment in business services, rather than throwing resources into traditional sectors or dispersing them across the city's neighbourhoods. This prioritisation of the city centre made for uncomfortable reading within Labour's left.

The strategy was maintained despite there being no short-term political gains and with most voters and many commentators being initially sceptical. Undoubtedly, however, the impact and success of the International Convention Centre (ICC) and the Symphony Hall concert venue, which opened in 1991, built with public, private and European funding and a catalyst for both the city centre renaissance and promotion of new business sectors, began to shift opinion. This helped to maintain the strategy, despite a change of Labour leadership in 1993, until its success became widely accepted and acknowledged in the late 1990s.

Through the remodelling of the city core, Birmingham became established as a leading international conference and business services centre – an objective regarded a decade and a half earlier as hopelessly unrealistic. In the initial years the changes had required substantial public investment, but the leveraging effect meant that projects gradually required fewer public resources. By the early 2010s, Birmingham was becoming one of the main destinations for business investment in Europe. In terms of employment, 'business, financial and professional services' have become three key employment sectors in the city responsible for almost a quarter of the total workforce and employing 115,000 people. These sectors have attracted a number of key players to the city including Deutsche Bank and the Royal Bank of Scotland, not just for back-office roles but for a wider range of significant services. Large insurance companies and major offices for all the main accountancy firms have relocated to the city, while the presence of a strong legal service has emerged with the Birmingham Law Society, the largest in the UK. Thus there has been a crucial pivoting of the local economy and this reorientation has helped to move a significant element of it onto a more stable, longer term footing.

The strategy also had a significant impact on retail and leisure, which grew to become the second major sector, accounting for a quarter of the workforce. Birmingham is the largest city economy outside London and has developed both as a major retail centre and also a significant tourist destination, having become the fourth most visited city by international visitors in the UK. The impact of the National Exhibition Centre as well as the ICC has been crucial here. Shopping has been boosted by the renovation of the Bull Ring with major stores such as Debenhams and Selfridges along with a revamped New Street Station which now houses John Lewis as its anchor store.

It has opened up job opportunities for migrants in the city. Samera is in her late thirties and has worked for the last sixteen years at a main high street store in the city centre. Her father originally came from India but had to move to Pakistan during the independence upheaval in 1947. He came here in 1960 and worked for years at GKN. Samera didn't fancy following in his footsteps and instead went into retail. She is employed as a sales and shop assistant. She began in the Foods section, then went to Menswear, back to Foods, and is currently in Home Furnishings. She likes the job; she is happy there with the pay and conditions and the people. There is a good mix of staff – black, white, Asian – who get along well. There is the occasional bad egg, but no real problems. She has no career ambitions and doesn't want to go into management. She is just pleased with her job as it is. With her straight black hair and brightly painted fingernails, as she stands by the counter taking the orders and chatting busily with the shoppers it's obvious that she likes her work. The Bull Ring is one of Birmingham's multicultural hotspots, its youth and diversity visible at every turn. Samera likes the mix of people who come into the city centre to shop.

'It's good to have a mixture. I don't like it when you just have one group of people. I like the city: it is cosmopolitan.'

The public sector including hospitals and universities represents the third key sector and accounts for a third of total employment in the city. Local councils are often a first port of call for migrants looking for employment. A decade of austerity has drastically reduced their employment function and the services they are able to offer. However, they still play a key role both in terms of the numbers they employ and the example they set. For the last thirty years Birmingham City Council has monitored the ethnic composition of its workforce and over time it has begun to reflect more accurately the ethnic make-up of the city.

Daljit has worked there for over two decades. A quiet, unassuming woman, she was born in 1969 and grew up in Derby. Her parents came from the Indian Punjab. Her dad worked at Rolls-Royce as an engineer and her mum as a machinist in a textile factory. Her parents saw education as very important, and made sure that when Daljit came home from school she went up to her room to do her homework. And she wouldn't come down till it was finished. She went to college and took an NNEB qualification in nursery nursing but wasn't really sure that was what she wanted to do, so she studied for a BTEC qualification in business and finance. Then she got married to Harpal and moved to Birmingham. Harpal's dad worked in a factory but he took the education route and, like Raj, studied at Loughborough University before he found work as a computer analyst and programmer. The company transferred his post to London, so Daljit moved there and got a job at the Department of Transport. She was there for three years. When Harpal came back to Birmingham, Daljit was able to get a transfer to a position at the Department of Transport's office at Five Ways. Then she saw an opportunity with the council in an administrative and secretarial post. This lasted for several years, including her first maternity leave. She was promoted to manager and currently provides project and funding support to the departmental team, supporting projects and submitting their financial claims.

'I am quite happy in the role that I am in . . . the role suits me . . . I have a great team I work with, there is flexibility in the council and I am drawing on the skills I acquired with my BTEC.'

She has particularly benefited from the equal opportunities policy which the council has operated. It has meant that she has been able to combine her job with having children.

'I had three months off with my eldest; took a six-month break with my second daughter; and then with my son I took two years off as part of the council's flexible maternity leave policy.'

Hasan grew up in Nuneaton, a relatively small town with a tight-knit Asian Muslim community, where his parents moved after his father suffered a serious industrial accident while working at the Vauxhall car plant. He did well at school, got good GCSEs and A levels and then studied business systems and information technology at the University of Central England, now rebranded as Birmingham City University.

'My mum and dad mapped out my life along with my two elder brothers. We never had a choice or even a discussion about dropping out of school at sixteen. My dad was clear. I was not going to end up working at Vauxhalls.'

His first substantial job was with the Islamic Relief charity. Founded in Birmingham in 1984, Islamic Relief had grown rapidly. Hasan became the project officer looking after Eastern Europe. He worked there for three years and enjoyed it, even if the pay scales were not great and the field visits meant he was often away for a week or ten days at a time. He moved to the public sector and for almost a decade has worked on policy and project issues for the City Council in cooperation with its various partners. He has run a series of project activities, firstly, around crime and community safety, then on an anti-graffiti campaign; initiatives to tackle fuel poverty; and then combatting gang violence. A broader role on performance management followed and from there he has moved on to procurement and sustainability issues. The common thread has been project and partnership working.

In all of these cases the rupture from the world of their parents is stark. Changes in the character of work meant that Raj, Samera, Daljit, Harpal and Hasan – just as with Salma and Sam in the previous chapter – could leave the factory floor and go to the office or shop, whether in the private or public sector. This was the shift that most of their parents dreamed of. Hasan is explicit.

'Dad knows that none of his children are working in factories. My younger brother is working with the Highways Agency; my eldest brother went into sales and now has set up his own company; my sister works part-time on mobile phones; and my other brother is a high-flyer at Ernst and Young advising on health. When I went to university, Dad said, "You have to work all the way through university and by that I mean manual work, so that you understand where I came from and so you know what hard grafting is." So from age of sixteen I worked in a range of labouring jobs, packing in a warehouse, working in Homebase. It did ground me and made me appreciate the difference between manual work and being in an office.'

Another familiar path in this transition from manual to mental labour is teaching. The changing political and legislative framework created openings here. The Local Government Act 1966 provided local education authorities with extra resources to meet the needs of minorities. In particular, Section 11 entitled the education authorities to establish special courses designed to overcome language deficiencies in the children of Asian migrants with central government covering the cost. This was followed in 1976 by the Race Relations Act, with sections 35–37 and 76 recommending that local authorities take 'positive' actions to improve the community relations and proportionate representation of ethnic minorities in employment, education and health institutions.

Kalsoom was an early beneficiary of Section 11. She had arrived in Britain from Pakistan in 1969 as a young bride in an arranged marriage. Her husband worked as a machinist at the Hardy Spicer machine tool factory. They lived in Small Heath and she had four children when she was very young. In contrast to the classic tabloid stereotypes of passive, stay-at-home Muslim mothers, she went to study once her youngest son was at nursery. Her husband was 'very open-minded' and encouraged this. She did voluntary work at the nursery first of all and then went to East Birmingham College on an adult education course. From there she applied for the role of classroom assistant on a Section 11-funded post, which illustrates the way it served as a stepping stone into teaching as well as benefiting the pupils. She worked as a bilingual support teacher in schools with students from India, Bangladesh and Pakistan. Her mother tongues were Urdu and Punjabi, having learned English with her children and by watching TV with them. Her managers recommended that she got further qualifications, so she went to Handsworth College. 'It's never too late to study. I didn't want to waste my talents. There was something inside me, telling me that I wanted to do something. I didn't want to just stay at home.'

She got a teaching qualification at the University of Central England in the mid-1990s and proceeded to work for the next twenty years as a language teacher at a secondary school. At the start there were hardly any Asian teachers, even though the majority of children were Asian. Once she was qualified she had full responsibility as a teaching instructor in Urdu, working with different teachers and classes, helping the students with their language. She stopped in 2012, mainly for health reasons. She felt that she had achieved as much as she could be expected to in her work in a big secondary school.

Nazir found his professional opening through an offshoot of the Race Relations Act. Born in a village in Mirpur, Azad Kashmir, Nazir's father had joined the British Merchant Navy, travelled all over the world and then settled in the UK in the early 1950s, opening his own corner shop with his brother in Saltley, east Birmingham. Brought up in Kashmir by his maternal grandparents, Nazir joined his dad in the mid-1960s hoping to do a degree. Instead he earned a living by working in factories over the next fifteen years; improved his English; joined the Open University and the Workers' Education Association (WEA) doing foundation courses and evening classes; and played an active role in the Kashmiri Workers' Association and like-minded anti-racist movements. He entered full-time education in 1980 at the University of Birmingham. He was engaged by Leicester City Council in 1983 as an Equalities officer as local authorities began to address the requirements set out in the 1976 Race Relations Act. The following year he got a teaching job at Handsworth College as a lecturer on Industrial Language Training. Organised through the Manpower Services Commission, this was geared to enabling employers and their staff to have the necessary skills and capabilities to respond to the needs of a multiracial workforce. He became Head of Unit until he quit and decided to run a Kashmiri restaurant.

There has been an ebb and flow to race relations within the UK throughout the whole of this period: spells of relative social peace, suddenly disrupted by riots, disturbances and upheaval – from Notting Hill to Tottenham via Toxteth, Handsworth, northern towns, Lozells and Brixton. The 1976 Race Relations Act followed by the Scarman Report, arising from disturbances in the early 1980s, and the Macpherson Report in 1999, following the death of black teenager Stephen Lawrence, were concerted attempts to establish a new consensus on race relations. In particular, they

encouraged both public and private sector organisations to address inequalities within their own ranks, to record the ethnic
composition of their workforces and to avoid any systemic or
institutional racism.

One side effect of these developments was the opening up of
new employment opportunities for migrants in the police and
criminal justice system. The West Midlands Police, like other
authorities, were very aware of the negligible numbers of ethnic
minorities within their ranks. One of their initiatives was to
recruit special constables from the local black and Asian communities. At the age of nineteen Adam stepped up to the plate.

Born in 1980, with three sisters and a brother, Adam lived in
Balsall Heath, had gone to Moseley School, enjoyed it, but failed
all his GCSEs. After he failed his retakes he just started working
with the local mosque providing pastoral care as a kind of un-
official, untrained youth worker. With his genial, chubby smile
and bubbly enthusiasm he looks the part, and in this role Adam
would organise activities such as orienteering, paintballing and
football tournaments – entirely for the boys. He says the mosque
is more enlightened nowadays! In 1999 he applied for the post of
special constable based at Police Headquarters in Steelhouse Lane.
It was an unpaid officer role but one in which the individual had
the powers and the uniform of a normal police officer. He did it
for ten years, working sixteen hours a month mainly doing
high-visibility patrols as a bobby on the beat. He progressed
through the ranks until he became a district officer

'It was the best thing I ever did. I always wanted to do public
service. I learnt so many skills, including how to mix with people
outside of the Asian community. Broad Street was an eye-opener

for me. What the hell is this? I had never seen this, vomiting, fighting, pissing on the street on Friday and Saturday night. I got into the heavy music, felt I was exploring life but I didn't drink.'

Yet after a while he became bored and uncomfortable. 'The "land of the zombies" was how I described it. It made me ashamed of being a Brummie. But I do miss it.'

Rashda works at the Magistrates' Court. She lives in a modern, small Barratt-type home not far from Spaghetti Junction. The motorway rumbles in the distance. One of her working sons still lives with her. She settles me down on a comfortable settee, offers me a cup of tea and recounts her journey. Born in a small town near Multan in the Pakistani Punjab, she came here in 1976 via an arranged marriage. She always wanted to work but was hampered by having five children, an unsympathetic husband and the fact that her oldest child was severely brain damaged and required a lot of attention. Like Kalsoom, she got her break-through via Section 11 when the deputy head at her children's school said there was an opportunity for a classroom assistant helping with the children and their language. 'They wanted someone from the community, so I was lucky. I got the job in January 1991 and it lasted seven years.'

Rashda wanted to become a teacher but her daughter's condition was too serious. The child's social worker suggested interpreting as a more flexible option. Rashda acquired training at the Magistrates' Court and started working there in 1999. She enjoys it a lot, working with a range of agencies helping translate into Punjabi and Urdu. She translates and interprets in the magistrates' courts, county courts and police stations. The pay varies: £15–20 per session depending on the agency. Sometimes she has three sessions a day and at others she has to work in the evenings and at night. The work is irregular and she is often called upon at short notice. She had to rearrange the interview with me twice because of new requests. She feels she has been able to make a bit of a career given that she had to look after the children, but she still hopes that she will be able to study and get a degree.

For six years Kashan was the Home Office's race equality manager for West Midland prisons. This was a new senior role created to address the race relations issues and controversies that had arisen in the prison service post-Macpherson, which had been followed by the Zahid Mubarek case at Feltham Young Offenders Institution. Kashan got the job in May 2006 and as Head of Equalities and Human Rights his task was to tackle the equalities issues affecting the 8,000 prisoners and 6,000 staff across twelve jails in the West Midlands. He had both to develop policy and ensure its implementation. He was really young to get this senior post: it was post-9/11; he had a big beard; and he had a rebellious past.

Kashan's parents were very keen for him to progress through education. He went to Bishop Vesey's Grammar School in Sutton Coldfield but he was not very successful there. He got just a couple of GCSEs and wasn't allowed to go into the sixth form: the school wanted rid of him as he brought down their overall grades. He went to St Philips Sixth Form College, spending three years there, resat his GCSEs, took some A levels and got a place at the University of the West of England studying bio-medicine.

However, as Kashan recalls, in his teenage years he was a wild boy. His love of driving and fast cars got him into innumerable scrapes with the police and his own father. After he moved to Bristol, he acquired quite a petty criminal record portfolio. At the end of the first year he failed his exams completely. His dad issued an ultimatum: sort yourself out or leave home for good. This tempered his deviant tendencies enough to enable him to get a degree in psychology at Luton, which he followed with a two-year masters in Criminal Justice at the University of Central England. That was the moment he decided he should look for a career in the prison service. He worked on a project for the resettlement of offenders and then went into prison education at HMP Blakenhurst, Redditch, where he built up his capability for delivering programmes. A two-year stint at the Birmingham Race Equality Action Partnership gave him a taste for policy: 'I realised the importance of issue-based interventions rather than ethnicity-based ones.'

This approach stood him in good stead for the challenges of the prison service. He knew that lots of the staff were really sceptical about him; they thought of him as a 'liberal lefty' who had probably got the job because of his ethnicity. In response he adopted a really pragmatic position. He used a rights and responsibilities framework and pursued a broad equalities approach which took in being overlooked for promotion; health and safety issues arising from back strains and disabilities; issues of pensions; as well as behaviour towards black members of staff. He worked across the range, from listening to prisoners' complaints to delivering management training programmes for staff. He began to work on equality and focus on this more than diversity. Race issues were conceived as part of a broader agenda.

Gay rights was one of the equality dimensions he worked on. They set up a staff support network, Gays and Lesbians in the Prison Service, with the wonderful acronym of GALIPS. He got sponsorship from the staff groups so that when he climbed Mount Everest for Islamic Relief he wore a GALIPS T-shirt. He recalls one of his fellow mountaineers quizzing him about this, saying that, as a Muslim, like the other theist religions he should see it as a sin or an aberration, to which he replied, 'You must not discriminate against anybody or treat anyone differently at work. Our approach is one of no detriment. You can have prejudices but certain ones you have to park at the gate. It is the same if you are a racist, or opposed to immigrants. A huge proportion of our prisoners are foreign nationals. You need to leave your prejudices behind and understand why equality works for all of us.'

He feels his achievements were not sustained once he left, partly because the post was not replaced. After six years he decided this was not going to be his permanent career, because there is a dark side to the prison service. 'We lock people up well but are not so good at their rehabilitation. The life there can be very grim.' So he left and went into a Walsall law firm.

Birmingham is seeing an expansion of both voluntary organisations and independent social enterprises – the so-called third sector. This sector comes in all shapes and sizes: from local, community groups with no permanent staff and minuscule budgets; through those with a handful of permanent staff and a budget ranging from £25,000 to £250,000; to those with a larger staff, providing more services and with considerable budgets. A number of second-generation migrants have found work within this sector.

Chris works for one of the more established organisations, Friends of the Earth (FOE). He didn't follow his Irish parents into the medical profession but, rather, saw higher education as a way to self-improvement in a much wider global perspective, which is why he has worked for FOE for the last twenty years. His wide experience with a degree in applied and environmental chemistry; a series of jobs in industry; and seven years with an environmental consultancy where he used his skills as a trained chemist to investigate scandals such as the use of anti-freeze in Austrian wine and the infamous case of benzene in Perrier water have given him a depth of knowledge that serves him well as FOE's regional campaigner. He does a mixture of tasks; he is Jack of all trades, master of none, one day on fracking, then climate change, food policy, air pollution, traffic and transport, then bees and pollination. At the moment the organisation is stable in terms of membership and income with twenty-two local groups doing a wide variety of tasks. Chris offers them campaigning expertise and support. He sees that environmentalism is growing but acknowledges that, 'I am the wrong side of fifty so I need to see how I can pass my skills on to the next generation. And I am not as digitally and IT aware and those are the skills that people will need in the future.'

The largest non-governmental organisation (NGO) in the city is Islamic Relief which, over thirty years, has grown into one of the world's largest Islamic NGOs. Founded by a group of concerned postgraduate students in Highgate, Birmingham, in 1984, it has grown so that today it operates more than a hundred offices in forty countries worldwide – from Afghanistan to Albania, Pakistan to Palestine, Somalia to Sudan. As well as disaster relief, it carries out sustainable development work to provide water, food, shelter, health care and education in the long term.

Islamic Relief is not the only Islamic NGO in the city. Fatima has worked as an orphan officer for an international, faith-based NGO for four years and continues to work even with a young child, as her husband shares the childcare. She was born and brought up in a strong Mirpuri community in Lozells. Educated and encouraged by her teachers at Holte School, she went to Joseph Chamberlain Sixth Form College and then on to study social policy at university. The NGO was originally a small Birmingham-based charity running two schools in Pakistan. It received a major boost after an enormous earthquake in Pakistan in 2005 killed 85,000 people. With a huge influx of funds, it realised that it had to become a fully fledged NGO. By 2009 it was raising £5 million a year and had extended its range of activities from schools into orphan care, environmental and water projects in the countries in which it operates.

The thirty staff in the office based at a mosque in Sparkhill support 2,000 children across Asia, the Middle East and Africa. Orphans are defined as those without a parent, usually without a father, so that they have no access to financial support. Most, but not all, of the orphans are Muslim. Fatima has responsibility for much of the organisation of the scheme and linking the placement child to the prospective donors. Other staff raise the money and the charity has placement officers in each of the countries. She works in a team of three people, to ensure all donors contributing £30–£40 per month have a child allocated to them. These donations are used to support the child with the money channelled via the charity's staff in the countries where the orphans are living. To support a child costs £360–£480 a year. The majority of the charity's donors are Muslim and its donor base has spread across the UK.

'It is really interesting work but I feel now after four years that I have reached my limit.'

Zubeda works in the burgeoning social enterprise sector. Her dad came with her grandfather from Gujarat in the early 1960s to work in the textile mills, following a call-out from the British government for the work that white British people did not want to do. He was fourteen at the time. Zubeda's dad married young and then her mum came over. They moved around in the north of England before settling in Bolton. Zubeda was born in 1975, one of seven children, and grew up in an Indian area, a mix of Hindus and Muslims with just three or four white kids in the primary school. Her secondary school was more mixed and she encountered considerable racism there but she did her GCSEs, A levels and then went to Manchester University for her degree followed by a masters in Middle Eastern Studies. Of the seven children in the family, five went to university. She had to go to Manchester because she wasn't allowed to stay away from home. Her parents were quite explicit about this. Fortunately, her older sister had gone before her.

'Education had two advantages. It was the one way we could keep our parents happy and not get married. The Islamic texts say that the prophet encourages education and this was the one way to convince our parents to allow us to go to university.'

When she graduated she got a job with the Labour Party for eighteen months as a local organiser. She had always been political through her dad, who had been involved in the factory and the trade union movement and used to sign passport applications.

This was followed by a job with Bolton Council in housing, but she was afraid of simply getting married and assuming a role that was expected of her, so she went abroad, to Egypt, Jordan and Syria, without her parents' permission. It was her first time away from home and she loved it. 'I knew when I came back, that I had to move out of Bolton. I love it and the North West but after Cairo I knew I needed to live in a big city.'

That is how she came to Birmingham. She worked for the City Council in a number of different jobs on urban policy, in the Equalities Division, and then was seconded to the West Midlands Police to help with the recruitment of community mentors where she created a regional mentoring programme. In 2013, she set up Connect Justice, a limited company and independent social enterprise designed to build trust between the police and ethnic minority communities. Zubeda emphasises that they are not a charity beholden to others, but, rather, an independent enterprise not reliant on grants. Connect Justice functions as a business, which wins commissions and projects funded by different organisations ranging from the West Midlands Police to the US Embassy. They have three core staff and then draw on half a dozen consultants. Zubeda is a founding co-director.

Over their first four years they have got the organisation off the ground with a voice and a presence in the extremism/radicalisation arena in which they undertake a lot of their activity. She feels they have bridged the gap between minority communities and state agencies as they are not funded through the Home Office. To show their independence they list all their funders on the website. They are transparent. When they hold events with the police, they stress that Connect Justice is not an agency of the government.

They reach into parts that others do not. When they ran an EU project, they had access to both far right and Muslim extremists, as they did when they had a crowdfunder and raised £8,500 to produce a video in order to hear the stories of former extremists. That gives them a distinct niche in their field. They are now looking to deliver online training for schools and others to work on radicalisation issues in ways that avoid the stigmatising impact of the government's Prevent programme.

Connect Justice work across a range of equality issues. One of their reports, 'A Tale of Three Cities', addresses the responsiveness of leading public institutions in three major cities – Bristol, Birmingham and Manchester – to the challenges of gender, race and disability. The findings make for uncomfortable reading for, while significant progress has been made on the gender agenda, progress on race and disability remains slow.[2] As Zubeda says, 'There are big institutions in the city where diversity is not reflected in their organisations. Some of this is shocking.'

Yet she retains her optimism. Zubeda's organisation is based on justice and civil rights, not on ethnicity. Her co-director is a white convert to Islam; her third director is a hardcore secularist. They want to avoid the divisiveness that treats minorities as homogenous blocs and pits one community against another. Like Kashan, she believes there has been too much focus on ethnicity, giving money to people because of who they are rather than what they do or the issues they are tackling. Connect Justice explicitly allies itself to the wider Birmingham community, which is why they are based at the Impact Hub social enterprise centre.

The Impact Hub is one example of where the 'diversity advantage' is favouring the city. As Aliyah, one of the support staff of

Irish/Barbadian descent, says, 'This is definitely an intercultural space. All people come here. It is shared innovating space for the social good with a common ethos.'

The Hub hosts micro-businesses and social enterprises and is growing fast with members from all backgrounds drawn from Birmingham and surrounding areas. It is the brainchild of Immy, a young, second-generation Indian Sikh woman, born and bred in Birmingham, whose first main job was with the Tony Blair Faith Foundation in London.

'London was the place to make it, but I then found it was not the place that I thought it was going to be, so I came back to Birmingham and worked at Bromford Housing Association. I used it to find out about the realities of life in the city and then left it all to start my own entrepreneurial journey with the Impact Hub.'

Immy is short and slim, wears a headscarf and exudes energy. She was doing TEDx and she met people who told her to use the TEDx group to build something new.

'We used a range of platforms, social media and events to develop the Hub momentum. In December 2014 we launched a crowdfunding initiative and had an amazing campaign linked to building a better city. In thirty days we raised £65,000. And then the Barrow Cadbury foundation agreed to match us with £50,000. We fitted out the building by going out to the community and drawing on their support.'

This is a reflection of wider trends finding prominence across Europe. In the Netherlands there is a growing emergence of such initiatives which illustrate the potential of civic crowdfunding not just as a fundraising mechanism but also as a powerful tool to promote actions at the grass roots.[3]

The Hub has three main sources of income: membership; events where it hires out the rooms to organisations for meetings; and running its own programmes. Its focus stretches beyond social enterprises. As Immy explains: 'We want to build a better city and a stronger economy and need to have all sorts at the table including big corporates, individual freelancers, local institutions as well as social enterprises and the Big Lottery. We see the Hub as a place to talk to a cross-section of organisations so that they can contribute to building a vibrant economy. That is why the Chamber of Commerce has a membership here too; they don't need the space.'

The Hub is based in the renovated redbrick factory of a Victorian manufacturer of marine instruments and is located close to the city centre in the old industrial quarter of Digbeth. This is the emerging creative nerve centre of the city. The Hub is just one of a string of venues that have taken root here over the last two decades, including Maverick, a burgeoning TV and media production company; Fazeley Studios with its forty-five neatly designed offices aimed at creative and digital companies; and the Custard Factory, the former premises of Alfred Bird's custard powder plant, now housing scores of micro-businesses and small NGOs. All these are clustered together in Digbeth. The Hub is the conscious adaptation of an old industrial building to the needs of the new economy using European Structural Funds to promote social innovation and bring life to a dying quarter of the city. The onward march of automation poses a threat to a whole range of existing industrial and technical jobs. That's why the renovation of places like this and the creation of new businesses and employment in growth sectors of the economy is crucial to the city's future.

With its strip lighting, high work benches, plywood tables and open-plan workspace, this is innovation easy-style. Zubeda works here as does Sam and his health project team. He and others are grouped around the computer and worksheet discussing new projects. The whiteboard is littered with Post-it notes. The extendable plug points drop from the ceiling so that the teams can connect to the ubiquitous portable computers that cover the tables. Relaxed, easy-going, youthful and intercultural: this is cosmopolitan hybridity, the open city at work and at ease with itself. It's Birmingham's answer to London's Shoreditch. The task is to replicate it across the city.

# 4

## *The New Entrepreneurs*

People leave their homes, their families and their surroundings in the hope that they will be able to improve their lot and make a happier life for themselves in a new country. This drive to get ahead, together with their initial exclusion from the more traditional routes into mainstream society, are two of the key factors that explain why many immigrants set up their own businesses. It is a relatively straightforward, uncomplicated starting point. Furthermore, UK law makes this a lot easier than elsewhere in Europe. Compared to many other countries, in Britain there is comparatively little bureaucracy involved in opening up a shop or setting up a business. And immigrants have little to lose by giving it a go. If you arrive in the country with next to nothing, then the risks of striking out on your own are relatively low.

This is what many who came to Birmingham have done, especially those from the South Asian communities. They have given new lifeblood to the city's businesses. The 2011 census data shows that Indian and Pakistani ethnic groups in the city have the highest levels of self-employment, between 9 and 10 per cent, on a par with the national average, even though the figures for female self-employment are low. Their arrival and activity has altered the face of the high street, and the world of business beyond it, entirely. Over the last half-century Birmingham's small-business community has changed dramatically, whether in retail, manufacturing or services, with Asians especially prominent. This has not been either a simple or a straightforward process. Many have fallen by the wayside; others have struggled to survive. The never-ending processes of global change reach into every nook and cranny of the economy, threatening the precarious livelihoods of both aspiring and established small businesses. This chapter explores the trials and tribulations of some of the city's migrant entrepreneurs; how they have responded to the wide-ranging economic challenges that they face; and how they have altered and expanded the range of services and choices that are open to the citizens of the city.

The local newsagent selling papers and magazines, cigarettes and sweets has long been a feature of British urban and village life, a reference point for communities, the place to nip into for your fags and to pick up the evening paper. Over the years it has evolved, stocking milk and groceries, selling lottery tickets, so that those living in the nearby streets can use them as a local convenience store. Increasingly, this traditional British community icon has been run by migrants, above all Pakistanis. Of the estimated 30,000 independent newsagent retailers in the UK, more than 75 per cent are thought to be Asian. It is hard, unforgiving work.

Rehman's newsagent is at the end of a long row of neat, terraced, late nineteenth-century houses. It stands opposite a large, well-tended park, popular with kids, parents, dog walkers and joggers. Rehman has owned the shop for thirteen years. The long-term Irish owner had sold the shop to another Irish family, but they failed to make a go of it, so Rehman was able to buy it. Short and stocky, he sits behind the counter waiting for his customers. He has brief but friendly exchanges with them as they come in for a paper or cigarettes. At times, he exudes a certain weariness with life but comes alive when we talk football, his hopes for Liverpool and his gentle ribbing of my team, Arsenal. The tiredness is easy to understand.

'I get up at five thirty; go to the shop; sort out all the news-papers and deliveries. Then stay there all day. In the shop I sell papers and magazines, cigarettes, plus sweets, ice cream, food and drinks. I am on my own. I'm happy with what I am doing, it's basic stuff. The profit margins are quite high, helped by people going to the park. I close at four in the winter and stay open until six or six thirty in the summer. I am open seven days a week, every day apart from Christmas Day. I haven't had a holiday for twenty-three years. In the winter you get less customers, it can be very quiet and it's a bit depressing. In the summer with more custom-ers it is better. But if you have been doing it for a long time you just get used to it. It's okay.'

Born and bred in inner-city Birmingham, Rehman is one of five children born to parents from Chakswari, near Mirpur in Pakistan. His dad worked at a factory in the Black Country until an industrial injury forced him to retire.

'Growing up was very, very hard. We had to walk to school and everything. We didn't have no money. We were living in Balsall Heath and went to school at Queensbridge [two miles away]. It was on the 50 bus route but we had no money for the bus fare.'

At school, he got educated to A level, did a BTec in business and finance followed by a Higher National Diploma but then dropped out. The family had bought a newsagent's shop in a rundown shopping precinct on a mainly white, working-class tower block estate on the southern edge of Birmingham, so he had the opportunity to apply his business and finance skills in real life.

'Dad had burnt his back at the foundry and couldn't work no more, so he was looking for opportunities. My dad bought it and gave it to me and my brother. It wasn't that much. It was a lease, the rent was very cheap. The business was very good. Supermarkets didn't open on Sundays in them days. But it was a very rough area. We had lots of trouble but that was not so much racial as that they wanted to rob the shop. Four or five break-ins. Me and my brother ran the shop. We done that for thirteen years. Then I decided to give up. I had had enough by then. I got knifed once. I don't like telling people. Me and my dad was there and they tried to rob us. They didn't take anything. That's life. Nobody helped us. We had CCTV cameras but the police couldn't find them.

'Then I had a break. I didn't want to do this sort of work no more. I didn't want no pressure. I tried to find a job but nobody would employ me because I didn't have no experience of office work. I tried for many supermarket jobs but they wouldn't employ me. I couldn't get a job for about a year. Then I bought this place.'

The fast-changing nature of society and the impact of global-isation and IT reach into every corner of the world of business. Newsagents and corner shops are no exception. Rehman's business is affected in several ways. Firstly, the kid's paper round has gone. It used to be a basic way for youngsters to get some extra pocket money. That's what Rehman did when he was a kid. But kids don't want to do it now. They're just not reliable. They won't get up in time so he has to rely on pensioners.

Secondly, the big supermarkets are setting up small, local stores which are direct competitors to the corner shop and newsagent business. His brother moved to Ward End (east Birmingham) but he has now closed his shop. A Tesco Express opened there and he decided he had had enough.

Thirdly, and most dramatically, the internet is rapidly transforming people's reading habits and the newspaper industry along with it, as the immediacy of the online world takes its toll. National newspaper sales are declining sharply, while the local *Birmingham Mail* dropped *Evening* from its title in 2005 and now only prints a morning edition, so there are no evening papers to deliver. Rehman is pretty pessimistic about the future as his main newspaper clientele ages.

'Young people don't buy newspapers. It's only the older generation who buy newspapers. Once they die, there'll be no newspapers. There is no future because the people who distribute the papers and magazines are likely to get out of it. They are diversifying into parcels and other things.'

He knows the changes that could be made to his business but is not looking to diversify. He owns the shop. The top floor could be rented out. There is scope for other things: mobile top-ups; card payments; electricity and gas payments. That could attract more people in but he has had twenty-six years working at this and he doesn't want the extra hassle. He is taking things a bit easier. There is less money in this game now. You have to be like Nisa or Costcutter and sell everything. That requires big investment and he doesn't want to go into that.

Rehman works on his own. It is harder for sole traders. He knows what is needed to respond to the changing circumstances, but he does not have the energy to do it.

'I still make a decent living but it's hard work. I want to enjoy some of my life. I may have one or two more years here. I have worked hard and I have enough money. I will want to do something afterwards, but something less stressful.'

After twenty-six years of work, twelve hours a day, fifty-two weeks a year, you can't blame him.

Pam stands bespectacled, straight-backed and erect behind the counter with the bearing and aura of his military father, dispensing charm and bonhomie to his regular flow of customers. They are waiting to download and print their own photos off digital phones and cameras; buy picture frames; request portraits; as well as ask for detailed restoration and artistic work. This is no down-at-heel high street business. There is the feel of cutting-edge technology within its tight confines, for the shop is a tribute to the restless spirit of innovation that a hard-working migrant has brought to his trade.

Pam's father arrived here from India in 1956 and Pam was born two years later. The family lived in Smethwick on the western edge of Birmingham. Pam went to a specialist photography and cinematic college in Wednesbury where he began his interest in the trade that he has followed his entire life. His first shop was in Wolverhampton. He built up the business with six shops doing film processing and enlargements. He then decided to open a small factory in Smethwick so that he could manufacture his own frames. At its peak this employed thirty people and they had regular orders from the big companies like Kodak, delivering

20,000 frames a week. Then the twin forces of globalisation and the ICT revolution hit his business.

'The business system changed and we opened up to China and Korea. Our small business sector was sacrificed. Kodak decided to buy from importers. My business was sacrificed. We were devastated. Our factory with its thirty staff was forced to close.'

It was not just Pam's business that suffered. The largest similar producer in the country, in Telford, employed 170 people. They had to close down, too. Pam lost a lot of money. He was really down, uncertain what he was going to do. Some people even suggested that he should declare himself bankrupt, a temptation he resisted.

But the biggest blow was yet to come. That was the digital invention which killed off the big giants in the imaging industry, Agfa in Germany, then Konica and then Kodak. Thirty-five Kodak minilabs closed down in the Midlands alone. Pam sold some of his shops to their managers. Two of his ex-managers run them and are still trading. He kept just one shop. But he was keen to survive and adjust. Following a visit to Prague and seeing the artists on Charles Bridge, he realised that the digital revolution had to open up new opportunities. He reckoned that people are taking millions of pictures, more than ever before when they were limited to cartridge film. So he thought, 'Okay, can we do something with those images that they cannot do at home?' He saw the potential and established a new line of online artistic digital pictures. With a new website set up in 2004, and establishing a business in India to undertake the digital work, he has managed to survive and flourish. He describes the development of the new business.

'We are producing personalised art from those digital pictures: can we convert that picture into an oil painting, into a character, into pencil? I found that there was interest. How can I make this bigger? How can I supply a new service to other shops? My project was to receive a digital file; convert it into art which the shop can download and print onsite. With that idea I went to the world's largest photographic exhibition at the Cologne Messe and I launched this idea over there.'

He is now supplying this service in six EU countries. He faces many competitors. He produces art from customers' pictures. If, for example, a child likes American wrestling, he can turn him into Hulk Hogan. In the shop he gets customers from around the world plus the requests for this from the six EU countries. He cannot extend the business as he does not have sufficient capital. He makes around £150,000 per year just by turning around these digital files. He has joined the globalisers, having sent these jobs to forty to fifty people in southern India. He also does photo restoration online. A shop in Germany will email the damaged photograph to him; he'll get it to India where it will be restored; and then back to the customer in Germany. Sixty to seventy per cent of his current business is based on this internet work.

'My shop is an office. Internet business is website business. The shop on its own has no future now. The high street is totally dead. As a small businessman I feel idiots rule the policies here. First they made China and its cheap labour ruin our business. They became so powerful that we couldn't stop them. Then we started to follow an American system of shopping areas, totally forgetting that we aren't a big country like America. We started to open big malls out of town, away from the high street. We killed the high street, by opening superstores, big malls and all that. All the big stores started leaving the high street. In our area we have eighteen charity shops. You cannot save the high street now.'

This is perhaps overstated. His shop has a steady flow of shoppers – and not just on Saturdays. The remarkable fact is that in the face of the challenges of the digital revolution and globalisation Pam did not give up. Instead, he altered and adapted his business. He found a new niche that kept pace with technological change and offered new opportunities to his customers.

Zahoor is a typical small shopkeeper, an indispensable feature of any decent high street. He has been in his present shop since 1997. Set in a side road off the main suburban high street, it is a multipurpose electrical store. The shop sells a range of electrical goods and products: the small traditional supplies and accessories such as plugs, extensions, electrical wires and cables, screwdrivers and tools, batteries; a range of basic digital equipment; and then products such as radios, TVs, kettles, heaters, etc. At the back lies the workshop, where Zahoor is often to be found crouched over his tools carrying out electrical repairs. Being a skilled electrician and engineer means that Zahoor offers the kind of knowledge, skill and on-hand service not usually found when you walk into Currys, Dixons or PC World. For those who do not want to chuck away every electrical product the first time it goes wrong, Zahoor offers a local, accessible support service. 'I do repairs which many people don't. This helps a lot for my business. It's two in one: retail and servicing.'

That is his niche. It is not huge; it will not make him rich, but it is a role which earns him a respectable living and retains the diversity of the high street.

Zahoor's father was a member of the Pakistan Air Force and in his childhood Zahoor travelled a lot around the country. After studying to the age of eighteen, Zahoor wanted to pursue his further education in the UK. His great-uncle, who had been living in the UK since the 1930s, arranged Zahoor's admission into the Cornwall Technical College in 1969 on an apprenticeship paid by the company, a large mining equipment company near Redruth in Cornwall. There were hardly any people from Pakistan in Cornwall, and he had very little English for the first year, but he got on very well with the others.

Zahoor was one of fifteen of the thirty apprentices who were offered a job in the company. They took him on within their production line in different departments and then sent him to East Kilbride, Scotland, followed by two years in Tehran (abruptly ended by the Iranian Revolution) and then a spell in Saudi Arabia as a customer support engineer. In 1983, the company decided that he should leave Saudi Arabia. He tried to settle back in Pakistan but didn't like it. So, as a skilled engineer he ended up running his own businesses in Birmingham, working from home. Electronics had been his hobby and he began by doing outdoor markets at the weekends; the first one in Long Marston, the second at Wellesbourne in Warwickshire. He got a lot of business at these markets; then started doing indoor markets, first one in Kings Heath, Birmingham, selling electrical accessories and goods. Things developed from there. At one stage he had three businesses. For a while, when he was at the markets, his wife looked after the shop. As with almost all shopkeepers, things are never as good as they once were. He no longer does markets and now operates with just one shop.

'Overall trade is not the same as it used to be. The main reason is the internet setup and normal shops are open longer, so there is more competition. Initially I worked really long hours, especially in the markets. Now my opening hours are nine to five-thirty, six days a week, so it is still long hours. But I make a decent living, yes.'

Not all have been so fortunate in their business ventures. Ajay came over from Gujarat, India, when he was twenty years old in 1967. He was a tailor. He came because he wanted a better life: 'It was as simple as that. It wasn't easy. It was a hard life, everywhere. I was lucky as I was a sewing machinist and I got a job straightaway.'

He started in Coventry and then found work in Birmingham. He worked in a shop for three years and then decided to set up his own business, making and selling children's casual wear and anoraks. He admits that the business didn't develop much. He had eight or nine ladies working as sewing machinists in their homes. He outsourced his work to them. He operated for ten years but it didn't really work out. There was a lot of competition and when he had young children in the early 1980s he decided to stop.

He had been operating in Sparkhill, in inner-city Birmingham. After a few years working with British Rail he wanted to give his own business another go. He thought it was worth another try. He tried the business for a couple of years but again found the competition was just too much for him. He ended up in debt and had to close the business down.

After working in industry for more than fifteen years, mainly at the Lucas lighting and motor components factory in east Birmingham, Mashood and his brother started an engineering company in 1980. It lasted until the financial recession of 2008–9.

At first, it was very hard. They didn't have a workshop as they had little money and no capital. They concentrated on engineering design and started by winning specific designs for contracts such as prisons. They then developed expertise in the design and manufacture of very heavy industrial products. One of their major jobs was to make the industrial staircases for the renovated Bull Ring shopping centre in the middle of Birmingham. They gradually built up their capital and were able to run a company with more than twenty employees.

It was satisfying work. They were players in a niche market with other major players as clients such as Balfour Beatty, Taylor Woodrow and Wimpey's. They established a factory in Ward End, but they were unable to withstand the impact and knock-on effects of the financial crisis.

'We lost everything in 2009. The banks gave me no credit and the company we were working for, a branch of a big multinational, closed down and when they closed we went down with them. They owed us something like three-quarters of a million pounds. Their parent was a giant company worth 1.2 billion pounds but their corporate lawyers hived off this loss-making branch and we got no compensation. We were halfway through the project and we couldn't survive the waiting. It was a sad end to my working career. I did bits of freelance for three years after that and then called it a day.'

Many migrants start up a business and see it fold quickly. Others like Ajay struggle to get by, hang on for a while and then fall into abeyance. Then, when he tried again, the business crumbled and left him with significant debts. Mashood's is a different story of the small company getting along nicely until it became collateral damage to a big company's economic troubles in the financial crash. Others survive. Pam, Zahoor and Rehman have had their ups and downs; all have had to confront the changing nature of modern business, but each has managed to hang on in there and make a decent living.

Some fail, some succeed. That's the general picture. However, there are those rare figures who hit the big time. Wing Yip is one of them. His oriental food grocery business now stretches across four business sites in the UK: the main one in Birmingham is a ten-acre business park. Here and at the others in Manchester, Cricklewood, north London and Croydon, south London, he stocks and sells a vast range of oriental grocery products. In the last two decades the company has extended the range from just Chinese food so that now it has become a pan-Asian grocery business with products from Vietnam, Thailand, Malaysia, Korea and Japan. Annual turnover is more than £100 million and the company employs directly 370 staff with a steady 4–5 per cent profit on turnover. The company has plans to open two more sites in Cardiff and Nottingham. In addition, the sites act as a commercial and business centre for Chinese-focused companies, not just restaurants but also banks, solicitors, hairdressers, etc., with £3 million rental income coming from these other companies on the sites. Wing may be approaching his eightieth birthday but with his short, slim build he remains as restless and proactive as ever. He tells me: 'We are always planning to expand. So we are not just a Chinese grocery but deal with Chinese and oriental products. We have got a range of Chinese-based companies on our sites; and we are now looking to sell old-fashioned, traditional

Chinese goods and products – porcelain, tea and silk – which the Chinese brought to Europe in Victorian times. The Chinese product line is still not that good, but the idea is draw on our history and reintroduce these three types of products. I am optimistic about the future.'

So how did the poor boy who left Hong Kong in 1959 with £50 in his pocket end up like this? Wing was born in 1937 along the coastal shores of southern China, close to the area which is now Shenzhen. His family originally came from central China and were Hakkas. They migrated to Hong Kong when he was born but after the Japanese occupation in late 1941, his family went back to China. He lived under nationalist Chinese rule but after the Communists took over in 1949 the family returned to Hong Kong, where he went to school. Prospects were limited for a young man growing up in Hong Kong, but Wing had a British passport so in 1959, at the age of twenty-two, although he had no family connections in Britain he decided to migrate to England.

As Hakkas – which translates as 'the guest people' – Wing and his friends were used to the idea of emigration. They knew there was a Hakka Association in Liverpool who would look after them and find them jobs and somewhere to live. Of the fifty on the boat to England in 1959, forty were Hakkas.

They sailed to Marseille as the French boats used to go to Vietnam and then on to Hong Kong. The boat they travelled on was a troopship with bunk beds. The trip cost £100.

The Hakka Association put Wing up first in Liverpool. He began by making tea and coffee in a restaurant. The Chinese restaurants included accommodation. A three- or four-room terraced house, each bedroom had two double bunk beds, which meant four people sharing a bedroom. Then, when someone left, he got a job washing up in one of the three Chinese restaurants in Hull. When the owner saw him reading the newspaper he asked him to be a waiter as he could speak a bit of English. After a year, one of the chefs moved to Ipswich and there was a vacancy in his restaurant, so Wing moved there. They talked about setting up their own restaurant, so he bought a scooter and drove around. He found a place in Clacton-on-Sea, owned by two elderly sisters who ran a light lunch and afternoon tea shop with lots of elderly clients. They bought the lease and turned it into a Chinese restaurant. It went well. It was luck. By the early 1960s Butlins had opened a new holiday camp at Jaywick Sands. So, in the high season you got 7,000 people, all the Redcoats, plus lots of day-trippers. The local fish and chip shop closed at 9.30, so after that they all ran to his place. This worked for two summers. In winter it was very quiet, so he went to buy something else in Ipswich, an old bakery shop. The owners were elderly and he bought it for £5,000. Wing kept the restaurant in Clacton. Ipswich worked 'very good', so well that they bought seven further properties over the next few years. They also opened a dinner and dance place.

It was the period of the Cold War, and there were lots of US military personnel at the air bases nearby with plenty of money to spend. They would stay on the base during the week and then they came out and took the Suffolk girls to the pub. The young English local boys got jealous. Every Saturday there were fights between Americans and the locals. There were invariably three or four military vehicles around the pubs, so when Wing opened his dinner and dance restaurant, instead of taking their girls to the pub, the Americans took them there. So the English girls learned how to use chopsticks. For the Americans from California, they were used to Chinese restaurants on every corner. The English boys couldn't afford to go to this type of restaurant with the higher prices; they went more for fish and chips. And so the business took off. Next, Wing sent for his brother Sammy from Hong Kong. They talked it over together but they knew they could not cook and so they always needed chefs as partners. Then a family friend said to him, 'Why don't you start a grocery shop supplying the restaurants?' They thought that was a good idea. By now the Chinese restaurant trade was well established in Britain, although there still weren't any takeaways. He looked at the map. He went to the library in Ipswich and looked at the history of big companies. He was really surprised by what he found.

'Look at the main companies. None of them start in London. Marks & Spencer – Leeds; Boots – Nottingham; Barclays Bank – East Anglia; and Lloyds – Birmingham. I looked at lots of others, none of them from London. So I asked a young man who came into our restaurant and he said, "London is like the jungle; it only has big trees, they don't have grasses. London is a place you finish up, not how you start up. Very simple logic." So I said, my God, we must not start there.'

So he studied the map again and all the main roads seemed to go through Birmingham. So he started looking in Birmingham and then opened up in Digbeth, at 5 St Martin's Place, just down from the Bull Ring. The shop is still there. It used to be a record shop but business suffered when people started using tape cassettes rather than vinyl. He opened up as a grocery business and lived upstairs. There was no need to deliver as people could park outside the shop. He still kept the businesses in Ipswich but gradually sold them so that they could expand the grocery business. They then moved to Meriden Street, a one-acre site beneath the railway arches. In those days they kept both the shop and this new warehouse store. They kept expanding. They became the main supplier for Chinese and then oriental goods in the West Midlands. After a few years Wing's other brother came over from Jamaica and they opened a new store in Manchester.

Wing thrived and grew because he had hit on a wider social trend: the emergence of a cosmopolitan food culture in the UK. In 1950s Britain, the diet was pretty staid and stodgy. It could fairly be called traditional and limited in range. Roast beef and Yorkshire pudding was the common culinary highlight; wine was unknown in most ordinary British households; and spaghetti was such a rarity that millions would be taken in by Richard Dimbleby's April Fool's Day spoof on BBC's *Panorama* in 1957 about Swiss women carefully plucking strands of spaghetti from a tree and laying them out in the sun to dry. As the BBC explained at the time, 'Spaghetti is not a widely eaten food in the UK and is considered by many as an exotic delicacy.'[1] Half a century later globalisation and migration have changed the country's culinary landscape beyond all recognition: every supermarket sells wine from across the globe; all stock endless varieties of pasta; there is barely a small town or village in the land which does not have either an Indian or Chinese restaurant – usually both – and chicken tikka masala has become the nation's favourite dish.

Birmingham has been at the epicentre of this culinary revolution. There are more than two hundred curry houses in the city:

that's one for every 5,000 citizens. They are often clustered in the main Asian neighbourhoods but many more are scattered in the suburbs all around the city, some offering a cheap, simple meal, others catering for a more upmarket clientele. The city created its distinctive hallmark with the Birmingham Balti,[2] the original Balti dish invented by Pakistanis living in Birmingham. The curry is cooked and served in the dish, a small, lightweight wok-type vessel made of thin stainless steel, which was invented for Pakistani chefs by a Sikh living in Smethwick. The Balti explosion took off in the mid-1980s when the Balti belt or triangle developed in inner south Birmingham in the area of Sparkhill, Balsall Heath and Moseley, bounded by sections of the Moseley and Stratford roads. More than fifty restaurants and curry houses are packed into this area. Balti quickly became Birmingham's most famous culinary dish, typically prepared with vegetable oil rather than ghee, and cooked quickly over a flame in the same bowl. The quick cooking process with the caramelisation of the onions, the use of tomatoes, ginger and garlic and other spices gave it its distinctive flavour, while the price helped its popularity. It remains a relatively inexpensive dish.

As with Wing Yip, accompanying the restaurant sector has come the emergence of Asian food distribution grocery businesses supplying the growing market. Starting in Wolverhampton, the Indian-born Wouhra brothers developed as suppliers of South Asian spices, lentils and rice. They expanded their operations into Highgate, central Birmingham, in 1972. They set up to supply independent retailers, family-owned stores and the growing number of Indian restaurants. With the increasingly popularity of Indian food they have expanded their business so that they now have a national distribution network and supply to a wide range of shops, pubs and supermarkets as well as their traditional markets. Today East End Foods has three distribution centres in the Greater Birmingham area, supplying over 1,250 'ethnic food' lines sourced from across the world and giving an annual turnover of £180 million.

Then there are the single-street traders. Moses does not follow the stereotype. His parents came from the West Indies at the end of the 1950s. His dad worked on the railways and his mum as a nurse. Mo has been employed in youth services, for charities, in fundraising and bid writing and has run his own holistic services and aromatherapy business, but for the last decade he has followed his passion for food and built up Kuskus Foods. With his natty flat cap and razor-sharp patter, Mo makes the ideal street trader. The words just flow off his tongue. His commitment to his vocation runs through his conversation but producing West Indian food is not for him.

'If you love food, why would you narrow yourself down to just one genre of food? It is just ridiculous, absolutely ridiculous. I produce all vegetarian food, North African and Middle Eastern food. I sell at farmers' markets, family fun festivals, on university campuses. I do three or four stalls in the winter periods, then four or five a week from spring to November . . . Sometimes I make a loss but what is important is that I am happy with what I have done. I employ some people on a consultancy basis. The business is aimed at meat eaters, to give them an understanding, an appreciation of good, wholesome food. It is not trying to change meat eaters into vegans, it is not trying to create tens of thousands of vegetarians but to reintroduce into people's lifestyle, handmade natural food.'

He works as a sole trader. He prefers it this way. He started by making the food in his own kitchen but now has a unit in a converted hayloft and old stables in the north of the city, where he prepares and cooks the food. For his sanity and welfare, it helps to have that distance from his home. While coy about his turn-over, there is no doubt that he has created a successful niche in the marketplace.

Mo eulogises about his work. He sees it in a broader context, talking with passion of how life and food flourish from mixing and hybridity.

'Food isn't an inanimate object. Food is a constantly fluid thing that moves. Therefore, the concept was to be inspired by the Middle East. I make the food to be vegetarian but in fact it is all vegan but I don't use that word as it is too niche. Falafel, mezes, tagines, tabboulehs. My food trail helps to tell people about the origin of the food, how it has been developed over 2,000 years. Food has always had a trail, a journey, and I want to explain that.'

Which he does with vim and vigour to the often unsuspecting buyers at his market stalls.

Wing Yip's grocery business is part of this kaleidoscope. There are around 2,000 Chinese restaurants in the UK and a further 2–3,000 Chinese takeaways. Wing is quite clear about why Chinese restaurants have become so popular.

'Firstly, we offer a big choice but not a fancy price. Secondly, our food is not too spicy, so it is suitable for most palates. Thirdly, we invite all the family. We cultivate eating as a whole family from a very early age. If you go to a Chinese restaurant you see the whole family. You go to other restaurants and they say even on the menu, "we don't do half portions" which means children are not welcome. We are different. If there is a little boy or girl you bring them a dish and they have what they want.'

As the restaurant and takeaway sectors boomed, so did the need for knowledgeable suppliers of Chinese food products. This is where Wing and his brothers scored. As he says simply, 'we know the business'. Recognising the growing interest in food with the boom in TV shows and celebrity cookbooks, Wing's stores are open to anyone keen to experiment with Chinese and oriental cooking. Today his stores stock more than 6,500 products.

This transformation of British food habits is one of the most significant features of the post-war migrant influx. It has opened the British palate to the tastes and delights of food from other cultures: it has excited people's curiosity and their willingness to try something new and different. It is one of the most tangible benefits of the post-war migration, which has transformed the food culture of the country. Unsurprisingly, barely a word of this phenomenon emerges from the never-ending stream of negative, anti-migrant stories that form the staple diet of the news and feature pages of the *Daily Express*, the *Daily Mail* and other parts of the tabloid press. Yet the reality is that migration has transformed the eating habits of the majority of their readers. What is more, this has occurred by free choice. People have simply decided that they like Chinese and Indian restaurants and gone there in ever increasing numbers. Just as they go from time to time to Greek tavernas, Italian bistros or Spanish tapas bars. Never has the British palate been so diverse and varied, nor so willing to experiment with different food cultures. And this has only been possible because foreigners have come here, brought their food culture with them and made a living from it.

This cosmopolitan culinary entrepreneurship has proved infectious. With its Frankfurt German Christmas market staged for six weeks prior to Christmas every year, Birmingham City Council has got in on the act. Whenever I get asked by local people about the work that I have done, the one thing that they'll always know about, whatever background they come from, is the German Christmas market.

Locals, commuters and visitors take the train to New Street, come out of the station and walk up to the Council House. There before you are the sights, sounds and smells of an authentic German Christmas market. There are more than a hundred stalls. They sell hot Glühwein; frankfurters; pretzels and Bratwurst; fresh fruits covered in chocolate; Stollen and Lebkuchen; homemade jewellery; delicately crafted wooden toys; intricate multicoloured candles; salt crystal lamps; tableware; dolls; decorations and lots more. Across Germany there are 1,100 such markets set up in front of town halls in great cities and small villages every Christmas. It's an ancient Germanic tradition. In partnership with its twin city of Frankfurt, Birmingham has brought that tradition to Britain. In less than two decades this six-week event has grown from scratch to attract several million visitors each year. Birmingham has successfully transferred a European custom and made it an intrinsic part of the local Christmas scene.

This was no easy task. It was one component of a wider project by politicians and policy-makers to rethink the city, open it to new influences and find ways to bring life and activity to the city centre. Birmingham began to look to Europe from the mid-1980s, not just for funding but also for new ways of urban development, anxious to break from its post-war legacy of six-lane highways and a core city centre dominated by huge flyovers and dark, dingy pedestrian underpasses. Many Western European cities were turning away from the lure of this American urban model and in its place were developing a compact, smart growth model, which looked to retain, modernise and humanise dense, urban areas. This more human-oriented view of city development placed conviviality and cosmopolitanism at the heart of urban life. This broader thinking laid the basis for the Christmas market experiment. It was an early example of intercultural policy making.

Discussions were held with Frankfurt politicians and the council events company which arranged Frankfurt's own market. In December 1997 an initial pilot market was established with eleven stalls. It was not a great success. Inevitably, there were teething problems, especially with the licensing justices horrified at the thought of adults drinking hot spiced wine in public spaces. In the aftermath, the Frankfurt company decided to try their luck elsewhere. However, the idea remained part of the city's strategic thinking. There came a renewed call to re-establish a traditional German Christmas market in Birmingham and, on a visit to Frankfurt, the new Council leader Albert Bore, the Chief Executive Michael Lyons and I hammered out a deal. This was to be a five-year partnership which would grow the market gradually. Birmingham would provide the venue and logistical support as well as undertake publicity; the Frankfurt company would organise the market and bring the stallholders.

This took some time to put in place. Frankfurt had to organise a sizeable enough group and convince them that this was a viable business proposition. On the Birmingham side, with Jim Kelly, the city centre operations manager, we drew up a five-year business plan with the goal of the project being cost-neutral at the end of the period. Learning from the 1997 experience, early discussions were held with the police Operational Unit Commander on drinking arrangements. Subsequently the licensing magistrates permitted a much more flexible arrangement for the new market than they had allowed before. The Council's European team, which I headed at the time, advised on accommodation for the stallholders; helped them with the banks; gave detailed language support so that the queries raised on some stalls by health and safety officers could be resolved. And with twenty-five stalls the new market was a bigger venture which the Council press team was able to publicise more effectively. The event went well and in consequence Frankfurt was able to attract forty-seven stalls to Birmingham the following year. A number of first-time stall-holders had enough confidence to come with additional stalls and with different kinds of products.

Already at the end of its second year, the pull of the market was evident both by the size of the crowds, especially at weekends, and the breadth of those attending. Importantly, for the retail and shopping appeal of the city centre as a whole, the market was already attracting visitors from a wide geographical area. Two thousand and three saw a further steady consolidation of the market with fifty-five stalls. A large proportion of stallholders were returning, a sign that the market was a sound business proposition for them, despite having to cover their travel, accommodation and living expenses.

There were a number of key factors in the market's success. Firstly, Birmingham had the imagination necessary to appreciate the potential for a good product to be transferred into another setting. The city understood the attraction of the Christmas markets in Germany and felt they could also appeal to British people. The city's openness to Europe also meant that they were not afraid of adopting ideas from continental cities and trying them in Birmingham. They did not let insularity narrow their horizons.

Secondly, both officers and politicians ensured that the market fitted into and reinforced the wider strategy of animating the city. A wooden bandstand was designed to complement the market stalls and an entertainment programme inaugurated for the six-week period. This provided an opportunity to showcase local musical and school talent and promote 'civic pride'. The Frankfurt Christmas market showed Birmingham's capacity to use public space to stage a long-running event which generated life, enthusiasm and joy from across the whole demographic spectrum. As Jim Kelly put it, 'This is an event that crosses over all generations. It attracts a wide range of people across all ages, races and classes. It is not a niche event, unlike most things in modern life. And that helps create a calmer atmosphere, even though people are drinking.'

Thirdly, the city had the committed politicians needed to drive change. There were risks involved, an inevitable accompaniment to innovation. Some costs had to be found; officer time had to be allocated; and as it was a German event, wider Euroscepticism had to be countered. From the outset this project had the general backing of the Labour leadership but above all it benefited from the drive and engagement of a senior politician, Albert Bore. He had lost an election for Labour leadership of the Council in 1993 but whatever the disagreements within the group he was recognised as its European expert and given broad support on European issues. This was reinforced after he became Council leader in 1999. A clear agreement to the market from the Council's political leadership was crucial. It provided heavyweight backing to the project and gave the officers the time and resources necessary to establish the project. It also meant that politicians handled the adverse criticism in the local *Birmingham Evening Mail* when the Eurosceptic municipal affairs correspondent tried to arouse opposition to the market.

Ironically, the biggest political test came in 2004 when the market was already well established. Following that May's elections the political leadership of the council changed and a Conservative–Liberal coalition under Conservative Mike Whitby took control. When Whitby went on holiday in August, the Conservative cabinet member for Leisure, Sport and Culture, Nigel Dawkins, announced in the local press that the German market was to be axed. Giving voice to the deep vein of anti-European hostility within his party, Dawkins declared: 'The Conservative group has never been too happy with the Frankfurt market because we think there can be a British market with Birmingham traders. We are thinking of setting up a new quality Dickensian market, which would have a very British Christmas feel to it.'[3]

The *Birmingham Post*'s editorial pointed out that 'there may never have been such markets in the Victorian era' but 'the Conservatives want to take us back to basics'.[4] The *Post* noted that the Frankfurt market had become 'a local institution and the new council might think twice before throwing them out entirely'. The astonishing public response guaranteed it did. Letters and emails in support of the market poured into the local press and onto radio phone-ins, pointing out that Birmingham people had a chance to sample local produce all the year round at the Bull Ring markets; why should they be denied a once-a-year chance to sample produce and products from Germany? This kind of political ruckus was the last thing a new leadership wanted, especially as the German-speaking Whitby was anxious to promote Birmingham as an outward-facing city. Snubbing the Mayor and city of Frankfurt – Europe's main financial centre – was not the best way to pursue this objective. Whitby returned from holiday; gave a radio interview outlining his general support for the market; discussed with his party and coalition colleagues; and then bit the bullet. On 2 September he announced that the Frankfurt Market would continue. Dawkins lost his job.

Since then, the market has gone from strength to strength. By 2008 it had ninety-five stalls in place. The official cameras monitoring footfall over the market area estimated more than 2.8 million visitors to the market over its six weeks of operation. Over the period more than 650 coaches ran specific trips to the Birmingham Christmas market from as far afield as Southampton, Durham, Norwich and Wrexham. An independent survey indicated that more than half the visitors to the Christmas market came from outside the city.[5] Indeed, not only had the Birmingham market become the biggest Christmas market outside Germany and Austria but in terms of visitor numbers it had burst into the top ten rankings list of German/Austrian Christmas markets. Since then it has continued to grow steadily with more than one hundred stalls and now a footfall of around five million individual visitors.

The episode showed that the influence of old-style anti-German feeling based on wartime stereotypes was waning. The Birmingham public was prepared to try out the German market; liked what it found; and when its existence was threatened had voiced its opposition. A grassroots pro-Europeanism had won out. But it also showed the diminishing impact of a traditional appeal to parochialism – 'our' traders; 'our' traditions. Birmingham's migrant influx meant local people were aware that there were now other traditions to value and celebrate; other foods and cultures to enjoy, and, indeed, to take to one's heart and embrace as one's own. What they know and recognise is that the market's sheer *joie de vivre* has become a Birmingham hallmark, a distinctive feature of the city's life, one of the new traditions that an openness to the outside world has brought to the city. The Frankfurt Christmas market joins the Chinese quarter, the Ladypool Road, Lasan's and Jyotis, East End Foods, Kuskus Foods and Wing Yip. They all represent the cosmopolitan face of Birmingham. Fifty years of entrepreneurial endeavour that have changed the taste buds of a city.

# 5

# *The Global University*

'The global university at the heart of an ambitious city' is the University of Birmingham's strapline. Compared to many brand statements this one has a ring of truth. It reflects one of the emerging realities of globalisation. As substantial urbanisation and industrialisation extends swiftly across the world, with it comes the emergence of millions of skilled, technical and office-based jobs that require people with the skills, language and knowledge to do them. There is a vast and growing demand for university education among the world's young and the UK is one of its primary destinations. The number of overseas undergraduate students rose from 50,000 in 1995 to 230,000 in 2015, 13 per cent of the total with another 200,000 postgraduates representing a huge 40 per cent of the overall postgraduate cohort. Birmingham and all its other universities want to be part of this trend.

The University of Birmingham is the city's oldest and most prestigious higher educational institution, founded by the City Council leader Joseph Chamberlain at the end of the nineteenth century. It forms part of the group of redbrick city universities of the Victorian era, even if its distinctive tower and architectural layout harks back to the classic Renaissance heritage of Siena. For decades it was Birmingham's only university. Yet, with the increasing importance of the knowledge economy and the shift to white-collar employment in an increasingly computer-dominated age, the economic and cultural, as well as educational, significance of universities for urban metropolises has increased.

In 1966 the Aston College of Advanced Technology was given university status. Since then Birmingham Polytechnic has become Birmingham City University (BCU), the College of Food and Tourism has become University College Birmingham (UCB) and the Newman College of Higher Education has become Newman University. Employment at Birmingham's universities has been growing steadily with the three largest institutions – Aston University, Birmingham City University and the University of Birmingham – all increasing staff numbers. Universities in Birmingham now employ more than 10,000 people, making the sector one of the most significant in the city.

A distinctive and common feature of all of these universities is that they now conduct their operations and activities on a global basis. Aside from the general impact of global urbanisation and industrialisation, three factors have prompted this shift. Firstly, the pulling power of English as the global language of the computer age means that universities can attract aspiring students from the growing middle classes from all over the world. The high regard for British universities in world ranking comparisons, with thirty-four in the top 200,[1] gives an additional advantage to British universities. The second factor is the increasing mobility of intellectual labour. Unlike a company, there is no capital investment or plant which ties an academic to one place or makes upheaval prohibitively expensive. This means that academic recruitment now takes place in a global marketplace. I have friends who have left Birmingham for jobs in Florida, Karlsruhe, Durban and Melbourne. Thirdly, the sharp cuts in government funding for universities have accelerated these trends as universities have increasingly had to diversify their income streams and look to overseas students as a crucial source of revenue. All have looked abroad for fee-paying students. BCU has links with recruitment agents and representatives in seventy-eight countries, while of the 8,000 students at UCB, more than 1,100 are international students who come from sixty-five countries around the world. These trends are common to most major universities in the big cities. In 2017, Manchester had 10,640 overseas students out of a total student population of 39,700, 27 per cent of the total.

There are downsides to these developments. The removal of core government funding, the embedding of a high level of fees within the basic student offer and a long-term loan repayment system have profound consequences. It shifts the notion of higher education from that of a public good to a private asset. This reduces the opportunity for many middle and low-income students to go to the university best suited to their interests. It also encourages a purely instrumental attitude to education on the part of students while diminishing the scope for academics to engage in independent research – the very opposite of the critical minds and innovation a knowledge economy requires and that higher education as a public good should be designed to promote.

These underlying trends have made the support and promotion of universities a key aspect of the economic development programmes of all the older UK cities, as they try to overcome the decline of their manufacturing past. To prosper and grow universities have to be open to the world and able to bring people to their city. In return, the cities themselves have to be attractive to newcomers. They need emerging economic growth sectors, able to exploit and benefit from the innovations, spinoffs and new companies emerging from university research departments and adjacent science and business parks. Thus the university sector is one of the main globalising forces within the city, opening it up to new waves of migration from all over the world.

The 2011 census showed the growing importance and significance of Birmingham's universities to the life of the city. The bulge in the age group around the early twenties is due largely to students coming to the city's universities. The number of full-time students aged eighteen and above living in Birmingham during term-time grew from 48,227 in 2001 to 78,440, an increase of 62.7 per cent (30,213). This is a truly enormous rise within such a short period of time.[2]

Within this overall total there are a growing number of international students studying at both undergraduate and postgraduate level. Birmingham University has the fourth-largest population of international students at any UK higher education institution. As of November 2014, there were around 5,000 non-UK domiciled degree students registered at the university, representing more than a sixth of the total student body. Of these, by far the largest number came from China (1,923). The university's international postgraduate community is the largest in the UK.[3]

One key indicator of the attractiveness and prestige of the institution is its capacity to recruit high-quality staff and increasingly this has meant going global. Over the last decade Birmingham University has enhanced its profile so that currently almost a third of its academic staff were born outside the UK and are foreign nationals. This internationalisation trend is evident across the university. It affects the medical school, engineering and physical sciences departments as well as the social sciences. Nikos and his team are a good example of the trend towards internationalisation.

Nikos is in his mid-fifties. He has worked as a senior academic in Greece for most of his life. In 1998 he became a professor of engineering at Thessaloniki University running a department with 105 staff. During his career he has spent short periods in Italy and at the Humboldt University in Berlin, but in 2011 he applied for and was appointed to a senior post within the College of Engineering at Birmingham University. The university wanted to appoint a top specialist in the field of wind energy.

Nikos is a specialist in steel structures. Over the past decade he has moved to a specialisation in all the engineering issues relating to wind power: how to construct different types of wind turbine towers; the potential of much smaller wind turbines with designs appropriate to urban settings; the most efficient ways to harvest wind energy and maximise its output; how to reduce public concerns over wind energy. He and his team are at the cutting edge of this technology and reducing the barriers to its widespread introduction. The new designs and rotary systems mean that there is a growing potential to develop small and medium-sized wind turbine systems. These can operate effectively at lower average wind speeds and also be used in urban settings. There is an emerging small turbine sector within the UK and provided the regulatory framework can be clarified Nikos sees significant potential for the sector to grow in the next few years.

Nikos draws on both national government and EU-funding programmes to develop his unit's work and recruited his team from far and wide: other members of staff come from Italy, Thailand, Egypt and Mexico as well as Greece. His postgraduate students have a similarly diverse international background. They all appreciate the positive atmosphere they find in the university and the city.

His Egyptian colleague previously worked in Sweden and found that the local students there tended to sidestep him and were more likely to approach a Swedish lecturer for advice. In Birmingham, he finds that the students are more open and come to him with their questions. As Nikos remarks, 'There is a very international environment here amongst the academics and with the students. The UK has become like the USA.'

The university has actively encouraged these developments, marketing the attractive environs of the campus; undertaking significant new investments; and being an active player in Universitas 21, a global network of leading research universities. At the same time it has consciously fostered its links with European universities and made sustained efforts to access more EU research and development funding. Xavier is a Frenchman who took a master's degree in Town and Country Planning at Bristol, fell in love and has lived in Britain ever since. After a spell at the University of the West of England he became the European regional and funding officer at the University of Birmingham at the turn of the century. He describes the approach that the university had at that time as 'parochial', giving support to only a few individuals. But the big universities were recognising that they had to get their act together. Xavier's was a new post in the Research Unit and the aim was to spread information about both funding and learning exchange opportunities across the university. His team has grown so that he currently manages seven people. They help university staff to apply for European Union research funding, essentially accessing EU Framework programmes, rebranded for the current period as Horizon 2020.

'Over the decade we have moved so that we are now one of the top players in the UK for EU funding. In terms of resources we have done pretty well accessing projects and resources across the whole research programme.'

At the same time his team promotes the active collaboration of university staff and researchers with European counterparts. EU funding is often an enabler which brings researchers on short-term placements to Birmingham and sends Birmingham staff on secondment to their counterparts abroad. This has been the research equivalent of the Single Market, with intensive collaboration occurring among a population of 500 million rather than just sixty million.

Pragmatic and very focused, Xavier is aware that the withdrawal of the UK from the EU could affect this collaboration. While not a big fan of the EU, he recognises that withdrawal from the mobility and the freedom of movement clauses would throw a big spanner in the networks of long-term collaboration that have been built up. It is not just losing research funds that is at issue, although the net loss of £1.1 billion per year that British universities and research institutes receive currently from Europe's Horizon 2020 R&D programmes would be a severe blow. As troubling is the possibility that, as Xavier puts it, 'If we don't comply with the free mobility of people that will impact on our participation in programmes.' This explains why the Russell Group of universities feels that any exclusion of UK universities from the European Economic Area, and hence their capacity to engage with Europe's research and development programmes, would be severely detrimental to their future prospects and their continuing ability to attract quality staff.

The university's growing openness to the outside world is partially reflected by a gradual willingness to open up to migrants on its own doorstep. The university employs 1,275 staff from black, Asian or minority ethnic (BME) backgrounds, equivalent to 18 per cent of the total staff population. This figure has been rising slowly and is the highest proportion of BME staff that the university has employed to date.

The number of BME academics increased from 378 staff (16.2 per cent) in 2011 to 473 staff (18 per cent) in 2014.

Yet there are many capable researchers who remain on the fringes of the institution. Ozlem is a quietly spoken, multiskilled woman in her forties who has yet to gain a secure footing. Her parents were migrants who moved in the early 1970s from a village near Erzincan in eastern Turkey. Her dad was a peasant farmer who left the land to work in a leather factory in Istanbul, while his two brothers tried their luck as *Gastarbeiter* in Germany, where they still live. Her story is similar to those who came to

Birmingham from rural communities in Ireland, the West Indies and Asian subcontinent.

'My parents were at the bottom of society, very poor, living in a working-class environment. The way to get out of this was to be educated. We lived in a community who had migrated from the same village. There was that sense within the community that if the children got educated there would be a better chance in life for them. I was encouraged and so were my four sisters.'

Ozlem went to university in Bursa, four hours from Istanbul, and after studying econometrics then worked in a bank for three years. She found it rather limited, felt she should learn another language and open up wider options, so she came to the UK as an au pair in Solihull. She earned £35 per week looking after the children; she got free accommodation and food, and earned enough to go to college. At the start it was really hard with the family. It took six months to get her English to a basic level. After two years she went back to Turkey but before she left she met her boyfriend, whom she later married. After having a child, she did a sociology masters at Birmingham and then started teaching. For the past ten years she has been a freelance researcher and interpreter with a portfolio of short-term contracts in and around the university. These research jobs have required survey work followed by the analysis of the findings; in-depth interviews, setting up and running focus groups; drafting reports; and presentation of findings. Topics have included a nationwide study on the exclusion of young people from education; an analysis of police responses to antisocial behaviour; religion as a source of resilience, where she had to find the participants and interview them; an assessment of the impact of the Syrian and Iraq wars on British Muslims; and an analysis of attacks on Muslim women, where, again, she had to find participants and undertake interviews. Her migrant and cultural background and understanding means that she is able to undertake this work with an assurance that many others would not possess. Generally these have been temporary contracts of six months to one year and she has now undertaken this multipurpose portfolio research role for a decade. As she acknowledges, it is 'totally insecure' filling in on the margins of academic life with a daily rate that is rarely above £100 a day. University life is not immune from the casualisation of the economy discussed in the following chapter.

While data from 2004 onwards indicates that the number of black and minority ethnic staff is on an upwards trajectory the University support staff population continues to be under-representative of the BME population in the City of Birmingham as a whole. The support staff population is predominantly recruited locally and currently stands at 20 per cent BME staff. Mandeep has been here for eighteen years. Her parents migrated from the Punjab to a small Midlands town where she grew up. After leaving school, she followed her sister's example and trained as a PA on a one-year secretarial course. She then went on a Youth Training Scheme programme working in a big engineering company, as an office junior. After this she was appointed as a junior secretary in the local council. She stayed there for two years but moved to Birmingham when she married. She applied for an administrative post starting off as a secretary and then got a job as postgraduate administrator. The job involves working a lot with the students as well as the staff. She really likes it in the department. The people are very nice. They have been very good at helping her with the children and enabling her to work flexibly. There certainly has been some career progression but perhaps when she looks back she has not moved on as much as she would have liked. She still has work ambitions. She has taken on more voluntary roles. She has been a harassment adviser for ten years for both staff and students.

'I am very good with people. If you push yourself you can do things. I have found it harder here. With the university as the employer there are fewer black and minority ethnic staff than comparable organisations like Birmingham City Council. And there seem to be bits of indirect discrimination. People are far more comfortable with their own kind.'

The university's own report acknowledges the issue and has identified the under-representation of BME staff among its locally recruited staff as an area of concern. Another issue of concern is the fact that among academic and other related staff, while the proportion of BME staff in more senior roles is increasing slightly compared to previous years, there is still a clear trend of BME staff representation decreasing as seniority increases. Top management, as with most public and private sector organisations in the city, remains heavily white.

These globalising trends are also evident at the city's other universities. The ethnic mix of staff at Aston shows a higher pro-portion of black, Asian and Chinese staff than the national picture. The Asian and Chinese staff are largely contract researchers and academic staff, while the black staff are mainly in the lower grades and manual workers. The overall proportions are broadly similar to Birmingham University but, again, there is a significant lag in seniority and in the upper echelons of management with only 11 per cent of staff at grade 10 or above. At BCU the overall numbers of black and minority ethnic staff are higher with a third of all staff drawn from these communities.

However, the student data shows two strongly emergent trends. Firstly, the international composition of the student body. The 8,000 undergraduate and 2,000 postgraduate students at Aston University comprise an astonishing 142 different nationalities. The main countries of origin are China, India and Nigeria. In two of the university's five schools overseas students now outnumber home students. Aston Business School has the highest number of overseas students with 1,291 in 2013/4 compared to 732 home students.[4] At Birmingham City University the student intake of 23,500 comes from more than eighty countries.

Secondly, what is remarkable at both universities is the way they are responding to the presence of second- and third-generation black and Asian heritage students who were born or live within commuting distance of the city. Forty-five per cent of Birmingham City University students are from black and minority ethnic communities, while the student ethnicity information shows that Aston has a very high population of Asian students (35 per cent) compared to other UK universities, where the average is 8 per cent. In addition, 10 per cent of its students are black and 9 per cent Chinese, who are mainly drawn from overseas.

## UK-domiciled Students at Aston[5]

| Ethnicity | 2012 | | 2013 | |
|---|---|---|---|---|
| | Aston % | National % | Aston % | National % |
| White | 43.21 | 81.61 | 36 | 81.09 |
| Black | 9.96 | 5.94 | 10 | 6.04 |
| Asian | 35.16 | 7.79 | 35 | 7.87 |
| Chinese | 2.20 | 0.88 | 9 | 0.87 |
| Mixed | 2.89 | 2.75 | 3 | 2.92 |
| Other | 4.83 | 1.02 | 2 | 1.05 |
| Not Known | 1.76 | 0.01 | 5 | 0.16 |

The highest number of Asian or Asian British students are in Life and Health Sciences. Pharmacy, Optometry and Biology programmes attract students from Asian or Asian British backgrounds more than Language and Social Sciences programmes. Both BCU and Aston have undertaken recruitment programmes geared to local ethnic minority communities; a large proportion of their students continue to live at home; and the figures show that this recruitment activity is paying off. Aston's Equality, Diversity & Inclusion Annual Report 2015 proudly notes that 60 per cent of its total student population is from black, Asian and other minority backgrounds, many drawn from the local area, the highest proportion of any UK university.

A similar but not so pronounced trend is evident at Birmingham University where black and minority ethnic students represent 26 per cent of the UK-domiciled undergraduate population. Across the higher education sector over the decade, the proportion of UK-domiciled BME students has increased from 14.9 per cent in 2003/4 to 18.8 per cent in 2012/13. This indicates that black and Asian students are able to progress in mainstream schools. For Birmingham, it is tribute to the efforts of the three main universities and the local schools that the proportions of black and Asian students accessing these universities is far above the national average.

As well as welcoming second- and third-generation migrants into their lecture theatres and classrooms both Aston and BCU are welcoming postgraduates from all over the world. Tall and languid, Ben came from Nigeria to BCU to study for his Ph.D. He knew nothing about Birmingham before he arrived other than an awareness from watching a Premier League game between Birmingham and Aston Villa – those were the days! – that this was not just a regular game but there was something else behind it in the atmosphere and the aggression. His dad was a senior official in Nigeria's Central Bank, who had 'reached the top of his game'. Ben spent most of his secondary education in a military boarding school and then went to university where he studied chemical engineering. There was a big stress on rote learning rather than skills acquisition. He got an upper second and then worked for Exxon Mobil for two years in the Niger Delta region in crude oil extraction and processing at an off-shore facility. It was a well-paid job with good conditions of service but after a while a bit of tedium set in. He thought about doing further education in a part of the world where education is 'well known' and has a high reputation. He moved to the UK in 2008 to do a master's degree in project management at BCU. He had initially applied to Imperial College London but their processes were too long-winded. Ben looked around and decided to go for a more applied course and the Engineering, Design and Management Systems programme at BCU attracted him.

There were sixteen students on the course, three of them from Nigeria, the rest being quite a mixture but with very few British students. Ben did well, got his degree and then returned to Nigeria for a job with another oil company. But before he left he put in for a Ph.D. on sustainability and social issues. He liked the concept of a broader approach to economics embracing the need for sustainability. To his surprise his application was successful, he gained a studentship funded by the university and started properly in February 2011, finishing in June 2014 with his thesis entitled 'How SMEs can manufacture in a more sustainable manner, a new environmental business model'.

Alongside his research, he did bits of teaching; co-published a few articles; and towards the middle and end of his work began to meet other overseas students and make a wider set of friends – nurses, City Council employees, a lawyer, etc.

'You need to experience the new culture if you move to a new country . . . it has been really interesting for me to mix in this way. I did some voluntary work with a Community interest company called BLISS based in Kings Norton and Rednal. We organised community programmes for young people, afterschool clubs, vocational training and social events.'

He hasn't experienced much racism, just one or two incidents. He feels that in terms of racism, Britain does better than many other cultures. 'Overall Britain does a good job of managing it.'

He has stayed and found work in Birmingham since completing his Ph.D. Currently he has a work visa but feels British and would like British citizenship somewhere along the line. He has grown fond of the city.

'It is cosmopolitan but not as big as London. I like the urban feel of Birmingham but it is not too big. I am happy here and want to work in the low-carbon-sustainability field.'

He is more comfortable living here. The country is less conservative than Nigeria. He is able to go out with people from a range of different backgrounds without any hassle.

'The way I look at life in general, and overall, I identify with British values and how things are here. I feel more comfortable in the society here. I love Britain and its approach to things as against places that are much more conservative. My parents would like me to come back. Economically, that would be simple and I could earn more money. But life, experiences and people keep me here.'

His quiet, thoughtful manner offers a measured rebuke to those who are forever critical of the British experience of multiculturalism. This was a guy who knew nothing of Birmingham before he arrived but who now wants to make it his home. Yet in the wake of Brexit there are repeated calls to cut sharply the migration flows into the country, including the number of students. The proposal to remove students from the overall net migration figures on the basis that the large majority return home after study has been rejected by the government, while it has also focused on tightening its student visa application procedures in India. As the Chancellor of Birmingham University, Lord Bilimoria, has noted, this type of negative publicity will only help to drive potential students to universities in Canada, Australia and elsewhere.

Universities need to manage the influx of international students and ensure that they have adequate English language skills. At the same time they should be actively supporting an inflow of talented youngsters from low-income households in the UK in danger of being deterred by the high fee levels. But to pull up the drawbridge and block the flow of European and international students would be to turn UK universities against one of the main trends of the contemporary world. This is no time for barriers. Birmingham's universities benefit from their presence economically and culturally, as does the city as a whole. Global universities are a crucial ingredient to the development of an open, lively city.

# 6

## *Doing the Work that Nobody Else Wants to Do*

Ashraf lives in a long line of redbrick, narrow-fronted terraced houses. Tall and slim, he sits with me as we sip tea in his living room, where the front door opens straight out onto the pavement. There is a row of streets here that stretch in parallel lines down to the main road that slices its way through inner-city Sparkbrook. This used to be the heart of manufacturing Birmingham. The former Birmingham Small Arms Company was based at the bottom of the road, which in turn became the main centre of motorcycle production in the UK. Those days are long gone, along with most of the indigenous white working class that used to live in these Victorian terraces. Today, the owner–occupied houses are full of people who originate from the Indian subcontinent and their children, along with more recent arrivals from the Yemen and Somalia. A few Irish remain. Ashraf's mother lives across the road from him, while two other brothers live further down the street.

Ashraf's parents came from the Mirpur area of Pakistan. His dad arrived in the 1960s and was employed as a steel worker in

Sheffield; he went back and forth to Pakistan. At the time lots of people were coming to the UK from Pakistan, many relocated because of the building of the Mangla Dam, so his dad saw the chance to earn money and do better for his family. That was the reason for emigrating. He saved money on housing by living, like many other migrants, in shared accommodation. As soon as the night shift finished, they would swap beds with the day shift. House sharing meant a lot of mattresses on the floor. In 1977 his mother got her visa and the family settled in Sparkbrook. His father got a job at the Fort Dunlop tyre plant where his manufacturing career continued until he was made redundant in the mid-1980s.

Ashraf was born in 1977 in Sparkbrook. He went to the local nursery, junior and secondary schools. His father died while he was still at school and he and his eight siblings were brought up by his mother. Education wasn't the priority at the time among kids of his age unless the parents pushed you. His mother came from a rural, peasant background so there was no strong pressure on him to get on. He went to the local technical college but lasted only four months.

The first generation of post-war migrants to Britain had played their part in Britain's post-war manufacturing revival. Ashraf's dad was one among many: he had worked in steel plants, foundries, brickworks and then a big tyre plant. The Thatcher era saw the wholesale demise of vast swathes of these manufacturing giants. From 1979 to 1984 Birmingham lost more than 200,000 manufacturing jobs. The era of stable, steady, semi-skilled manufacturing jobs in large plants and factories drew to a rapid close. Their sons and daughters either looked to the white-collar service sector for jobs, which usually required some examination qualifications, or else they applied for the 3D jobs: the dirty, the dull or the difficult, the type of jobs that nobody else was that keen to do.

There have always been low-paid and casual jobs in the economy. It is just that a more casualised, non-unionised, deregulated economy generates more of them. They are a growing feature of twenty-first-century Britain. Carers, cleaners, cooks; van drivers, delivery drivers, taxi drivers; fruit pickers and food processors; packers and shelf stackers; waiters and washer-uppers; security men, porters, warehouse staff: many often working long hours, usually at the minimum wage, sometimes with irregular shift patterns and increasingly on zero hours contracts.[1] These jobs are rife within and around the Birmingham area. They require few qualifications, are relatively easy to access and often require only a short CV. In the city 17 per cent of the working age population have no formal qualifications, the highest figure of all English major cities and way above the national average. These are the types of jobs where many migrants are to be found, jostling with poorly qualified locals. This chapter looks at migrants' experiences in a number of these areas.

The assured, steady manufacturing jobs of Ashraf's father's era are long gone. Instead, he has had to find a series of 3D jobs in order to earn a living over the last twenty years. He started working as a labourer, followed by a stint as a lacquer sprayer. He did some packing where there was decent money, followed by security work at the former Pallasades Shopping Centre in town. He then had seven years as a minicab driver which he liked but 'was very, very flexible' on hours. A spell of unemployment followed. He now works as a delivery driver for Asda.

'It's good. I enjoy it, being out, no one watching you. The wage isn't brilliant, it's about £7 an hour but it's about how comfortable you are in your job. If you don't enjoy the work, it's not worth it. As long as I can pay my mortgage and provide for my children, money doesn't have a massive significance. I am not ever going to be a millionaire, but I can support my family. I have regular hours and a set contract, which are two of the advantages of working for a larger, established company.'

His wife is careful with money; she'll start looking for work soon, once their youngest is at school. In the future Ashraf would like to be self-employed again. He likes being independent, so he is looking to start a small business, but he'll start slowly and build it up.

Ajay had come to the Midlands from India. When his small clothing business failed he got a job at the Post Office as a casual worker. That was his foot in the door. After two years, he got a full-time job with them at the main Mailbox sorting office in town. The work wasn't too heavy. He was sorting parcels and letters. It wasn't boring but it was relentless – lifting, checking and shifting with a manager looking over his shoulder all the time, supervising what he and the others were doing. The basic pay was low, but he made it up with overtime.

'I did lots of overtime and shift work. On average I did twenty to twenty-five hours a week overtime. It was the way we made up our money. At the Post Office I usually worked sixty-five hours a week. Sometimes a bit less, but from September to December I would often work double shifts.'

They moved the workplace twice and both times he went with them. The office then moved again to Daventry, which would have involved a lot of commuting each day. Ajay felt this would be too much for him, especially after long shifts, so after fourteen years he took early redundancy. He found a temporary job shifting goods in a big warehouse at Hams Hall on the edge of Birmingham and then found work as a driver for Ring and Ride as part of the Special Needs service provided by the West Midlands Transport. He did that from February 2004 for the next ten years until his retirement. Ring and Ride was a better job, as he found driving a bit easier and there was no manager looking over his shoulder. The pay wasn't high – £250 a week by the time he finished – with no overtime. Looking back over forty-five years of work, once his clothing business had failed he had done a series of manual jobs, none of them well paid, but he had grafted hard enough to look after and bring up his family and earned enough for him and his wife to now have their own house in one of Birmingham's outer suburbs.

Driving is one of the classic areas of work where migrants congregate since the core skill is easily acquired. Across the world's cities taxi driving is done by migrants. Getting 'the Knowledge' is hard work (now eased by the ubiquitous GPS systems), while the long hours are hardwired into the migrant DNA. The Birmingham taxi business used to be dominated by Irish; now it is predominantly Asian and above all Pakistani. There are over 1,600 registered taxi drivers in the city and a large majority are of Pakistani heritage. Within the main Taxi Owners' Association nearly 300 of the 450 members have a Pakistani background. Akram and Yasin are two of them.

Akram has been a driver for twelve years. His parents came to Birmingham from Mirpur in the 1960s. His dad worked in the paint shop at the British Leyland car plant in Washwood Heath for twenty years. Akram was born and brought up in Birmingham. Before becoming a taxi driver he worked in a series of industrial jobs, his last one making radiators and heating equipment. He left there after a bout of redundancies. As the redundancies began and his job started changing he began learning 'the Knowledge' so that when he lost his job he was in a position to take up taxi driving. He works days, renting the vehicle from a mate. He is on the road twelve hours a day, seven days a week, apart from Friday when he takes a two-hour break to go to prayers. After all the costs are accounted for, he earns £450 a week. In other words, he works twice as long as a normal worker but still gets less than the average UK wage. Akram takes three weeks' holiday a year. He plans to take a week in the Mediterranean, maybe Egypt, or if that is a bit too risky he may try Morocco. Then he'll go away for two weeks in January when the prices are lower. It's a hard life but he gets by and it earns him a living.

Yasin has been driving taxis for ten years. Before that he had had a decade on the buses. Like Akram, his dad had come over from Mirpur to work in factories in the 1960s. He works out of the airport transporting holidaymakers. About 300 taxis ply their trade from there. 'There are lots of Pakistani drivers, but others who are English, Indian, Sikh, Bangladeshi and Somalian. Just never any Chinese.'

He gets about four or five journeys a day; things always vary but over a month he clears around £2,000. He likes the flexibility that taxi driving gives him as compared to the set shifts he had to work on the buses. But even with the long hours he doesn't earn a great deal and he has to support his children as they go through university and college. That's why he has not been on holiday for ten years. 'You have to make sacrifices for your kids.'

It is not just Pakistanis who become taxi drivers. Others, like Abdul, find their way in there, too. Born in Somalia, he and his family left the country after the collapse of the government in 1991 and arrived in Germany. Abdul grew up in Bonn and he speaks fluent German. The family moved to the UK at the turn of the century and he has lived in Birmingham for the last fourteen years. He studied at Aston University but has been driving a taxi for four years. He likes the freedom and the flexibility despite the long hours he works. 'The reason most people migrate is to get a better life for themselves and their family. In that sense they are economic migrants, even if they are fleeing persecution and repression.'

As a job, driving often has flexibility, which means that migrants can combine it with other work. Arron's family had grown up in East Africa, returned to India and then migrated to the UK. His dad worked as a car mechanic and then became one of the emerging generation that taught itself about IT. At the start of the dot.com bubble he was able to get work in a school as an unqualified assistant teaching kids about computers. But to make up his wages and support his family, at the same time he worked as a self-employed driver delivering newspapers to businesses all over the city in the middle of the night. He would work from midnight till five in the morning in a large warehouse full of 'freshies' – newcomers to the country. This was hard, physical work, sorting the papers and delivering to petrol stations and shops. He would arrive home, sleep for an hour or two and then teach IT for the rest of the day. This helped with the family finances but did little for domestic harmony or father–son relations. As Arron ruefully recalls, 'He did that newspaper job for eighteen years which had a big impact on his family and on his relations with me.'

Some of these 3D jobs are more gruelling and exploitative than others. Often, it is newcomers, desperate to earn some money and make a living, who accept these jobs. For more than a decade, this has been the East Europeans.

The fruit and vegetable picking industries and food processing are notorious for some of the worst conditions. Tomasz is a young Pole from Wrocław, who studied at university there. Like many of his generation, he was eager to see the world, earn some money and improve his English. He got work via an agency in Poland and went strawberry picking on a large farm in Tamworth, just to the north of Birmingham. He didn't last long. The farm used lots of Bulgarian and Romanian labour, secured on a contract basis. To get around minimum wage regulations, the farm stipulated how much fruit they expected to be picked within an hour. Tomasz found that he was only able to pick well below the required weight within a given hour. The farm assessed the wages based on the overall weight of produce that each person had picked, so if it took you eight hours to pick the weight of fruit the farm expected you to pick in four hours, they paid you just for four hours work and the other hours were put down as 'rest'. This is the type of shady practice that is rife in casualised labour markets. When Tomasz objected to this practice, he was told that he had the option to leave. The Romanians overseeing the site said it suited them as they would be able to pick more fruit later in the season, when the strawberries were bigger, and reach the targets more easily. The Romanians and Bulgarians would stay for the full eight months and hope to achieve higher quotas and pay in the peak growing season.

Anita's first experience with the food processing industry was brutal. She is a working-class woman in her early fifties who has lived and worked all her life in Gdynia, a seaport on the Baltic coast of northern Poland. Her husband left her when her daughter was two years old and gave her no financial support, so she brought up her daughter on her own, working at the same time. Anita worked in industry with her main job being on an assembly line making lamps for a German company. With her daughter at university, she emigrated after she lost her job and applied for many others with no success. After a two-year spell of care work in Greece, she returned to Gdynia but still found no work; did three months working on a mushroom farm in the Netherlands; and then saw a job advertised in England. In December 2007 she flew into Stansted for a promised job in the pottery industry. However, the contact at the airport did not materialise and she realised she had been conned. But she had friends already working in Birmingham, who told her to get a bus to the city.

Anita arrived in Birmingham on Saturday and on the following Monday morning she had a job as a food processor, sorting potatoes. In the 1950s and 1960s, the British government advertised for foreign labour in the local press from Kingston to Karachi via Co. Cork. In the twenty-first century, this role has been replaced by the internet and private recruitment agencies. Anita got her work via GB Resourcing, a 'temporary recruitment provider' based in Birmingham. GB Resourcing was established in 1999 and offers recruitment services throughout the Midlands.[2] It was taken over in December 2012 by Staffline, a national outsourcing organisation which claims 'to provide people and operational expertise to industry'. It offered Anita a job straight-away. The workforce met in town and they were taken by bus to a factory outside the city more than an hour away. The potatoes were being washed on a tray and the workforce then separated and sorted them. 'The working conditions were appalling. We were standing in water up to our ankles, or had water dripping down our backs or on our heads. We were wet all the time.'

There were no technical requirements for the job apart from stamina. As far as Anita could tell the main criterion for employ-ment was that none of the workforce spoke English, so they could barely communicate with each other. They normally worked twelve hours a day at the factory, sometimes fourteen, for six days a week. Anita got £1,000–£1,200 a month, which was good money compared to what she was used to but amounted to a fraction of the legal minimum wage.

She eventually got a transfer to a factory based in Aston, Birmingham, packaging food and vegetables for sale by the big supermarkets like Morrisons and Tesco. Compared to the previous job it was like working in heaven: there was no standing in water; less travel; and more sociable working hours.

Thirty miles to the south of Birmingham lies the Vale of Evesham, one of the agricultural centres of England. There are a number of quite large family farms here that concentrate on two or three crops such as spring onions. The really big players are a couple of agribusinesses with farms of 4–5,000 acres. Three-quarters of the plums grown in the Vale are produced by one business. There are now relatively few small producers left in the Vale. Roger is one of them. He farms just over seventy acres here, of which he owns fifty-five. He has been here for nearly three decades and grows a lot of veg all the year round, notably potatoes, asparagus, peas, beans, purple sprouting broccoli and cabbages, with tomatoes in the greenhouse and strawberries, redcurrants, blackcurrants and cherries in the early summer before the plums – his main crop – arrive in August. Eighty per cent of his plums go to the wholesale market but he sells the bulk of his vegetables directly through the forty local farmers' markets that his business attends every month, including several in south Birmingham. Most market gardeners have a few crops that they grow on a large scale. Roger does a lot of crops on a small scale. That works very well for him. On one thing Roger is absolutely clear: 'We could not survive without migrant labour. This is central to my business. And it is similar for other smallholders in the Vale. We couldn't rely on local people. Locals want to do other stuff, especially in the summer. According to the official figures in Wychavon the unemployment rate is 1 per cent. Therefore, there are no local sources for labour.'

Seasonal labour has changed over the last three decades. Roger has always used it. In 1982 it was either local or travellers, with little in the way of foreign labour. Then for a while there were Asians bussed in from Birmingham, who were very badly paid. After 2000 they began to get more East Europeans. who are now the dominant source of labour in the Vale. For a while he used the government's Seasonal Agricultural Workers Scheme but when they put their fees up for small producers he opted out and now employs his foreign staff directly.

He knows that not all the people on these schemes have a written contract that sets out hours per week and wages. 'Some of the farms are a bit naughty. If they don't need them, then they limit their working hours. And sometimes they charge a lot for accommodation.'

Roger uses four Bulgarians for six months of the year with the manager staying all the year round. He has three or four regular part-time workers who are local and do two or three days a week all the year round. For the East Europeans he provides accommodation onsite, two caravans for which he charges £15 per week. The working hours vary, something over forty-five hours a week, sometimes rising up to seventy. He pays £6.50 an hour. Other smallholdings pay similar wages. He has been very satisfied with their work; a number of the people have returned the following year, and there have been relatively few problems with the language, partly because Roger has often recruited university graduates who understood some English, even if at the start they did not speak it so well. Furthermore, over fifteen years there have been almost no incidents in town with the locals.

Christo has been working on Roger's market garden in Evesham since 2009. Originally a management student from Veliko Tarnovo, a town of 70,000 people in central Bulgaria, Christo came to England on a Seasonal Agricultural Workers Scheme in 2008 after completing his management course. He now stays for the whole year and manages three other Bulgarians who work half the year on the farm. It is arduous and sometimes dangerous work. Christo has been in hospital twice, once when he fell from a tree while picking plums. But there was no problem with the health service, no request for papers. He enjoys the work and it means he can put his management training to good use. 'I do not want to return to Bulgaria, I am keen to stay in UK. I like the job I have.'

Simona came to Britain in 2014. Her family is happy for her to be working in the UK. She estimates that she works sixty to seventy hours a week. Both she and Christo are able to save money each month and both earn a lot more here than they would in Bulgaria. She contacts people at home every week using the internet, Skype or Weibo. The reality of modern communication technologies means that 'We can keep in touch easily now. The gap of being away from home is a lot less than it was. Sometimes we send some money home.'

They often go into Evesham on a Sunday and meet some locals. They echo Roger when they say, 'We find no trouble.'

Cleaning and caring is typical work for female migrants and refugees. It requires no written qualifications and the locals are not clamouring to do it. It is the kind of work that is mushrooming all around the city. The growth in business and professional services in Birmingham; the expansion of the banking, finance and insurance sector; its emergence as a major retail centre; and the growth in business and leisure tourism all mean that there are a growing number of office blocks, premises, shops and hotels to keep clean and tidy. In addition, with a rising elderly population there is an increasing number of people who need full-time residential or nursing care. This is not automated work: it is almost entirely non-unionised, especially as home care services are privatised or contracted out. Cleaning is dull and dirty work and when it involves frail, elderly people it can be difficult, too.

Hies works for an agency that services offices. Clad in her black wraparound scarf, white top and trousers she cuts a striking figure. She works as a cleaner. When I meet her she is busy cleaning the corridors and toilets of a modern office block. She has lived in England for thirteen years. Originally from Harissa in Somaliland, she fled the civil wars along with her brothers and sister. She got out via Djibouti and then went to Moscow, from where she made her way to Norway. She speaks decent English and is hoping for better things. But for the moment, the cleaning job earns her a living.

Magda cleans hotels. She came to Birmingham with her young son in 2012 as she could get no work at home. Her husband stayed in Poland. She started to work in a city centre hotel and her sister helped with the child care. She got the job via a recruitment agency; it was on a zero hours contract, for minimum wage cleaning rooms and toilets. She usually got work each week as it was a busy hotel and on average worked about seven hours a day. She stayed there for nearly two years.

After stints working in food processing and engineering, Anita returned to the care work that she had previously done in Greece and took a job as a care assistant at a nursing home with nearly forty residents.

'I do everything. I am a care assistant, I clean the apartments; I do the laundry. Sometimes I have to wash and toilet the residents. I have to lift them. I am properly trained to use the hoist. The job is hard especially when people are dying. Sometimes it is physically challenging when people are heavy; sometimes it is hard when people are suffering from Alzheimer's or dementia and they can be aggressive as well and they hit you. They are ill and you just have to understand that.'

Anita has had a proper contract from the first day she has been employed. She works thirty-five hours a week and then every other Sunday. Occasionally she is asked to do some extra hours and she is paid just a notch above the minimum wage. When asked if she saves money, she laughs. The rent for her sixty-square-metre flat is expensive. 'It is very difficult to save with this job. I have my additional jobs such as sewing, cleaning and extra cleaning jobs for households, two each week and then a third every fortnight. Otherwise, I cannot save.'

This use of migrant labour is common across the cleaning and care sector. At my mother's nursing home in north London more than half the staff were Romanian or Polish. In Birmingham, more come from Poland and Lithuania as well as the local Asian and black population. The working conditions vary. Anita may have a proper contract, but the low pay means she has to make up her wages by taking on additional jobs. The newsagent Rehman's wife works as a carer in the south of the city for a company that has two residential homes and also offers community care to frail people in their own homes. She washes people, provides support and gives them their medicine where necessary. She gets the minimum wage and travelling expenses but does not get paid for the time she has to spend travelling between people's homes. She likes the work and is good at it but is on a zero hours contract with no holiday or sick pay and only gets her work rota at the start of each week. This is the ignored underbelly of Britain's labour market, where crucial work is often done by first- or second-generation migrants for low wages and with few employment rights.

Dariusz and Magda had both studied at university in eastern Poland but found no work after getting their degrees. They got married in 2002 and went to Jersey, in the Channel Islands, working in a hotel. They were in their early twenties; they had to get a work visa, which was needed then; they spoke no English. Dariusz worked as a kitchen porter, cleaning the ovens and machines and washing the dishes, Magda as a chambermaid, cleaning the rooms. He recalls that it was a short contract – March to November in 2002, then March to December in the following years. They went back each year till 2006. It was twelve hours a day for him; ten hours for her, six days a week. They did it so that they could save money for the house. Once a child came, they stayed back in Poland but with little work they became frustrated. Magda joined her sister in Birmingham and got a job, then Dariusz followed. He had a 'really crap job' at a warehouse in Erdington, but then got a job through an agency, working at a busy period for John Lewis. Then it was made permanent.

'It was very, very busy before Christmas. Then we had three shifts. Now we get the bad news that fifty-five people will be sacked as we stop the night shift. In the warehouse I have responsibility for the logistics of the floor. I am the duty assistant responsible for logistics and to direct material. I get a bit more than the minimum wage. £7.50 an hour. I work thirty-seven and a half hours a week, sometimes I get some overtime. I got many English, Irish and Somalian friends from the job, but I don't see them socially.'

Magda managed to move to John Lewis from her zero hours hotel cleaning job. She started off as an agency employee working on the minimum wage; then after that it rose to £7.00 an hour. She works there on the computers, checking the items in and out of the warehouse.

Currently question marks remain over the future of the site as there are plans for it to close and move to Milton Keynes. But Dariusz anticipates no problem getting any future manual job, since 'Three years in John Lewis is a good recommendation. They have a good reputation; everybody knows about them. It is like working for the Queen.'

Both feel they are doing better here than they would in Poland.

'Life is easier here than in Poland, it is better economically. We can buy more things and better quality food than in Poland. Compare petrol. With one hour's work here I get seven and a half litres. In Poland, for one hour's work, I get two and a half litres.'

They want to remain in the UK for their future. They are trying to sell their apartment in Poland and use the proceeds as a deposit to put down on a house in Great Barr, north Birmingham. They currently rent a former council house in Kingstanding for £600 a month via a property agency but for them and their two kids they have an eye to the future. 'We don't want to be paying rent for the next twenty years.'

There has always been casual work in bars, cafés and restaurants. In the 1950s, once marriage had brought an abrupt end to Peggy's career in nursing, she had a job in the social club at the Dunlop factory. Initially she was a cleaner but they said she was too fussy and cleaned everything too well, so the manager put her behind the bar.

'I then worked for the same pub gaffer for the next twenty years, moving around to various pubs. It fitted in with the kids.'

Nowadays, these jobs form a much larger part of the economy with fast food a growing segment of the market. After his experiences as a fruit picker, Tomasz had a spell doing car valeting before he took a job with Subway at the National Exhibition Centre on the outskirts of the city. A couple of dozen worked at this venue: Birmingham-based Indians; some Indian students; some ethnic Russians from Estonia and Latvia; all overseen by a Polish manager. This is the classic McJobs territory. The hours were long and irregular; the work required you to be speedy and efficient; you got just above the minimum wage. You had to work as required, so that when a big conference or show was on Tomasz would work for five or six days consecutively, for up to seventeen hours a day. He would often have to do two weeks' worth of work in one week. You could pack a lot of hours into one week and then you would have nothing the following one. But in that week he would get no money. The job involved preparing the vegetables; baking the buns; cleaning; sorting out the bar and the tables. It wasn't too exhausting, but he had to be quick and accurate, good with the customers and careful on hygiene. To prepare the sandwiches, he had to stand in a line putting in either tomatoes or cucumber slices. 'For this I got called "the sandwich artist". It was the job title my manager gave me as a bit of humour.'

This chapter reflects the tough realities, the long hours' culture and the increasingly casual, unregulated nature of work at the lower end of the labour market. Traditionally, this has always been the place where newcomers start their working lives. The last decade has seen a major influx of Poles, Lithuanians, Romanians and others into the city following the entry of Central and Eastern European countries into the European Union. In the 2001 census for Birmingham Poles came sixteenth in the list of the twenty most reported countries of birth outside UK. In 2011 they were sixth. This accelerating rate of population change and the consequent increased competition in the labour market and for scarce public services has occurred at a time of recession and austerity. This combination has aroused widespread public concerns about the rate of migration and its social impact, issues magnified by much of the tabloid press.

These issues played a decisive part in the EU Referendum campaign in June 2016 and were a major factor in the decision by 52–48 per cent for the UK to leave the European Union. The city split 50/50 but the socio-economic realities of the vote were stark. Almost all the outer ring wards and those where there are large concentrations of white working-class voters voted decisively for leaving. All twelve wards which comprise the constituencies of Northfield, Yardley and Erdington – all currently held by Labour MPs – recorded clear majorities for Leave with the Shard End ward recording a 76 per cent leave vote. All the anecdotal evidence from canvassing confirmed the polling data that showed that concerns over immigration were a crucial factor in influencing people to vote to leave.

There was a real variety of opinions expressed on immigration by the interviewees for this book, but it undoubtedly troubled many. Daljit, the council office worker, saw migration from EU countries as problematic.

'When my parents came you needed people to help work in manufacturing. Now you have high unemployment in areas and I don't think this helps.'

Pam, the photo shopkeeper, supported the UK being a member of the EU but said, 'There are obviously some policies where I'm not happy, immigration policies. I do not agree that we should allow 400,000 people to come from Eastern Europe or Syria or any of the other Muslim countries and flood this country.'

Mo, the market trader, opposed the EU rules from another standpoint.

'Today it is downright exploitation from private companies who want to export jobs and import labour. People are enticed to come and undercut labour costs here. When you have corporations that see themselves above democracy that is what is going to happen.'

Others were more relaxed. Ajay said: 'We don't mind. Just like us. I came from India. I wouldn't criticise them. Everybody wants a better life.'

David, the product engineer with Jaguar Land Rover, was similarly relaxed: 'For me that is fine, people coming here to work. That is fine.'

As was Adam, the charity worker: 'I don't have a problem. Who am I to say no if my own father did the same thing?'

However, there is no doubt that the pace of change and its impact have influenced the thinking and views of many second-generation immigrants. While the Birmingham electoral wards with the main concentrations of immigrant population showed solid majorities for remaining in the EU in the Referendum, the figures were not as high as would have previously been expected. Newspaper reports found significant elements of 'Leave' sentiment among black and Asian Britons, often linked to migration issues.[3] Mandeep, the administrative officer, was clear that immigration policies have been causing big problems. In an interview held well before the Referendum campaign, she expressed concerns that became commonplace during it.

'There is the feeling that people are taking their jobs. Because there has been no control over immigration, local people have got annoyed and restless, fed up with the whole situation. Things are out of control, the NHS is out of control . . . people are thinking, "why should they get services rather than me?" This is causing so many problems, whereas twenty years ago there was a lot of integration.'

In the discussions on race and migration, too much of the focus has been on culture and identity; too little on the economic and social. For both the twenty-seven countries remaining within the EU and for the UK heading for the exit door, this is an issue that will not go away. How can the needs of both indigenous and migrant workers employed in 3D jobs be addressed?

Any discussion has to start with the reality that the past sixty years have fundamentally changed the face of both Britain and Europe – and there is no going back. The future of Europe is multi-ethnic. The political issue is how to manage the processes of change and where necessary deal with them on a cross-European basis.

When Jacques Delors was President of the European Commission, Europe's mantra was to combine economic efficiency with social justice, an updated version of the post-war German commitment to the creation of a social market economy. However, with the turn to the market in China, the productive surge unleashed by the ICT revolution and then the collapse of the USSR and its satellite states, the world experienced a headlong rush to globalisation. Ronald Reagan and Margaret Thatcher formed the vanguard. The abolition in 1987 of key controls on the City of London gave a huge impetus to the financialisation of global markets. Temporary hiccups were overcome; economies boomed; Tony Blair boasted of forty successive quarters of UK economic growth; and the EU gradually dropped its social commitments and adopted a neo-liberal path – with some distinctive German characteristics for the new euro currency and the European Central Bank. The consequence was the pursuit of a naively optimistic – not to say Panglossian – version of globalisation. All was to be for the best in this best of all possible worlds.[4]

This had profound consequences for the European labour market. British policy-makers and politicians followed by their European counterparts went for wholesale liberalisation, oblivious of its social consequences. One of the founding principles of the European Union had been the guarantee of the free movement of people for work, but in fact, since 1957, labour mobility between EU countries had been relatively limited as compared with the United States. The collapse of the Berlin Wall showed how that could change, with a massive surge of East Germans to the West that left swathes of former East German towns derelict and empty. That was a sign of things to come. The extent of the wage differentials between East and West meant that West European labour markets would be a huge temptation to young, energetic East Europeans after their accession to the EU. But the British political establishment took no notice. They completely failed to recognise the size of population movement that would follow the entry into the EU of eight former East European states in 2004. One Home Office estimate put the probable number of new-comers at 13,000.[5] More cautious EU policy-makers imposed a seven-year transition period before general labour mobility could apply but the UK government, along with Ireland and Sweden, ignored the ruling. To make matters worse Tony Blair refused to sign up to the European Working Time Directive which set a maximum forty-eight-hour working week across the Single Market. The Labour governments of Blair and Gordon Brown rejected this as unwarranted interference in the natural workings of the labour market, a policy which got the full-throated support at the time of both the Conservative Party and the tabloid press, so vocal in their complaints a few years later about uncontrolled migration.

Unrestricted working hours were the magnet that drew East Europeans to the UK – not welfare benefits. Since 2004 very large numbers have come to work in the UK and Ireland. As this chapter shows, they are employed in a wide variety of jobs, often arduous and dirty, and have gained a reputation for being consci-entious and hard-working. Employers in a range of low-wage industries have been absolutely delighted. They have acted as a reserve army of labour within the UK economy and their presence has reduced the pressure for higher wages as Mervyn King, former Governor of the Bank of England, acknowledged.[6]

Since 2011, following the end of the transition period, these migratory pressures have built up in other EU countries. They have combined with more long-term migratory influxes from beyond the EU – such as with Latin Americans and Northern Africans into Spain and Italy; Ukrainians into Portugal – and the pressures of refugees fleeing wars and persecution in Syria and across the Middle East to produce a volatile mix of pressures and resentments.

However, on intra-EU migration the neo-liberal mindset has frozen political thinking. Political debate has been paralysed by the belief that globalisation is inevitable and that you can do nothing about it. It has been presented as a binary choice: either accept globalisation as it is or turn your back on it and retreat into a nationalist bolthole. There is a Third Way: neither accept it nor reject it, but tame it.[7]

At the moment, across the Single Market the free movement of labour brings with it substantial economic advantages for employers in terms of a skilled, cheap workforce. For the individual migrant, the large wage differentials between Eastern and Western Europe mean that they get new work opportunities and higher wages than are available in their own countries. But the social and cultural costs of large-scale people movement are not picked up by any public authority. They are just experienced by citizens living in the areas where migrants congregate – additional kids in schools, where they often do not speak the local language; extra pressure on housing; more people in doctors' surgeries. When combined with the added competition in the labour market, with East Europeans prepared to work for long hours at much lower wages than locals, this adds up to a dangerous cocktail. Things cannot continue like this in Europe or the UK. Policy-makers and politicians have to show how these situations can be managed and that the problems which arise can be tackled. A managed migration policy with Europe is perfectly possible and should be a central aspect of future relations.

Economics, geography, culture and security mean that a close working partnership between the UK and the Continent is in the interests of both parties, whatever the rhetoric of the 'hard Brexiters'. After the Referendum, the EU remains the UK's major trading partner by far; Britons make over fifty million journeys to Europe each year; the country remains just twenty-two miles from Calais and 3,000 miles from New York. The UK needs a partnership and cooperation arrangement with the EU across a whole range of areas from climate change to terrorism where we have vital interests with our closest neighbours, as they have with us too. The precise form of those arrangements is a matter for negotiation but a recognition of our mutual interdependence is the essential starting point. For instance, on the economy the central issue is not trade but the fact that modern production flows across borders. The reality all European nations face is that the optimal economic area is now continental in scale. In Europe, all the main production processes rely on integrated supply chains operating across Europe. Just ask Airbus, BMW and Nissan or look at the Port of Dover.

However, for there to be any accommodation from the EU to those arguing for a soft Brexit, progressives have to face one big question: how to resolve the wish of the majority of the UK electorate to control migration with the EU rules on freedom of movement. The free movement of people has brought substantial benefits to many citizens in European countries, including Britain. These are particularly welcomed by young people for whom it offers increased horizons and opportunities for travel, study and work. However, the unexpected size of the flow to the UK after 2004 has brought real concerns and difficulties to the fore. These problems are largely of the UK's own making. In 2004 the Labour government waived the seven-year transitional controls on migration from new EU member states and refused to sign up to the EU Working Time Directive. The effect was to create the ideal conditions for a swift, unexpected surge in East European workers into the UK, legally able to work very long hours at low rates of pay.

If the UK is to negotiate seriously with the EU, it needs to change this situation. The least damage to the UK economy and wider relationships depends on the UK remaining in the Single Market. To secure that requires that the UK signs up to the Working Time Directive and imposes a mandatory forty-eight-hour working week; applies the EU rule[8] whereby any person here for more than three months who has no job can be sent back home;[9] significantly increases the number of factory inspectors so that minimum wage and health and safety regulations are properly enforced and removes the legal obstacles that obstruct trade union recognition in the workplace; and introduce a substantial Migration Impact Fund to provide additional funds in areas of high migration to address pressures on schools, housing and health services.[10] Taken as a package these measures would stop migration being used as a Trojan horse for Dickensian working conditions at the lower end of the labour market of the kind highlighted in this chapter.

By ending the advantageous conditions that the UK has offered to East European migrant labour since 2004, the UK would see a decline but not an end to European migrants coming to the country and also more opportunities for local workers. Productive businesses would cope with the maximum working week limits as they do elsewhere in the EU and those operating on the basis of cheap, sweated labour would have to adjust their business model. The unmanaged flow of migrants from Eastern Europe arose from the Blair government's excessive neo-liberalism. The 'fair movement' policy set out here would lead to a fall in migration numbers without infringing the EU rules on free movement or depriving key sectors of the economy and the NHS of vital labour.

Such an approach would go some way to meet the concerns of Ashraf who says he understands why immigration is required but is clear that it needs to be managed.

'I wouldn't say control to a point you have to drip-feed people in because they can do certain types of work, like a doctor, but I wouldn't be comfortable with an open door, no borders society. As a society we need to be responsible for the amount of good immigration we can get in. My father wasn't a doctor but he contributed to society through his own work . . . I think there's a limit. It needs to be managed but not in a discriminating way. We still need labourers and non-skilled workers.'

Roger certainly agrees. He knows that his fruit and veg business along with many bigger enterprises in the Vale of Evesham cannot survive without European labour. The nursing and residential care homes, the hotels, the fast-food outlets and many companies and businesses in and around Birmingham know that, outside the EU, they will continue to need European migrants. That is one of many reasons why the terms of the UK's future relationship with the EU – close or distant – is so important. What is needed is to reshape the terms on which migrants come and the conditions in which they work and live. This is a 3D story that will run and run.

# 7

## *The Changing Face of Racism*

When my grandparents were driven out of their homes by the ethnic cleansing of Jews in the Austro-Hungarian Empire they settled in the narrow streets of Aldgate, near the docks where they landed and next to the Tower of London. My grandparents and their seven children grew up in a two-bedroom terrace in Alie Street. That was their enclave. It was nearly half a century before my mum and her brothers and sisters began to move and disperse across the suburbs of London.

New migrants cluster for shelter in the cheapest housing that mirrors their poverty; for familiarity in a strange land; and as protection against racism and discrimination. That is why ghettos and enclaves emerge. In the sixties there were plenty of reasons why newcomers found their way to Handsworth, Lozells, Saltley, Sparkbrook and Balsall Heath. These were tough times with open and explicit racism, as Peggy, Mashood and many others experienced. When Enoch Powell as a senior Conservative in April 1968 gave voice and political respectability to this racism, many local politicians followed. The Conservative leader of the Council, Alderman Frank Griffin, convened a high-level conference of City Council chairmen and chief officers the following month which agreed that the city was 'full up' and called on the government to divert new immigrants to other parts of the country.[1] At the time it was estimated that there were 82,000 'coloured immigrants' in the city. It was already known that the population of Birmingham was falling sharply as people moved to the surrounding shire counties – the 1961 census figure of 1,179,352 was to drop to 1,097,960 in the 1971 census – but facts were not the core issue. The *Birmingham Post* did point out that a dispersal programme would require the introduction of South African-style pass laws but that did little to stop the racist bandwagon.

Amidst the mayhem there were some voices of sanity. The Conservative chair of Housing, Anthony Beaumont-Dark, presented the city's housing strategy two months later. He pointed out that 75 per cent of migrants lived in sub-standard property or slum areas and that they would get a larger share of the planned new council housing as most would have met the five-year residence requirement that Birmingham set at that time. He asserted that they were Birmingham citizens like everyone else. 'I don't think the problem is insuperable. Birmingham people are realists.'[2] This was an era when councils still built tower blocks, maisonettes and houses and both David's family and Sam's moved into council accommodation during this period. A major study in 1977 found a marked increase in the number of West Indian families moving into local authority housing after 1970 while Indian and Pakistani households tended to remain in private renting or owner-occupation, often drawing on resources from their own social networks, as both Salma and Ajay recall.[3]

The cycles of racism have ebbed and flowed since then and different migrants have experienced discrimination and hostility to varying extents. When Kalsoom came here in the late 1960s and lived within a strongly Asian area she never felt any racial harassment. But when in the late 1970s she and her husband moved out of the protected neighbourhood into a predominantly white area, even though it was only a mile or two away, then it was a different story.

'When we moved to Yardley we had improvements done on our house. Double-glazed windows, a new garage. The next day I went out taking my children to school. And there chalked on the pavement was the sign, "Don't burn coal, burn a Paki".'

Later she recalls one day going to meet the children on their way back from school and a teenage white boy just ran up to one of her sons, thumped him and left him with a bleeding nose. And again in the late 1990s when she started to wear a headscarf she was going to the chemist and a teenager riding a bike pulled her scarf and ripped it off as she fell to the pavement. Over the last fifteen years she has had no further incidents with the headscarf. Today she feels there is more acceptance and fewer problems.

David's recollections of growing up in inner-city Birmingham in the 1970s illustrate an emerging co-existence combined with a certain wariness.

'You knew who your friends were. There was quite a mix with Asian boys. At that age, I used to walk home from school down to Saltley and Alum Rock and buy samosas. Everybody mixed, Asians, whites, there was no particular separation. But you knew there were particular boys who you avoided, I didn't want to mix with them after school.'

He also recalls a very specific incident in the first few weeks of his apprenticeship at Longbridge. Some of the other apprentices had never been together with a black boy before so their only way of mixing was to tell racist jokes. It got to a point where it was getting tedious and David was getting really fed up.

'In the end, there was one guy and I said to him, "look, I have had enough of this. You and me, outside now." He went into complete shock. It was in works time and could mean that we would lose our apprenticeships. He backed off. He came to me an hour later and said he was sorry, he didn't realise he was having such an impact on me. And it was strange. After that it stopped. They obviously talked amongst themselves as well and realised, "oh, he doesn't like it". The other apprentices all laid off me after that.'

Ashraf was born in 1977 in Sparkbrook. It was quite a mixed area with Irish, Yemeni and Pakistani. He recalls that 'you had your gangs as we grew up. It was a bit more tense than it is today.' Ajay had little experience of racism at work. 'Sometimes people had trouble when they went for promotion but I didn't go for anything like that so it didn't arise.' On trouble outside work, he and his wife lived a quiet life revolving around the Hindu temple so they 'haven't moved in that circle. We don't go to the clubs or the pubs.'

In the larger Midlands towns, people growing up in tightly knit communities got by. In Wolverhampton, the accountant Raj recalls that his parents and others faced a lot of challenges including racism when they first came here, so they were very close, lived in and out of each other's houses. But for Raj, it was a good time growing up, primarily with Asians at both primary and secondary schools, and he experienced no racism. Daljit's experience of growing up in Derby was similar. She lived in a close-knit community and she recalls playing in the streets and going to the local park with no trouble.

In some ways those brought up in smaller cities found life harder. Hasan grew up in Nuneaton and had some scary moments, particularly during his time at secondary school. There were eight Asians in his year and it wasn't pleasant.

'We regularly got hassled. My mum and dad didn't appreciate the aggravation we were getting. There were fights before or after school; people from the surrounding community; people shouting abuse from cars. The school did nothing much. A couple of kids got black eyes, but still nothing was done, partly because it happened outside school. We just kind of grew up with it, really.'

Mandeep, the university administrator, found it tough in her small Midlands town.

'My sister hated school and was very distressed there. She suffered a lot of abuse. At secondary school I had someone call me a horrible name and it really upset me. The school did nothing about it. My dad used to say, "just get on with it, there is nothing you can do". My brother got glassed in a nightclub in the small town with his cousin and a group of white friends. My niece when she was three, she came home from nursery one day and told us she had been hit with a ruler by another child. When asked why, she had been told, "I don't like you. You are a different colour." I grew up feeling quite embarrassed about my culture, my skin, my background. I wanted to be white like them. That lasted until I left the small town and its small-mindedness.'

When Mandeep got married and came to Birmingham, it was a real eye-opener for her to see how many positives there were to her culture, her religion, the support it offers and its values. She loves the support network and the respect for elders. She now tries to instil in her children all the goodness of each background, both the West and the East.

These accounts indicate a mixed picture, not one of unremitting gloom but where there is always an underlying unease. There is an uncomfortable edge to many people's experiences, an unmistakable ugliness that is sometimes very visible but elsewhere lies just under the surface. White British citizens may find it hard to empathise with the reality of living in a street where one of your neighbours has just chalked 'burn a Paki' outside your front gate. That is not the type of abuse that a white Brummie has to cope with.

One source of that unease and wider resentment arises from treatment at the hands of the police. When asked about his experiences, Mo, of Kuskus Foods, laughs. He describes growing up, being harassed by West Midlands Police when walking back from Small Heath, or being stopped by a Black Maria, put up against the wall and searched: 'That was our experience. You just took it as par for the course.'

It continued later when he was an adult and a qualified youth worker. Mo had a love of German cars and worked on youth projects in Frankfurt and Munich which developed his fondness for BMWs. They last a long time and are easy to maintain. He always remembers when he first bought a BMW. The amount of times he got stopped was absolutely ridiculous.

'I remember one night on the M6 coming back into Birmingham. We got stopped. "How does a chap like you afford this?" I started laughing and then said, "One goes to university, gets a degree and works bloody hard in order to afford it." "Don't be so rude and facetious," replied the police officer.'

Sam's story is almost identical. When he got his first company car with ICI, he used to get stopped by the police every few weeks. He recalls having conversations with police officers. One sat in his car for forty-five minutes. It was the ninth time Sam had been stopped that year. So he asked the officer, 'what are the chances of a driver being stopped by the police at random while driving along the road without causing an offence?' The officer didn't know so Sam told him that the chances are 0.4 per cent in a lifetime. It just doesn't happen. 'I didn't stop you because you are black,' the officer responded. 'I didn't say that. I asked you why do you think I have been stopped nine times this year?' He got no answer. As Sam says, that's how you experience the system.

These are classic stories, but they are not ancient history. The data for the first half of 2015 for the West Midlands Police area revealed the continuing bias in stop-and-search incidents.[4] Pakistani Asians and people of mixed race were more than twice as likely to be stopped as white British people, while black Caribbeans were nearly four times as likely to be halted. Two-thirds of the searches did not result in any official police action. While the overall use of stop and search is declining, this ongoing and persistent bias serves as a constant reminder of discrimination, along with the higher rates for the death of black people in police custody and for being subjected to the use of Tasers. In the early 1980s this persistent harassment was the catalyst for the social explosions and riots in Handsworth as well as London and Liverpool.

The gap between the police service and the city's ethnic minority communities remains today. It is sharply illustrated by the failure of the police force itself to reflect the demographics of the population that it serves. In 2014 the West Midlands Police launched its first recruitment drive since the austerity of 2010. More than 30,000 people registered an interest in applying for the positions. In spring 2015 the force announced its first set of recruitment results. The ethnicity of the first 162 officers revealed that 139 were white, thirteen were Asian, seven were recorded as being of mixed race, two were listed as 'none stated' and just one was black.[5] This remains an issue in other cities, too. For example, just 6 per cent of the police force in Greater Manchester come from ethnic minority communities and a mere 2.7 per cent in Bristol. The police are now under more political and community pressure to respond to these shortcomings from campaign groups, local MPs and the Police and Crime Commissioner. Its senior executives try to engage with the issue, but Mo puts it bluntly: 'I agree with Macpherson, the police are institutionally racist. When you draw your workforce from one particular area you are always going to have problems. If only one in fifty is black that is bound to happen. They need to respect communities.'

Throughout this era there were ongoing struggles to combat discrimination and racism in the political, workplace and cultural – as well as policing – arenas. During the 1960s and 1970s the Asian and Afro-Caribbean communities grew stronger in self-organisation with bodies such as the Campaign against Racist Laws, Black Peoples' Alliance, Indian Workers' Association (IWA), Pakistani Workers' Association, Kashmiri Workers' Association and Bangladeshi Workers' Association. They put pressure on central and local governments for policy changes. The Workers' Associations of South Asian origin, though organised and identified in terms of the country of origin, were strongly allied for the purpose of defending the collective interests of all involved. The source of their recruitment was the workplace. The leadership of these associations aspired to a secular, democratic ethos and were involved in the trade union and labour movements At that time the sectional (ethnic) identity was submerged in the collective, broader (class) identity. Nazir recalls that the Bangladeshi Workers' Associations (BWA) and IWA led the campaigns for equal opportunities for ethnic minorities under the rubric of 'black', not identifying themselves as Muslims, Punjabis or Sikhs.

'We were all Asians and worked with Afro-Caribbeans, working on campaigns against racist laws, against the National Front in east Birmingham. Tony Huq led the BWA and a charismatic leader Jagwant Joshi led the IWA.'

These movements campaigning against racist immigration laws and race discrimination had an impact on the overall political atmosphere. After the extensive riots in 1981 in protest at brutal policing in several English cities, the government set up the Scarman Enquiry. Its report recognised that 'racial disadvantage is a fact of British life' and set out proposals to challenge it, so that there would be equal treatment for all.

Another area of contestation has been the protracted battle for recognition of the cultural diversity of the city within its public spaces. The Irish St Patrick's parade began in 1952 and was the first of its kind in Britain. It was designed to reinforce community identity and ensure strong links with the home country. Several participants remember being refused the day off work to go to the parade. Those who risked it anyway found themselves without a job when they turned up for work the following morning.[6] The annual parade continued in a relatively low-key fashion until 1974 when a shadow was cast over Birmingham's Irish community by the IRA pub bombings. Two pubs in the city were bombed, killing twenty-one people and injuring 182. This caused a wave of anti-Irish sentiment and the St Patrick's Day parades were cancelled. It was to be more than two decades before the celebrations were revived in 1996. The festival has grown steadily since and attracts 80,000 people each year to the traditional Irish quarter of Digbeth. Chris as a second-generation migrant recognises the significance of the march especially as the second, third and fourth generation make their homes further out of the city centre and away from Digbeth.

'The march is very significant, especially after the Troubles. It is now the third or fourth largest Paddy's Day march in the world but whether it has now reached a peak and how to refresh it I don't know.'

Official recognition and celebration of different local cultures has occurred gradually over the last three decades. It was only with great hesitation and caution that the City Council engaged with communities and found the space and venues where they could display their culture. Yet slowly they have become an accepted part of the cultural life of the city; they have fitted into a certain type of multicultural story, each with their own space.

By the mid-1980s there was a formidable black music scene with local performers of national standing such as Steel Pulse and Joan Armatrading. Afro-Caribbean festivals were held in Handsworth Park for a decade from 1984 but proved controversial especially as regards the extent of council support. More recently it has been transformed into the Birmingham Caribbean Festival held in the city centre, designed as an event to celebrate and enjoy the diverse range of traditional African and Caribbean cuisine as well as provide a programme of live entertainment bringing together a range of black, Caribbean and African artists.

The city has two of the biggest South Asian festivals in the UK organised as free, public events in the main city parks to celebrate the diversity of the South Asian community through its culture, food, sports, art and entertainment. Attracting large crowds, the Mela is now in its sixteenth year and brings the sights, sounds and spicy aromas of South Asia into the city's public space along with traditional arts and crafts. In 2016, the Mela in Cannon Hill Park attracted up to 80,000 participants over the course of the day. In the winter, the city celebrates a flagship Chinese New Year festival in the Chinese quarter near to the city centre attended by 30,000 people, while in the autumn it celebrates Diwali, an ancient Hindu festival that symbolises the triumph of light over darkness and good over evil. Also known as the Festival of Lights, it is observed on the new moon that starts the month of Kartika in the Hindu calendar. The celebrations have been organised between the City Council and the Hindu Council of Birmingham for more than twenty years. Nowadays all these festivals are much more corporate, sponsored events that have lost much of the edge and rebellious feel of an earlier era. Thus Moneygram acts as the main sponsor of Diwali, while currently the Mela is sponsored by the fast food company, Big John's. The festivals are now an accepted, recognised part of the city's cultural scene. Each community has its own place in the city's public space but while there are efforts to open up to others, such as with the presence of Caribbean artists at the St Patrick's festival, basically each operates in a stand-alone framework.

The shift that has occurred reflects a much broader pattern of cultural change as society began to adjust and adapt to the realities of being a multicultural country. These developments within the city were helped by the wider adjustments that have occurred in two key cultural arenas: football and pop music. In both spheres, developments within the Birmingham area led the way.

The big significant breaks in both football and popular culture began in the late 1970s. There had been the occasional Jewish footballer over the years;[7] Irish footballers – from both North and South – were common; but until the mid-1970s there had been hardly any major black footballers aside from the South African Albert Johanneson who played for Leeds in the 1960s. West Ham started the trend with the selection of Clyde Best but it was West Bromwich Albion, located on the borders of north-west Birmingham, that established the phenomenon with the purchase and selection of three players – centre-forward Cyrille Regis, winger Laurie Cunningham and full-back Brendon Batson – who between them electrified top-flight football in the late 1970s. All were Londoners, signed from lower division clubs, Cunningham and Regis in 1977, followed by Batson the next season. The flamboyant Ron Atkinson had taken over from former manager Ronnie Allen mid-season and he quickly recruited Batson, who had been his club captain at Cambridge United. It was the first time a top-flight club had fielded three black players and their success squashed the classic stereotype that black players had 'no bottle'. Atkinson branded the trio his 'Three Degrees' after the black American pop band and their collective presence acted as the trailblazer for other clubs to follow.

I had seen the future ten years earlier. It was the classic wet winter's night in Walthamstow. I had gone to see Walthamstow Boys play in the national Under-15s competition, then the pinnacle of schools' football where all the top League scouts picked up the emerging talent. Two of our school were in the team – Harry, a solid centre-half, and Dave a centre-forward with two good feet, were already training with Queens Park Rangers – and I went along to watch them. But it was Brendan Batson from the nearby McEntee Tech who stood out. Tall and elegant, he ran upright in the manner Michael Johnson was later to make famous, able to control the ball in an instant. With an acceleration to take him clear of opponents, he stood head and shoulders above everyone else on the pitch. He ran the game from midfield. Through the winter and spring he ensured that the small London borough got to the final and shared the spoils with the mighty Manchester. I was even more impressed when I learned that Batson was on Arsenal's books, even if surprised to find that they saw him as a centre-half. I watched his progress through the youth team and reserves and then a handful of performances in the first team. But he was too far ahead of his time. It was to be another two decades before David Rocastle and Michael Thomas as black players could make it through the Arsenal youth ranks into the 1989 League winning team. Batson fell by the wayside: the rumours were that he was 'a bad influence'. After just ten League appearances, often as a substitute, he was transferred for a miserly fee to Cambridge United from whence Atkinson rescued his career.

All the black players, no matter how talented, received hateful and vicious abuse from opposing fans in those years. It remained a staple diet of football matches through most of the 1980s. It was to be another decade before the black breakthrough was confirmed and terrace racism began to abate. Aston Villa were to win the League in 1981 and then the European Cup in 1982 with a squad of fourteen, all white, mainly local players. Yet when they won the League Cup just a decade later – with Atkinson as their manager – it was to be with a black back four and a goal-scoring black striker, Dalian Atkinson, who tragically died as a victim of a police Taser incident as this book was being written. Today over a quarter of professional footballers are black and the local Sunday leagues and junior teams reflect the multiracial reality of the city. Yet challenges remain. While today black footballers have found their place on the pitch, they are rarely seen in the managerial hot seat, let alone in the boardroom. Their absence serves as a reminder that there's always another hilltop over the next ridge.

During this period black musicians began to make their breakthrough into popular music culture. Birmingham-based artists such as Steel Pulse and Joan Armatrading made it into the pop charts. In the late 1970s Rock Against Racism brought black and white artists together and their concerts achieved a wide following. The Coventry band the Specials developed their 2 Tone music combining elements of punk with ska music, a genre that originated in Jamaica in the late 1950s and was the precursor to reggae. Ska fused elements of Caribbean calypso with American jazz and rhythm and blues. The 2 Tone movement promoted racial unity; many Specials songs raised awareness of the issues of racism; while most of the 2 Tone bands had multiracial line-ups. The Specials had seven consecutive UK Top 10 singles between 1979 and 1981 and as mass unemployment hit the region, their unemployment-themed single 'Ghost Town' reached No. 1 in the UK Singles Chart.

At the same time, UB40 burst on the scene. An eight-strong mixed-race band from south Birmingham, UB40 played their unique brand of reggae alongside the emerging 2 Tone movement. Led by the Campbell brothers, Ali and Robin, here was a group steeped in the reggae tradition who sang about what they saw. Their name came from the number of the government unemployment benefit form. Both their name and their music reflected the times. Their debut single was released in January 1980; their debut album *Signing Off* followed in August. It reflected the sound of the inner city at a time of discontent with mass unemployment and extensive racism. Over the next three decades they became one of the most commercially successful reggae acts of all time with record sales of over seventy million, more than fifty records appearing in the UK Singles Chart and also achieving considerable international success. The band retained the same line-up for thirty years before they broke up in 2008 with some acrimony. UB40 broke the mould. Here were white guys in a mixed band able to play, sing reggae and apply it to their contemporary world and be a great success. They were a hybrid who went beyond traditional multiculturalism. Like 2 Tone, they showed that if you merge cultures together you can produce something new and qualitatively different. They symbolised a younger generation that was comfortable and at ease with its hybrid, multicultural reality. They were the harbingers of the mixed, open city.

These developments helped to create a more accepting culture within the city. When Albert Bore became leader of the Council he wrote: 'Great cities recognise cultural diversity as a real strength. It is the collective harmony of Birmingham people working together which makes it an exciting place to live and work. If we are divided we will not be able to take advantage of the opportunities of the new century.'[8]

It is inconceivable that his predecessor, Frank Griffin, could have uttered such words just three decades previously.

Yet profound structural inequalities still persist within the city. Often the product of a wider national and globalising world, they mean that the promotional and aspirational ambitions of the city frequently jar with reality. Tensions still remain and from time to time burst to the surface. Over this period the National Front has been electorally rebuffed; and the British National Party, too. But an undercurrent of division remains, often promoted by parties that pay lip service to multiculturalism.

Tensions exist not just with the white population but also within and between different ethnic minorities. In October 2005 there were sharp intra-ethnic clashes between black youth and Asian shopkeepers in Lozells which revealed the extent of bad blood between the two communities. Ashraf feels that the narrative on Muslims that you get in the media and TV creates divisions, but he is aware that incidents like a more recent shooting in Lozells showed problems between Bangladeshis/Pakistanis and Afro-Caribbeans. Kashan, the prison officer, recalls another example. He had left the gym and went over the road to the petrol station to buy some fags. At the counter a Pakistani man was serving an older Irish woman who had a lit cigarette in her hand while she was paying. The Pakistani man told her to put the cigarette out as it was a petrol station and they started having an argument. Once she had paid the Irish woman stormed off past Kashan, muttering under her breath, 'It is not as if you've never blown anything up.' Kashan burst out laughing. Fortunately, the guy didn't hear but given what this woman will have known from the Troubles about how ethnic groups get blamed for things they haven't done, 'for that to roll off her tongue tells me that racism remains a big fundamental issue in the UK now'.

This was even more the case in the EU Referendum campaign in June 2016 and was indulged in by politicians on the left as well as the right. In mid-May Conservative MP Boris Johnson demonised the EU and said its politicians were following Hitler and Napoleon in wanting to create a European superstate. The following day I was on a Radio 5 Live show at the Bull Ring market making the pro-European case. Gisela Stuart, a Birmingham Labour MP until the 2017 election, who co-chaired the official Leave the EU campaign was on air after me. I know her, so I approached her and said Johnson's article was an outrageous lie and asked what she was going to say in response. She shrugged and mumbled 'this is Boris'. I asked her again as a German-born female politician how she could allow such a calumny against Angela Merkel and her fellow German politicians. She looked embarrassed and started muttering about Ken Livingstone. She continued to share platforms with Johnson throughout the campaign and never once distanced herself from his comments or those of her co-chair Michael Gove when he stirred up the false claims that eighty million Turks were about to pour into Europe.

Here was a left-wing politician who remained silent as her colleagues peddled racist prejudice to win votes, yet who after the campaign wrote soothingly in the *Observer*, 'there is no place for racism, xenophobia and anti-immigrant language. This is unacceptable.'[9] Except that it was acceptable during the campaign to arouse anti-German feelings, racial fears and anti-migrant prejudice. These actions have consequences as the rise in racist attacks and xenophobic incidents after the EU Referendum illustrates.

Although reignited after the Brexit vote – hopefully temporarily – blatant, overt and nasty public racism has significantly declined. There is a broad acceptance of Birmingham's multicultural reality but still many parts of the city are not wholly comfortable in their own skin. However substantial the progress that has been made, there is still much to do. Over fifty years the public mood has shifted. There is a much more open, welcoming civic culture. There is less direct racism. Yet beneath the surface, an edge remains. Kashan says that people know there are laws against discrimination, so things are less overt now. But it still persists and shows itself in those small ways that serve as a reminder that if you are black, brown or just different, you are still not fully welcomed as an equal by many.

'Like in a dispute over a parking place when the other car driver gets out and shouts "this is England". It really unsettles me when this happens. They are saying, "You have a brown skin. We have always lived here. This is our place, not yours."'

# 8

## *Educating the Kids*

'It looked like a war zone,' says Ewa as she recalls the first time she went to the Polish Saturday school. There were five different classes taking place in one large room. The whole show was a bit of a shambles. The sharp increase in the number of Polish families in the city after 2004 had caught the long-standing Polish Saturday school – established after the Second World War by the city's émigré community – wholly unprepared. Mrs Wyszynska had been running the school for a long time and she was in poor health. Numbers fluctuated, which was difficult for the education of the pupils; the Polish club was reluctant to change; and there were problems with the insurance. Ewa stayed; began teaching Polish for GCSE classes; and quickly became involved running the school. It soon became clear that Mrs Wyszynska wanted to pass the baton on to her.

Ewa was born in Koszalin, a town near the coast of northern Poland. She took a degree in theology followed by postgraduate study in Warsaw. She is an expert on Augustine and 'The City of God'. She met Mariusz at university; got married in 2002; and had her first son in 2003. There were limited prospects for them in Poland; Ewa's sister had been living in Coleshill since the opening of the labour market in 2004; Mariusz's cousin, too; and they told them it would be easy to settle even though they had a three-year-old son. Sure enough Mariusz, who had studied mechanical engineering before turning to theology, landed a job on his first day through an agency. He quickly progressed through various construction jobs and for the past three years has worked as a painting inspector on major construction works. It took Ewa a little longer, having first to sort out nursery arrangements for her son, but after helping with a disabled child she became an integration assistant supporting autistic children. It is work that she both enjoys and fits in well with her children. However, she had not made the journey to Britain just to sit around and enjoy the delights of suburban Coleshill, and so got involved at the Saturday school. The school required a shake-up; the growing Polish community wanted a thriving educational and cultural centre; she set about securing it.

The school needed a larger, more purpose-built venue. Ewa sent letters to fifty schools asking for help. Eventually, she struck lucky. A former pupil of the Polish school worked at the Bishop Walsh secondary school in Sutton Coldfield and had got a positive response from the management, plus the agreement of the caretaker. When they eventually moved in 2011 they were down to just seventy pupils in five classes. Since then, with better conditions and bigger capacity, the school has expanded to ten classes, with up to thirty pupils in the younger classes. About ten to fifteen pupils take GCSE Polish each year. In total, the school engages fourteen teachers and half a dozen teaching assistants. The teachers are not paid; they just get expenses for their books and resources but Ewa has found plenty of Poles around who are quite happy to support the school in this way.

Ewa put the school on a more formal footing with a constitution and has involved parents more with its organisation. They have a small board of unpaid volunteer trustees which meets regularly, normally once a month and runs occasional fundraising events. Ewa is currently the chair of trustees, having previously been the head teacher.

However, the focus is not just on GCSEs. The school is a cultural body. It is a charity organisation registered with the Charity Commissioners. Parents pay a fee of £15 a month and the school's constitution states that it wants to advance education in Polish language, history, geography and culture and retain Catholic values. She stresses that part of its Catholic values is to be open to people of all religions and races.

'We are not a closed community. This is why we are doing all this. We want our children to understand where they come from and not to get lost in a diverse society, also religiously diverse and to be open. As long as you understand you can be open. If you don't understand, you get narrow and that is where the hatred arises.'

Ewa knows the Birmingham Polish Saturday school has come a long way. She admits that she used to be jealous when she looked at other supplementary schools – Muslim, Chinese – in the way that they could stay together and support each other. Originally, the Polish school was not like that. It had too many problems. But now the parents find it relaxing to be together and talk in Polish. At home many speak in English with the children. But they want their children to learn Polish so they can speak with their grandparents. The bulk of the parents are in working-class jobs and they welcome the opportunity for their kids to learn. Dariusz and Magda don't just send their son to the Polish Saturday school, they also pay for him to have extra English lessons at the Kumon Initiative. He goes once a week and he improves his spelling, writing and reading. 'He is now on the gold book at the school' they proudly tell me.

This commitment to supplementary schools is evident among other migrant communities in the city, especially where there is a combined link to retaining knowledge of a language and religion. Wing Yip's Birmingham store donates to both the local Birmingham Chinese supplementary schools, one organised by Chinese themselves and the other linked to the Church of England. On Sunday his grandchildren go there and learn to read Chinese and understand the signs. The children go for four hours, learn Chinese language and culture and meet other Chinese boys and girls.

The devout Muslim commitment is more substantial. Zubeda's mother was the driver on education. She and her brothers and sisters went to the madrassa from when she was four. They learned Urdu and Arabic as well as the Koran. The madrassa focused on the religious heritage and being a good person, but in those days there was nothing about politics. Hasan's two children go to the mosque for two hours every evening where they learn a whole range of topics: the Koran; Arabic; history; morals and character, their Islamic application and how you deal with important issues. His wife's cousin runs the madrassa in Aston. Compared to Hasan's own experience when he was growing up, today's supplementary schools are very different: they run course modules;

teachers speak English whereas when he went it was mainly in Urdu; and generally they are now much more professional. The extent to which there is a more ideological tenor to the scholarship remains an area of dispute.

However, even Rehman and his wife, who are not religious, have a tutor who comes to their home once a week so that their children can learn the Koran. All his older sons now know it. He insists that he is not pressuring them but it means they have learned about their religion. 'It was particularly my wife. She didn't want them to forget these things.'

I am reminded of my own strongly atheist dad. He agreed to me going to Hebrew classes for three hours every Sunday morning and being bar'mitzvah'd at the age of thirteen. The night before the ceremony he accompanied me to the synagogue – the first time I had known him go there – to meet the reverend and sort out the arrangements for the next morning. Once that had been sorted, he started a discussion with the reverend and before I knew it he was telling the guy why he doesn't believe in God. My sweaty palm pulled ever stronger on his hand as the discussion continued. As we were walking home, I said to him that I didn't understand, why was I going through all this palaver and effort if he didn't believe in any of it. 'Jonny, it's important you understand your culture, where you come from,' he replied.

Education is almost always important to migrants. You do not uproot yourself and on occasion cart yourself halfway around the world unless you have some optimism that life can be better, if not for you then at least for your children. This desire for a better life, above all for their children, is a common thread that runs through those interviewed for this book. That has been a recurring strand through the earlier chapters focused on work. Parents from working-class or, more usually, rural peasant backgrounds may not have known much physics or literature but they instinctively grasped the importance of education. They wanted to transmit to their kids the culture and ethic of learning. David's parents were out working before he got up in the morning. There were not many reading books at home. There were no bookshelves. His dad had an encyclopaedia on everything you ever wanted to know about welding. But the importance of education was communicated to David and his five brothers. It was a mixture of having to get your homework done and never being late for school. You had to be smart for school. You had to have clean school clothes. You didn't go to school scruffy. The whole thing about school was that it was an important place.

As first-generation Indians, Anu and Ajay had a similar approach to David's Caribbean parents. Anu says that for their children: 'We set them the boundaries, being on time, being respectable, choose your friends wisely because that makes you the person you are. We made sure they went to school but didn't force them to go into specific jobs. My son was a good artist and some parents said, "you should get your son into engineering, or medicine or be a lawyer". But we encouraged them to do the things that they wanted to do, not the things that we thought they should do. We told them to follow what they were good at. We wanted them to be happy in what they were doing. It had to be their choice.'

Zubeda's mum was learning English and a full-time housewife with seven kids. But she went to the headmaster to say, 'I demand that my kids have homework.' She had no access to it herself, was completely unable to offer any support to her children but she knew it was important for them.

This is not always the case, more especially among women from rural backgrounds. Ashraf's father died young and his mother was left to bring up nine children. She came from a rural, uneducated background and as a result there was no real support or push for him to stay at college. However, Ashraf is not repeating that mistake.

'Education is very important to me. My daughter is doing extra tuition. She is year 10. I don't earn a great deal but I put some money aside and pay for extra small class size tuition.'

When Fatima went to college and then on to university she met resistance from her mum who wanted her to learn how to cook and clean and be a good wife. She did not see education as that important. However, her dad was really excited about her going to university. He had travelled with friends from the UK to Pakistan by car; he enjoyed travelling. He always wanted to hear about any of her travels. He was generally much more open-minded.

Compared to other major English cities, Birmingham has a relatively low proportion of highly skilled citizens and a high proportion of its working age population with no formal qualifications. There are large differences in qualification levels between different parts of the city and between different ethnic groups. The unemployment rate for black and Asian communities is higher than the average for the white population; there are wide earning differentials in the city; and inner-city wards and some outer-city estates perform consistently less well on these criteria.[1] This is the difficult challenge that the city has to overcome if it is to prosper and grow in the decades ahead. That is one of the reasons why increasing efforts have been focused on education.

The recent picture is much more encouraging. GCSE attainment levels in the city have undergone a huge improvement since the turn of the century. From 2000 to 2013 the city's attainment rates for five GCSEs moved from being well below the national average to 4.5 per cent above it. The rise in attainment levels across the board was followed by a slight dip in 2014 and 2015, but the extent of the change remains significant even among the most disadvantaged. There is wide geographical variation across the city with poor performers found both in inner-city areas and in outer-estate wards with a mainly white working-class population. Ethnic groups that underperform against the city average include black Caribbean, Somali and, to a lesser extent, Pakistani pupils, as well as white working-class boys. But, even here, significant progress has been made. In 1998 the proportion of black Caribbean boys achieving five good GCSEs was just 13 per cent. By 2013 it had risen to 45 per cent. Over the same period the results for Pakistani boys had risen from 20 to 51 per cent.[2]

Albert Bore was responsible for economic development in the city from the early 1980s and then became leader of the Council in 1999. In these decades the council began to shift the employment profile of its workforce and pay more attention to service issues, in particular how schools were serving their black and Asian pupils. He compares the situation favourably to France where they do not keep any ethnic data and so are unable to record performance. The ethnic monitoring of performance is not a quick fix. He recognises that changes take a long time to work their way through the system, but he cites one pertinent example.

'For years Bangladeshis were at the bottom of the pile, in poor housing, with low-paid jobs and their children having low educational achievement. Our policy was to collect data, understand their position and then act. Over fifteen to twenty years we saw a remarkable change. They are no longer our lowest achievers. Our problems now are white working-class boys on outer estates and Afro-Caribbean boys. The Bangladeshi youngsters, many of them are now going to university.'[3]

Everyone with knowledge of the change points to the moment in 1993 when Tim Brighouse became its Chief Education Officer. Tall, gangling and dishevelled, Tim was an old-fashioned progressive who believed in the inherent ability of all children and that it was the task of teachers to unearth whatever talents lay within each child. He communicated this passionate belief in the value of education to teachers. Unorthodox and idiosyncratic, he was able to enthuse and motivate teachers with a stream of new ideas and initiatives. Backed by a solid management team he was able to lift the morale of the profession and improve pupils' overall educational experience. He also innovated on school governance: where national government wanted schools to compete, Tim offered a model of neighbouring schools collaborating. After a decade of achievement in Birmingham he took the same philosophy and outlook to the capital, where he became the London Commissioner of Schools in 2003. The London Challenge contributed to a similar sharp rise in educational performance among London pupils especially from disadvantaged backgrounds, so much so that some commentators are now writing about the 'diversity advantage' as the cities with high migrant populations begin to outperform other urban areas with fewer ethnic minority children.

Chris came to Birmingham to teach at a comprehensive school in east Birmingham in 1991. She has taught in the area ever since and became the head, responsible for a group of seven schools in east Birmingham grouped into an academy. In six of the seven schools at least 50 per cent of the pupils are eligible for pupil premium funding; while in five of the seven the majority of the students are of Pakistani heritage. As a white female teacher, she discussed how these issues had evolved. When she arrived, there was less understanding of the need to support ethnic minority students, less recognition that it was not an equal playing field. Things began to change in the mid- and late 1990s partly because of the changing local climate and partly due to the influence of Ofsted. Once both started comparing the performance of different groups of students and began asking schools why one group of students was doing less well than others, schools realised that they had to do something about it.

A number of elements were central to the transformation. As a first step, schools lifted the level of pupil expectations and told their children that they had real opportunities and the school was setting high expectations for them.

'Nobody was saying that to kids in Waverley when I went there in 2000.'

Brighouse's enthusiasm and the increased commitment from the council helped here. Eighty-five per cent of the pupils at Waverley were Pakistani Muslim. The level of expectation among the teachers was low. They lived in Solihull; had high expectations for their own kids; and then drove down the road into Birmingham and just did not expect the same of the Waverley pupils. Chris said this had to change; she told teachers they had to have the same level of expectation for these children as they did for their own.

This culture of low expectations was not just about race; it was also about class. Other teachers living in Solihull would also be going off to Chelmsley Wood – a 1960s Birmingham overspill tower block neighbourhood – and act in the same way there, thinking 'what can you expect of these kids?', 'what more can we do?' As we were talking I recalled similar discussions back in the mid-1970s in London, when supposedly progressive teachers decried the idea of teaching French or German to working-class pupils on the grounds that they would never use it.

These attitudes certainly affected the chances of black and Asian schoolkids. As a working-class, black Caribbean schoolboy David recalls that when he was in school in the late 1970s a lot of the teachers had a very stereotypical view of him.

'I only realised that later. Like, no one encouraged me to improve my reading which was very basic. Only a maverick maths teacher gave me and some others extra classes and helped encourage my interest in maths. The others didn't push me. So for the apprenticeship, I did the CV alone, went to the interview without any preparation and then got two offers. And the Careers Office was so surprised.'

It was similar for Adam fifteen years later. Since leaving school he has become the chief project officer for a sizeable international charity and done a master's degree as a mature student. But at school he failed all his GCSEs and all his retakes. In a matter-of-fact manner, he just says, 'I now know that I'm dyslexic. Nobody picked it up.'

This shift in expectations was accompanied by a new focus on performance and the creation of a climate that emphasised the importance of making progress. Schools looked at their results and then tackled the areas where there was under-performance. The leap in overall attainment levels from the mid-1990s until now tells its own story.

Initially, schools acted generically. They did not do it by focusing on race but by saying that for everybody who is under-performing in a subject like maths, we are having an extra lesson. And if the majority weakness was with black boys, the school tackled the shortcoming, not just for them but for everybody. However, there were some specific actions like the Windsor programme aimed at high achievers among the black and Asian students. That made some inroads. But the thing that changed everything was the Ofsted impact, with all pupils being measured. And more recently it has been about disadvantage with the pupil premium money introduced by the 2010 Coalition government. The consequence has been that Ofsted then asks what difference this has made for the pupils for whom that money was intended.

A further shift has been with the increase in the number of black and Asian teachers, which has risen significantly over the twenty-five years Chris has been in Birmingham.

'Numbers have increased, especially of Asian teachers and classically in maths, science and business. That's where the growth has been. If we advertise for a science teacher, the majority of applicants are Asian and here of Pakistani background. There are less when we advertise for history or geography.'

Chris sees this as very significant for the pupils especially for secondary school children for whom these teachers can often serve as role models.

Yet responding to the multiracial reality of modern urban Britain brings sharp challenges for schools, especially when they are confronted by religious fundamentalism. This chapter is not an analysis of the 'Trojan Horse' controversy – an alleged conspiracy by Muslim fundamentalists to take over and run a number of primary and secondary schools in the city in 2011–13. But the broad issues it raised are pertinent to this book.

The leading figure in the Trojan Horse affair, Tahir Alam, was on the governing board of Waverley School when Chris arrived there. She recalls him being rightly concerned about the need to raise standards and performance and complaining about the complacency of the staff. In many ways he was voicing the issues that Chris had been brought in to address. Tahir was also a member of the governing board of Washwood Heath Technology College in east Birmingham. In 2003, Tim Brighouse asked me to sit on the board as a council nominee when the school had been placed under executive measures by the government after upheaval between parents and the previous school management. Tahir did not appear as the stereotypical radical. He was a smartly dressed, courteous man, unfailingly polite and measured in his comments. After a couple of years he told me that he was a member of Hizb-ut-Tahrir, an Islamic group that believes in the peaceful refoundation of the Caliphate across the Muslim world.[4] And as a member of Hizb-ut-Tahrir, he had an agenda. He saw that the presence of parents on school governing bodies gave him and his followers a route to shape the educational agenda in the city.

At Washwood Heath, after all the upheaval, he was relatively circumspect but in 2007 he co-authored a document that set out his profoundly conservative thinking. Blandly entitled 'Towards Greater Understanding – Meeting the Needs of Muslim Pupils in State Schools',[5] this document was published with the official imprimatur of the Muslim Council of Britain. As a whole the document gives a fundamentalist interpretation of Islam. 'Boys should always be covered between the navel and the knee' – so no shorts – 'and girls should always be covered except for their hands and faces.'[6] 'In accommodating prayer requirements, schools need to allow pupils to use an appropriate classroom for the purpose of prayer. Care should be taken to avoid allocating rooms that may have displays with distracting imagery, such as posters of the human body.'[7] The document is particularly concerned about the expressive arts. Acting may involve 'performing in a manner that may encourage sexual feeling' while pupils may be exposed to 'potentially harmful forms of music'. Schools are asked to 'avoid studying forms of music and drama that may raise religious or moral concerns for Muslim pupils and parents'[8] – in other words no Shakespeare or classical music. On sex education it adopted a stance familiar to conservative Christians with the additional twist that 'girlfriend/boyfriend as well as homosexual relationships are not acceptable practices'.[9]

Reading the document, I was reminded of a Jesuit tract, above all with its obsessions with sex, women and bodily functions. Yet this specific literalist interpretation of Islam has been presented as the norm with the authority of the Muslim Council of Britain behind it. Across parts of Birmingham there have been some vocal parents and advocates who have sought to impose this interpretation on aspects of the school education system. A central challenge has been how to address religion in a country of multiple faiths, where a growing number have no religion at all and where the official law prescribes a daily act of Christian worship. In a haphazard, ad hoc fashion, a lot of schools have transformed daily acts of collective worship into short, general assemblies; gatherings that discuss ethos, values and behaviour, appealing to the spiritual side of life and what motivates people as human beings. However, they have no worship in them, thereby avoiding offence to any religious or agnostic pupils but also evading the letter of the law. The schools that Chris is responsible for recognise all the different major festivals observed by its pupils, but Chris does not think it is a school's role to promote a particular belief system. Pupils learn about different systems through their study in Religious Education.

Based on his experiences as a parent in Sparkbrook, Ashraf puts it this way: 'Respect the faith wherever they are from. But the children need to understand what the other religions are based on, so you see the common ground with Judaism, Sikhism, Hinduism, Christianity. A child learns that through participation in school and other religions.'

Every year Chris gets two or three parents who want to bring their religious belief into subject matter and object to dancing, art, music or sex education. These parents are wanting to proscribe what children do or learn, imposing a literalist interpretation of their religion onto a public institution. Chris finds truly alarming the idea that twelve-year-old boys and girls do not need to learn about music, dance and drama because it will have no part in their future life. She counters complainants by saying that it is all part of the national curriculum. When we speak she is dealing with a parent in a junior school who does not want her child to do swimming in Year 3. The national curriculum regards it as a life skill. The school makes sure that boys and girls are taught separately but there can't be any compromise on the principle. In the end, the parent accepted it. But she was trying to chip away; she said he couldn't do it because he was coming home too tired and couldn't go to mosque school afterwards. The school just said, sorry, this is when the lesson is. It was important not to give ground.

It is clear that these are not the only views among parents of Pakistani heritage. Yasin, the taxi driver, just disagrees with those Muslims who disapprove of drama, music and art. 'I loved drama at school. I got an A star for it,' he tells me proudly. He likes all kinds of music: pop, bhangra, classical, dance. And he watches lots of films too. He thinks that 'clerics who oppose these things are talking a lot of rubbish'.

Ashraf's son's school was involved with the Trojan Horse controversy. The leadership wanted to ban the school-leaving prom. They said it wasn't dignified.

'But my argument was that it had gone on for twenty years, so why shouldn't it continue? Religion shouldn't be the barrier for kids being kids. But religious kids should not be demonised. Nothing wrong if children don't go to the prom or if they do. You have to allow them to choose whether they want to go to a prom or not.'

In the end, a group of Asian parents organised it for the kids.

On occasions, different views on the Muslim religion are played out in staff rooms. Some of the Pakistani heritage teachers who have been recruited as part of the drive to rebalance the teaching workforce have themselves been fundamentalists. Chris had a group of teachers who tried to put pressure on other teachers to stop 'mixed socialising'. There were a number of Muslim teachers, men and women, who would be talking in the staff room or in the canteen downstairs, having a conversation about maths lessons or what they had read in the newspapers. The other group said they shouldn't be talking together like that. There should be no mixing and people should 'stand away from each other'. This presented awkward management issues and the need to confirm that men and women mix professionally – and necessarily – in the school environment. Once the group realised they were not making headway, they began to fragment. A number of them went to live and work in Middle East states like Doha.

Another issue that sometimes arises concerns dress. In Chris's schools teachers can wear headscarves but they have no teacher wearing a full-face veil. Chris is absolutely clear as to why this is the case.

'Teaching is about relationships and relating well to students. They need to know their subject, to be diligent but the best teachers are those who can relate to their students and that relates to how they communicate with pupils. If it wasn't, we could all do it by computer. But what is absolutely crucial for teachers is how they communicate directly with their pupils. In this interview I understand what you think and feel from your facial expressions. With a veil you are putting up a barrier between us.'

Kalsoom, having taught for twenty years, has a similar view. She wears a headscarf and did so when she was teaching. She sees wearing a full-face veil as a personal choice but she doesn't think it is necessary if you are working here and living in this society. She recalls that a lady with a full-face veil didn't get a job in her school. She was well qualified. The school gave some other reasons for her not getting the job, 'but the lady should have known that in teaching children it is about expressions and body language'.

Zahida comes at this issue from a different angle but with a similar conclusion. She was born in Birmingham but grew up and was educated in Pakistan. She returned in 1986 with her husband who found employment with the Royal Mail. Zahida had four children and then found a little work teaching English as a second language and within adult education. She became more religious, went to Saudi Arabia on a pilgrimage in the mid-1990s, and returned to wear a full-face veil until 2012. In her late forties, she reverted to the headscarf. As she explains it, 'the Koran says that when a woman reaches a certain age, it is OK to take it off'.

Despite various academic qualifications, she was unable to secure a permanent teaching post. She wore the full veil at interviews for jobs.

'I realised that the impact of wearing the veil is to give the message to others, "stay away from me; leave me alone". That was probably the reason I did not get the jobs. With the veil it is very hard for me to communicate to the children.'

So instead she has taught in Saudi Arabia and Malaysia for one- or two-year periods.

These issues are not going to go away. Chris is aware of a significant Saudi influence and a growing push for the study of Arabic, more than Urdu. She knows there are other pressing issues on the city's educational agenda, notably white working-class boys clustered in schools on the city's outer ring, who do not feel empowered. But it is this fundamentalist issue that troubles her most. The wish to be inclusive and egalitarian has resulted in some very regressive beliefs gaining hold. If someone says, 'this is my belief', they must accept that someone else can question it and ask why, without being accused of being racist. She knows that going down the French route of denying difference is not the answer. But the pressures of just doing the day job mean that she and her colleagues across the city have not taken sufficient time to discuss this and sort things out. She knows there is an urgent need for a new, progressive settlement.

# 9

## *God and the City*

Richard Evans was a big, burly man who had come up the hard way to become the Director of the Birmingham Social Services Department. He wanted me to sort out a problem. It was the mid-1990s and I was working as its Head of Policy and Planning. The Committee chair, Councillor Eve Brook, had had a complaint from a lesbian woman, who had applied to the Social Services fostering panel to become a short-term foster parent, caring for a disabled child at the weekends. The woman understood that she had been rejected because, as a lesbian, the panel had deemed her to be an inappropriate carer.

I went to see Councillor Brook. A feisty Yorkshirewoman, she had been the Social Services chairwoman for a couple of years. She explained the politics and sensitivities to me. There was no way that she could follow some of the Labour London boroughs and get a full gay rights policy through her committee. Her Asian members – those of Indian, Pakistani and Bangladeshi heritage – wouldn't stand for it. She had to approach these issues from a civil rights standpoint. She knew that some of the radical social workers wouldn't like this, but that was the political reality. With this brief, I went off to investigate.

Sure enough, the team manager complained about the Council's weak policy and failure to lead on gay rights. A three-person panel had taken the decision on this case, chaired by one of her social work team. I interviewed the social worker. I asked him about the panel's discussion. He was very straightforward. He said that it became apparent in the interview that the applicant lived with another woman in a lesbian relationship. The social worker was a member of a black Pentecostal church and as far as he was concerned she was living in sin. This disqualified her from being a foster carer.

I asked him whether he had been questioned about religion at his interview. He said no. I asked if he had been asked about politics. He said no. I said that was the deal. At the interview we, as the employer, ask you about your ability to do the job. We don't ask you about either your religion or your politics. In return, you don't bring your religion or politics into the job. I went back to the team manager and told her what had happened. I asked why she hadn't instructed her social worker to follow council policy – in this case just to test out whether the woman would be a competent foster carer. She had the good grace to look embarrassed. Here was cultural relativism being played out before my eyes: for the manager anti-racism had trumped gay rights. She feared that if she challenged her social worker, she would have been accused of racism. The manager had no overall framework by which she felt able to judge the validity of her staff member's actions.

My report pulled no punches. It stated the 'no politics; no religion' position explicitly. If a religious fundamentalist feels their beliefs are in conflict with the requirements of the job, then don't apply for it. Similarly, for an anti-Semite or a racist. As an employer, our job was not to inspect people's minds but to gauge their capability to do the job. That was the basis on which people were appointed. I reported back to the Director; the fostering panel was reconvened. I told Councillor Brook that her civil rights baseline seemed a pretty good starting point to me. Twenty years later it still does.

Most of the new arrivals to Birmingham brought religion with them. It was a common point of identity in a new land. Sam's parents were ministers at a Pentecostal church; David's parents went every Sunday to the central Methodist church; Kalsoom's husband negotiated with the City Council for the land for the Green Lane mosque. It was the same in my grandparents' time when new synagogues sprang up in London's East End. More recently, when refugees arrived at Calais, one of the first things they did was build a church or a mosque. But, over time, with the second and third generations, there is a more differentiated picture. The depth of religious commitment and intensity is weakening in a number of communities but at an uneven rate and this is counterbalanced by a renewed interest among some younger generations.

The signs of a weakening religious commitment are most evident among Irish and Afro-Caribbeans. Chris, the environmental campaigner, was brought up a Catholic. As a kid, he was confirmed, baptised, took Holy Communion and acted as an altar server. Today he is lapsed. He respects those with religious beliefs and those who come together on an interfaith basis to encourage people to live with each other and respect the environmental capacity of the planet. But he is also aware that the magnetic pull of the Catholic Church has been weakened by a series of profound sex and child-abuse scandals.

David, the car engineer, went to church out of duty until he was fourteen, when his parents allowed him to choose and he stopped. It is similar with Mo of Kuskus Foods. He was brought up as a Methodist, attended the local church and Sunday School, was part of the Boys' Brigade marching around Balsall Heath and Moseley but since then religion has played no part at all in his life. Sam used to go to church and still believes in God, but more as a spiritual connection that all people share. That is totally different from his Pentecostal parents. Yet while the religious intensity is weakening, it is not disappearing completely. Sam acknowledges that a number of his brothers and sisters retain their parents' Pentecostal beliefs.

Wing Yip, the oriental food entrepreneur, thinks religion is a good thing but should not be overdone. It is OK in moderation. He is not religious himself but he is not against it. He has some very religious people who work for him. It gives them peace of mind. However, as befits a successful businessman, this relaxed view has a material edge: 'My parents were Buddhists; my wife is a Roman Catholic: my religion is the Bank of England.'

A waning of strict religious belief is also evident among some second-generation Sikhs. Daljit, the council employee, is not devout. She likes to go to the gurdwara now and again just for that peace of mind. As a family they go on special occasions, more as a family outing. She has no intention of imposing her religion on her son. 'He has had his hair cut from day one. He has not had a topknot. In time that will be his choice. It is not something I am going to insist on when he is young.'

In contrast, Mandeep's attachments are stronger. Being part of a religious community gives her a sense of comfort and belonging, but the commitment is still shaped by the realities of contemporary life. Her parents and grandparents were not religious at all. It was only when she got married and found that her husband's family were religious that she became interested. She goes to the gurdwara every time there is a function, a birthday, celebration or a big event. But she sees limits to the religion. Her husband does not wear a topknot and nor does his father.

'We respect the tradition and adapt it to the world we live in. Although I wear traditional outfits at religious events I don't wear them for everyday life. I don't like it when people do it to go to the shops. I respect the religion but when I see men going to the shops wearing it, it just doesn't look right.'

Yet, illustrating that this is not a trend that moves just in one direction, Immy, the young director of the Impact Hub, has become profoundly religious, in contrast to her parents.

'My parents had to give up a lot of their cultural identity. That was not a good thing; they gave up their religious identity and I am the first of my generation to refind it. I saw how much they have given up and I have returned to it.'

Her religion influences her work.

'In the Hub, we don't shy away from religion. There are three baptised Sikhs in the core team. I don't eat meat or drink alcohol.'

Does this mean there is a distinct religious ethos at the Hub?

'No, but there is definitely a very clear set of protocols and we go out of our way to be a faith-respectful culture at the Hub. This is a secular space. There is no imposition but there is more space for beliefs. We have given people permission to be open about their religion.'

Her beliefs also shape her private life.

'For me, I would only marry someone of the same religion. A whole generation of Sikhs are going back. My brother isn't; he is married to a white woman and that is fine but if you are a baptised Sikh then you have to marry another.'

A similar contradictory picture is evident among Hindus. Religion does not play much of a role in the life of Raj, the accountant. He believes in God and that there is an afterlife. He went to the temple when he was young but not now. And he is happy to drink alcohol. There are some, like his mum, who say you shouldn't, but it doesn't worry him.

For Ajay, the postal worker and driver, and his wife Anu, Hindu belief remains central to their life and that of their children. They subscribe to a Hindu religious sect, Swaminarayan, which has members worldwide and their life revolves around involvement in its activities. Anu has helped in the temple as a volunteer for the past thirty years in the kitchen, preparing food every Sunday and for the festivals, as well as help with the cleaning. She goes to the temple every morning.

'It has given me a sense of calmness in my life. Whatever happens, we just cope with it. My children have been raised according to our values. No, we don't believe in converting people to us. You can convert a person to our values – no drinking, no gambling, be vegetarian, no addictions – rather than our religion.'

The temple pursues its self-contained, quiet existence within a Birmingham suburb, an example of the city's acceptance of a religious freedom that troubles few of its neighbours.

Contrary to some tabloid representations this mixed picture is also found within the city's Muslim population. The older generation exhibits signs of disengagement. Zahoor, the electrical shopkeeper, is by his own admission not a very religious person. He has only recently started going to mosque every Friday. When I ask why he says with a chuckle that he is getting older. He, his wife and his children are very open-minded.

'Of course you have got a faith, but we are not fanatical, we are not even ten per cent.'

And his other Pakistani friends see it the same way.

Religion is not important to Mashood, the engineer. He is not a believer in heaven, but his nieces wear a hijab. They like to wear it and that is fine by him.

Some second-generation Muslims are similarly relaxed. Salma, the NHS manager, is not particularly religious. It was part of her upbringing but not rammed down her throat. Samera, the shop assistant, doesn't wear a headscarf at work, only when she goes to the mosque as a sign of respect, just as there are signs in Catholic cathedrals asking for the arms to be covered. She likes to wear jeans and T-shirts but not short skirts. As she puts it graphically, 'You shouldn't wear a miniskirt or a boob tube if you go to a mosque or a church. You should respect your god.'

Yet generally the indications are that among the second generation of Muslims there is strong religious commitment, a trend clearly evident in a number of surveys which record much greater religious observance among Muslims than their white counterparts and other ethnic minorities.[1] Religion is important to Fatima, the charity worker. She started wearing the headscarf several years ago. She is more comfortable with it on. It feels more like her. She prays five times a day and finds peace in her prayers. Akram does not pray regularly because of his work, but he is still committed enough to take two hours off every Friday from his taxi driving to go to the mosque for prayers. It plays a very big role in Hasan's life. He goes to the mosque just two to three times a week but what is striking are his core beliefs. He does not just reject Islamicist extremists. He also 'massively disagrees' with those like the Quilliam Foundation which say that Islam needs to be updated, reformed and modernised. Why?

'Because when Islam was revealed back then it was finalised, it was the culmination of all the Abrahamic religions. The teachings of Muhammad basically reaffirm what came before. Islam was the pinnacle. No more messengers or revelations have come since. There is no room for those who say we need to modernise this and that in Islam because the rules were set then.'

This is an assertion of the eternal truths of a book written more than 1,400 years ago that would rarely be uttered with such conviction by a contemporary Christian in the UK.

Such theological certainty is not shared by all second- or third-generation Muslims. Adam has helped his own mosque change its attitude to women so there are now some mixed activities and women are members of the mosque board. He remains religious but is in a process of adjustment.

'At the local mosque we have grown up being taught the fear of God rather than the love of God. Or if you don't do this, that will happen. I am trying to cut off from that fear factor. Does that make sense?'

But there is a sharp reminder of the ugly side of religion when a person who lives within one of the more tightly knit communities, and who wishes to remain anonymous, tells me that they don't really believe in God but one is careful where one says that within the community. 'Some people might want to damage you if they heard you say that.'

The interviewees dispel the myth that there is a monolithic 'Muslim' viewpoint in the city. Rather, there are diverse views on the degree and depth of religious belief, as there are within all communities. But there is little doubt that commitment is much more extensive than that found among other religions. That is why there are now a hundred mosques operational in Birmingham and they get congregations at Friday prayers that churches can only dream about. At the same time over the last twenty years the signs of Muslim religious dress on the streets of Birmingham have become steadily more visible. Among women of all ages, the number wearing the headscarf has risen significantly and in addition the full-face veil is now a common sight on the city's streets. As Pam, the Sikh shopkeeper puts it, 'You'll see many women completely covered and you didn't see that ten years back; or men with long beards.'

These trends disturb old stagers like Nazir who recalls life in Kashmir in the 1960s.

'The entire population never wore a scarf, let alone a veil or a burqa. Working in the fields, or travelling or shopping, this was not seen. In the very remote areas or among the very pious, there were a few who wore the scarf.'

These changes can only be explained by international developments since the mid-1970s. Events far away have blown back to alter social behaviour within the city. It began with the popular revolt in Iran against the Western-backed Shah and his autocratic regime. This upheaval was not driven by the universal values of liberty and equality drawn from the Enlightenment and the French Revolution, as in many earlier twentieth-century anti-colonial movements, but was, rather, inspired by Shia religious leaders led by Ayatollah Khomeini articulating Koranic values. This placed religion centre stage.

At the same time, there has been the rise of Saudi Arabia as a power centre of the Arab world, its ambitions sustained economically by its oil reserves and petro-dollars and ideologically by its theocratic Wahhabi nationalism. Having unified the Kingdom of the House of Saud, Wahhabi nationalism has striven to exercise its domination of the Muslim world through boosting the role of its two holy shrines in Medina and Mecca and by a concerted training programme of Wahhabist clerics to serve as imams at mosques across Europe. These were also seen as the ideological shock troops designed to ensure Sunni hegemony within the Muslim world in the re-emerging bitter dispute with Shia Iran and to spread an austere, fundamentalist interpretation of Islam through the Muslim communities of Western Europe.

The Soviet invasion of Afghanistan gave renewed momentum to these developments. Resistance to the Soviet involvement in Afghanistan in 1979 was initially led by a Sufi movement wanting national independence, but the Saudis, along with the Pakistani security forces (ISI) and the US Central Intelligence Agency (CIA), marginalised these Sufi leaders and brought into prominence Jamaat-e-Islami, a Wahhabi group which they funded. Jamaat was and remains a reactionary organisation based in Pakistan linked with Wahhabi thought in Saudi Arabia and believes in the imposition of their brand of Islam by the state. This alliance invested huge sums of money, high-grade armaments and equipment in the hands of the militia fighters, the mujahideen. Over a decade they succeeded in securing the withdrawal of Soviet troops from Afghanistan and overthrew its puppet government. The mujahideen mutated into the Taliban and then into Al-Qaeda, led by Osama bin Laden, a scion of the Saudi establishment.

For a while these appeared to be faraway events which most of Birmingham and the UK could ignore. The first signs of change came with the Salman Rushdie affair when the publication of his novel *The Satanic Verses* in 1988 provoked outrage among Muslim clerics, a fatwa from Ayatollah Khomeini demanding Rushdie's death and a rowdy demonstration in Bradford ending with the burning of copies of his novel. Most people reacted with incredulity: this sort of thing was medieval, but now had the backing of a modern state behind it. Less dramatically, this was the period when Saudi influence grew in the city and elsewhere. As Nazir recalls, scholars from Kashmir previously trained in Egypt now went to Saudi Arabia and then came to Birmingham. They were educated along Wahhabist lines. Saudi money was made available for the building of mosques in the UK and elsewhere in Europe. Theocratic and socially conservative versions of Islam were being promulgated to Muslims across Europe.

The attacks on the World Trade Center in New York on September 11 2001 carried out by Al-Qaeda gave further crucial impetus to these changes. That was when Islamic identity became important. US President George Bush's call 'you're either with us or against us' had a negative impact on many Muslims, who felt it put them into the category of terrorists. Hasan states it baldly:

'9/11 was a huge game-changer, everything changed after that. I did not have a beard before then. I grew one. I needed to show what Islam was really like after 9/11.'

Zubeda, the social entrepreneur, explains, 'My mum wears a burqa, she wore it in the late 1980s, then she wore a headscarf and then wore the burqa again after 9/11.' Is it an identification with Al-Qaeda and the Taliban? I ask. 'Oh, God no. It's about being a Muslim.'

Since then there has been the US invasion of Iraq supported by the UK government with the overthrow of Saddam Hussein and the consequent chaos, bloodshed and civil war within the country; a series of major terrorist actions committed in the name of Islam in major cities across Europe, starting in London in 2005, followed by Madrid, Paris, Brussels, Istanbul, Nice and Berlin; uprisings against autocratic regimes across North Africa and the Middle East and their subsequent bloody suppression; and a huge upsurge in refugees as millions of people seek to find safe havens from this turmoil. These events have coincided with the most severe economic and financial crisis that the world has experienced since the 1930s. In this period of unprecedented upheaval, authoritarian nationalism has become the political flavour of the moment – Vladimir Putin in Russia, Recep Erdoğan in Turkey, Abdel Fattah el-Sisi in Egypt – while racist, nationalist parties have gained influence across Europe.

This lethal mixture of events has thrown traditional politics into disarray. All the existing European models of integration have struggled in response. In particular, left, liberal and progressive voices have floundered. Their inability to tackle issues coming from a pre-Enlightenment era has left them exposed. Some have fallen back on a 'live and let live' liberalism that has led them to turn a blind eye to illiberal practices under the guise of a cultural relativism. Others like Tariq Modood see religious groupings as homogenous and each should be given their distinct role in public life. The Introduction discussed the inadequacies of this communitarian approach. The interviews in this chapter show the wide diversity of opinion among migrants on these issues. They cannot and should not be shoe-horned into monolithic blocs.[2]

A more principled response is to apply the elements of liberty, equality and solidarity in ways that can enable both Birmingham and other cities to find a Third Way between French-style assimilation and closed, embattled communities. This is not easy in cities where the majority are not that interested in or excited about religion, while there are elements of the population for whom it is their motivating force. The issue is how to find a modus vivendi which gives space and respect to religion without permitting it to assume undue influence or special privileges and its more fundamentalist elements to hold sway.

The starting point should be a reaffirmation of civil and human rights. These are spelled out most clearly in the Universal Declaration of Human Rights drafted by an international panel led by Eleanor Roosevelt and proclaimed by the United Nations General Assembly in Paris on 10 December 1948.[3] For the first time it set out fundamental human rights to be universally protected. This should not be seen as the secular equivalent of a sacred, unchanging text but, rather, as the basic framework – a Magna Carta for humankind – which governments, cities and citizens should pursue as they cope with competing claims in a multiracial, diverse world. Even as pessimistic a philosopher and sceptic of the

Enlightenment as John Gray recognises their role. 'Universal human rights are not an ideal constitution for a single regime throughout the world, but a set of minimum standards for peaceful coexistence among regimes that will always remain different.'[4]

So how should an intercultural, open city secure these minimum standards in relation to religion?

The basic requirement is to have a place of worship. Without it, the exercise of the Universal Declaration's Article 18 is meaningless. With regard to the main religions of people who have come here, Birmingham has done well with few obstacles placed in the way of people wanting to practise. This is in marked contrast to a number of cities on the Continent. This religious freedom is welcomed and acknowledged. Abdul's family fled Mogadishu and he grew up in Bonn, before coming to Birmingham.

'One of the reasons we come here is because of the religious freedom. That's a big factor why we prefer the UK. It is harder in Germany.'

This commitment to religious freedom has to be combined with its essential corollary, namely the freedom to change one's religion and the right to dissent. This is expressed in Article 19 of the UN Declaration as 'the right to freedom of opinion and expression'. There are two dimensions here. One is the requirement to respect other religions and religious views. Enlightenment values were forged from the bitterness and blood of wars waged across Europe arising from the split in Christianity between Protestants and Catholics. Today, there is a similar schism within the Muslim world between Sunni and Shia. Then there is the smaller schism with the Ahmadiyya sect, which Sunnis deny is a part of Islam at all. There are signs that some of the sectarian fault lines on this issue within Pakistan are spilling over into the UK. That can only spell danger. Birmingham has promoted interfaith dialogue over the years: it needs to have the honesty and clarity to address such issues within its ranks. The other dimension is the right to respect differences being aired from within a religion. This is something strongly resisted by those of an authoritarian bent and a theocratic turn of mind of whatever religion. To them such thoughts are heretical.

These conflicts often arise in the cultural arena as happened in Birmingham in 2004. From time to time groups such as Christian Voice object to films, plays or musicals on the grounds that they are blasphemous to Jesus Christ and their interpretation of God. On this occasion they objected to a production of *Jerry Springer: The Opera* at the Birmingham Hippodrome, arguing that it blasphemed against their religion. They conducted their protest; they made their point; and life moved on. The two councillors, one Conservative, the other Labour, who attended the board meetings of Birmingham Hippodrome on behalf of the council supported the organisation's decision to present *Jerry Springer: The Opera* on the grounds of freedom of expression despite the threat of protests from Christian Voice.

A little while later, in December 2004, the Birmingham Repertory Theatre presented Gurpreet Kaur Bhatti's play *Behzti* (Dishonour).[5] The play by an emerging woman playwright, who is herself Sikh, sought to tackle the sensitive topic of sexual abuse within the Sikh community. The play referred to violent acts, including rape, taking place in the setting of a gurdwara.

*Behzti* presented an opportunity for Sikh religious fundamentalists. Two decades earlier, a radical group who wanted to split the Punjab from India and set up a separate state of Khalistan took over the Golden Temple. They were backed by Pakistan, in revenge for losing Bangladesh. The Indian government responded by invading the Temple. As Pam, the shopkeeper, recalls, in response temples in Britain were taken over by radicalised Sikh youths and the more peaceful Sikhs were pushed out. For a good ten years the Khalistani factions with their radical religious nationalism were dominant. Slowly, things eased in India and the radicals became less prominent within the UK. These people saw *Behzti* as a chance to revive Sikh fervour and identity.

Sikhs demonstrated in Birmingham against the play. On Saturday 18 December, initially peaceful protests outside the theatre turned violent as some participants attacked and broke into the building, smashing windows and disrupting not only a performance of *Behzti* but also a show for children taking place at the same time. Eight hundred people had to be evacuated from the theatre. Death threats were made against the playwright, forcing her to go into hiding. The police said they could not guarantee the safety of the building and the play had to be abandoned.[6]

The Birmingham Repertory Theatre is a major recipient of City Council funding. The Council's response was equivocal. Several city councillors gave comments to the press, but none of those quoted called for protection of the theatre's production of the play or of the audience's opportunity to see it. The Conservative leader Mike Whitby stated that 'as a practising Christian, I understand how the portrayal of religious issues or references to faith in art or drama can cause offence', an observation that he could have applied equally to *Jerry Springer*. One of the city's Labour councillors, Gurdial Singh Atwal, said the play 'has caused a great hurt and shows a lack of respect' and suggested that the theatre should have submitted to the demands of the Sikh representatives who had called for the setting of the play to be changed from a gurdwara. His colleague Chaman Lal argued that 'we understand the need for writers to have freedom of speech but that freedom should not be used to cause offence to a section of the community'.

This line of argument was vigorously pursued by the Roman Catholic Archbishop of Birmingham, Vincent Nichols, who said that the Sikh community 'has acted in a reasonable and measured way in representing their deep concerns . . . the right to freedom of expression has corresponding duties to the common good. Such a deliberate violation of the sacred place of the Sikh religion demeans the sacred places of every religion. People of all faiths will be offended by this presentation.'[7]

In contrast to the Council's prevarication, the *Birmingham Post* was firm. In two separate editorials it lambasted the Archbishop for wanting to curb freedom of expression, for apparently turning a blind eye to violence and for ignoring the lessons of its own paedophile priests within his own diocese.

A decade on, leading politicians like Albert Bore, who was leader of the Labour opposition, admitted that he ducked out of confronting the issue when interviewed for this book. Paul Tilsley, a senior Liberal Democrat figure within the Conservative-led coalition, reflects his ongoing unease when questioned on the issue.

'Looking back, I saw it as an internal Sikh issue and, like any family row, if you get involved you become the victim.' When it was suggested that it was not an internal Sikh issue, but, rather, about accepting dissent, he continues, 'I agree. However, [sighs]

. . . there have been a number of cultural events concerning blasphemy, plays at the Rep, taking God's name in vain. When you are dealing with Muslims and Sikhs you are going to something a little bit deeper, involving culture as well as religion and you know as well as me that dealing with religious fear, that goes a lot deeper.' Asked whether that challenges his core liberal beliefs, he responds, 'It probably does but as I said it was not just about religion but about culture. Now, ten years on, I might well approach it a bit differently but at the time, well, as I said . . .'

These issues are certain to arise again in one way or another. Birmingham has promoted a culture of openness, exchange and respect between its religions and with those who are not religious. However, this means recognising that religious institutions like all others must be open to enquiry and controversy. The crisis in the Catholic Church in Ireland concerning child abuse serves as a warning as to the fate of closed institutions. The *Behzti* affair shows the danger of allowing religious zealotry to determine public policy. The right of dissent is crucial to criticising and questioning tradition, the status quo or powerful interests. It is the grit in the oyster of democracy. Only time will tell whether Birmingham politicians have learned their lesson.

Alongside religious freedom and the right to dissent, peaceful co-existence means that religious beliefs must not determine access to public services. As Kashan described it in his work with employees in the prison service, 'You must not discriminate against anybody or treat anyone differently at work. Our approach is one of no detriment. You can have prejudices but certain ones you have to park at the gate.'

Or, as discussed earlier in the case with the social worker, 'keep your personal, religious beliefs out of your work'. These are both applications of Article 21 of the Universal Declaration, 'Everyone has the right of equal access to public service'. The social worker was trying to deny a lesbian woman that access.

That does not mean that public services should not address specific needs. Both Salma and Sam in their work in the NHS detail efforts to make services more responsive to the health needs of particular communities; Kalsoom's work funded by Section 11 money was designed to address the language needs of Asian pupils; Social Services provide halal or kosher meals for elderly Muslim or Jewish people. As discussed in the previous chapter, multi-ethnic schools have sought to address the conundrum arising from their obligation to provide a daily act of Christian worship to school pupils who are either increasingly agnostic or where many come from different religious backgrounds. Their answer has been to move to general assemblies in schools which highlight human values, morals and ethics. This infuriates religious fundamentalists,[8] yet, rather, it is a genuinely pragmatic innovation responding to the multicultural reality of Birmingham and other conurbation schools. This should be consolidated, extended and given proper legal recognition. It acknowledges the importance of communicating to pupils basic human values, helping others and ethics, while detaching the assembly from any specific religious faith. It retains space in the school curriculum for pupils to learn about different religions while leaving religious groups free to promote their faith through supplementary schools.

One of the core achievements of the Enlightenment is the establishment of a secular society where the state and religion are separated so that all beliefs, whether religious or not, are treated equally. The state is neutral with regard to matters of belief. This serves as a protection of religion, above all of religious minorities, as it restricts the state from interfering with religions and religious believers. As distinct from theocracy this enables pluralism and the practice of many beliefs rather than allowing only one 'state' religion. Moreover, the activities of public services are kept open to all irrespective of religion.[9]

Peaceful co-existence also requires the assertion that public space is free space. People are able to express their religious beliefs in public spaces, notably by establishing houses of worship or by proselytising in the street – as one sees and hears when walking around Birmingham city centre on a Saturday afternoon. A more complex area concerns how to respond to the full-face veil, where only the eyes are uncovered. Interviewees gave a range of reasons for its emergence. Some men 'have been imposing it on their women'; some women see it as a way to identify as being pious; some a sign that different kinds of Islam are coming into the country. Some see it as a kind of 'up yours', a way of saying we are Muslim and proud of it. Some wear it for two or three years and then stop. To Zubeda, 'It is all about identity. Not just in Birmingham but also in the north of England. For some people, the more they feel the community is being attacked, they withdraw. Unfortunately, they feel there is a belonging in that smaller community. These are women who don't have the chances to be part of wider society.'

A considerable number are uncomfortable about its emergence. Rashda, the interpreter and mother, doesn't believe in it.

'God has given us a face, an identity. Why should I hide it? Why should I cover it? '

As a newsagent, Rehman doesn't like it when customers come in wearing the veil.

'To tell you the truth, when they come into my shop I feel a bit uncomfortable. I think they shouldn't wear it. You like to see the person who you are serving.'

Samera, the shop assistant, puts it sharply.

'I don't like it when people wear the veil. I can't see them. It's not part of our religion. It's been brought in by the Arabs.'

The question this poses is how to respond. Is the more restrictive French route the answer? Nazir is one of the few who thinks it is.

'To say we are free to choose anything is nonsense, we are not. My choice is defined by an agreed legal framework. I cannot walk naked in the street. There are rights and responsibilities. You are putting a wall against the other. Wear it in your private space or in your religious space but not in public space. How can you communicate with people if they cannot see your face?'

Most take issue with such a stern stance. Ashraf says, 'It's quite fashionable. As my wife says, they don't have to wear it but do because their friends are wearing it. But, no, don't ban it. People should dress up in the way they choose to do so. If you start restricting what people can wear, that is too much.'

Zubeda is aware that the assertion of individual rights has social consequences. From conversations she knows that her mum would like to be able to interpret her religion in the way that she wants, but Zubeda is conscious that this makes wider engagement more difficult. She does not think things have worked well in France where they have banned it.

'I would defend any woman's right to wear what she wants but I also have an understanding that of course it makes it harder to communicate.'

Albert Bore, the former Labour council leader, pursues a similar line of argument.

'A more direct engagement is made more difficult by an individual woman wearing a full-face veil because face-to-face contact is part of communication. But there is an issue of choice here. If a woman for whatever reason – other than she has been told to do it, which is unacceptable – but if from her own volition she chooses to wear a full-face veil then I need to respect that. I would hope that we would find ourselves moving away from that but not by diktat. I think that is what is wrong in France.'

Salma, the health service manager, says the veil is a trend evident among some middle-class, wealthier Muslims. She sees its dangers.

'There is a group of women who think it is giving them freedom and that it is a choice, but I can't quite see how. I think it is a shame because they are isolating themselves and their children. This Muslim community does need to wake up to what it is doing.'

These are some of the challenges and tensions being thrown up in the twenty-first-century city. By and large there is an urban population unconcerned about religion living with a growing Muslim population in its midst, amongst whom there is a devout core. There is an asymmetry here which is being further tested by the separate but overlapping issues of Islamicist terrorism. This discussion indicates how peaceful co-existence can be promoted. The city has to see religious freedom as a core value but, in so doing, also support a culture of openness and dissent. The *Behzti* affair shows the danger of allowing religious zealotry to determine public policy. Its public services need to accommodate the specific needs of a diverse population, but their core function is the secular one of providing access for all without any discrimination. The development of general assemblies in schools which highlight human values, morals and ethics while detaching this from any specific religious faith is a genuine innovation, which should be consolidated and given proper legal recognition. Alongside this it needs to guarantee that public space is free space, so that the French attempt to coerce people in what they wear is avoided, while recognising that wearing clothing that hides one's face inhibits social contact and makes interaction between citizens much harder. The application of these standards will both grant religious freedoms but also restrain attempts by hardliners to impose their will on public spaces, services and institutions.

On the Birmingham train down to London, I was pondering these questions and the evident diversity of views they revealed. I was off to watch my team in the last game of the season. It was a warm spring day. Zainab was sitting opposite, wearing her short-sleeved Arsenal shirt emblazoned with Özil 11 on the back. It was good to talk to a younger member of the club. She'd been a fan since she was a young kid who had idolised Dennis Bergkamp. It is not that common to have Asian women who are football fans, but she had been introduced to the game by her brothers and had stuck with it. She managed to get to a few games a season, even though it was pretty expensive. Her parents had come to Birmingham from Pakistan and they, her brothers and her, all still lived in the city. She had trained as a teacher and now taught in a primary school in north Birmingham. So, I wondered, how come a Muslim woman was travelling down by train on her own, wearing a football shirt and jeans? Her rebuke to the communitarians could not have been clearer. 'Look,' she said, 'we are all different. There are plenty of different types of Muslim. I have my faith but don't need to parade it in how I dress. And no one stops me from going around and doing what I enjoy.'

Arsenal won the match 4-1. We overtook Spurs and finished second in the League. But with her assertion of female independence and cultural freedom, it was Zainab who had made my day.

# 10

## *Sex, Love and Marriage*

Rock and roll and the contraceptive pill were the emblems of the 'swinging Sixties'. The social impact of mass culture, sexual equality and greater individual freedom have reverberated around the globe ever since. This has not been a smooth, uncontested process. While the US has often led the way, its powerful conservative and religious minorities have successfully resisted the process in many states, most noticeably on the issue of abortion but also on matters such as sex education in schools and the active promotion of chastity.

Compared to the USA, resistance has been less effective in most of Europe. Parts of the former Soviet bloc vigorously oppose elements of this social upheaval with nasty homophobia encouraged in Russia and fierce opposition to abortion by the nationalist right in Poland, but elsewhere in Europe, including the Catholic south, the scale and scope of change has been truly remarkable. Despite the best efforts of the Catholic Church, divorce is now legal and accepted across Europe and in many countries beyond; sex is no longer automatically associated with marriage and children as the sharply falling birth rates in Italy, Spain and Germany testify; and the shadow of criminality has gradually been lifted from homosexuality. Here, as with abortion, the traditionalist right tries to check and halt the momentum, but over the last half-century there has been an unparalleled shift towards greater sexual and personal freedom, a trend reinforced by the result of the Irish referendum on abortion on 25 May 2018. The world that Peggy recalls in Co. Cavan as one of thirteen children, where the priest came round every year to check up on her parents to make sure they were having another child, has gone for ever.

Many, particularly among the older generation, have found this unsettling. The much more explicit sexual imagery used in advertising, in film and particularly now online disturbs many of those who support these overall moves towards greater liberty. Yet the direction of travel is clear. Today only one in ten of the British population disapprove of sex before marriage, while only a fifth consider homosexuality as always wrong, down from a half thirty years ago. For many from traditional working-class backgrounds this has been an unsettling transition. The culture clash is admirably captured in the film *Pride* based on the true story of a South Wales coal-mining community and the arrival of a lesbian and gay group from London to show their solidarity during the 1984–5 miners' strike. The 'Blue Labour' trend briefly prominent after 2010 gave voice to these socially conservative sentiments and tried to base Labour's future strategy on the revival of a past that had long gone. UKIP's Nigel Farage followed a similarly obsolete course. Post-Brexit, others like David Goodhart (see Introduction) are seeking to revive this route but there is no going back to a world where mothers stayed at home, sex was only for the married, divorce was stigmatised and homosexuality was illegal.

Yet these social and cultural changes have not just been unsettling for many Britons. It has meant adjustment for lots of migrants, too. For many of those who migrated to the UK, often coming from rural backgrounds with strong traditional family ties and religious convictions, these developments have also been deeply disturbing. The disruption of moving to a new country thousands of miles from home is profound, even more so when it means having to learn a new language. When the family customs and norms are being turned upside down by the wider world into which the migrants have entered, the unease and disquiet becomes even more intense.

For many from traditional, conservative cultures arranged marriages were the norm. Unlike intermarriage, there is no official data. However, it is clear that these broader social changes have been having a profound impact on the arranged marriage tradition. Most have responded flexibly and adjusted pragmatically to their changed circumstances.

The vast majority of first-generation Asian migrants to this country were in a marriage that had been arranged, sorted and decided by their parents without the prior agreement or consent of the children concerned. Yet whether from a Muslim, Hindu or Sikh background, it is clear that modern urban culture is rapidly dissolving this tradition. The information and communication technologies revolution gives second-generation migrant children access to the world and all its imagery at the click of a button. However enclosed many are within enclave communities, their children are just a bus ride away from meeting other youngsters at the Bull Ring shopping centre, the Central Library or Star City, where they can gaze at the glitzy world of Bollywood on one of its thirty cinema screens. Or else the click of a computer screen or iPhone. The norms, practices and protocols of village life in rural Pakistan or India appear to be from another planet.

That's the reality the first generation have to grapple with. Most have recognised that an absolutist resistance to change is neither feasible nor effective. This is very evident among those who themselves had an arranged marriage. It may have been imposed on them, but they are recognising that it can't be imposed on their own children.

Kalsoom was a very young bride who was brought over in 1969 and has raised four sons in Birmingham. The first sorted out his own marriage; the second, she and her husband arranged but with their son and daughter-in-law's consent. Kalsoom arranged the marriage for her third son but, when the girl came over from Pakistan, she and her son didn't get on so that was dissolved. Kalsoom knew it would not work. The fourth son she is leaving to find his own path. She recognises that the prevalence of the arranged marriage system is lessening: 'Definitely. And I totally agree with this. An arranged marriage with their consent, yes, but just arranged, blind, and then they go for it, no. Because at the end of the day, they have to spend their lives with each other and know each other.'

She also accepts the reality of separation and divorce. Her second son had an arranged marriage but is now separated. The couple had known each other for a year beforehand, everything seemed fine but after three or four years it wasn't working out. He has an eleven-year-old son and they are now both living with Kalsoom.

190

'Marriage means two people living happily with each other. If this is not happening, then you are allowed to get out of it.'

Zahida is a devout Muslim but on this issue she is not that strict. Her son and daughter have chosen their own partners. She sees it as their decision.

'I don't want them turning back to me if it doesn't work out and saying it is your fault. I am comfortable with this change in tradition. But my sister isn't. She has arranged the marriage of her daughter.'

Rashda was born in a small town near Multan, in the Pakistani Punjab. She came here in 1976 via an arranged marriage organised by her parents and her husband's elder brother. She had to bring up five children – one of them severely disabled – as a single parent when her husband left her. But she is very clear that who her children live with is their choice: 'It is for them to decide, not me.'

The difficulties of sticking to previous practice are evident in Adam's story. His mother wanted to follow the traditional path, so Adam's first marriage was sorted out by her. Adam had been brought up to be very respectful – probably too respectful, he now thinks – of older people and parents. So when his mother said that she wanted him to marry this girl from Pakistan he didn't argue. He didn't realise how tough it would be, not sharing a similar personality. They didn't fight or argue, but they just didn't have enough in common. She had been brought up in Pakistan, trained to be completely subservient to her husband. Adam was growing up in a more equal society. So when he asked 'what shall we do today?' she would say 'whatever you wish'; when he would say 'what shall we eat today?' the answer would be 'whatever you want'. It became quite tough for Adam. He thought she would grow out of it, but it just didn't happen. He talked to his parents and his mother would say, 'come on, Adam, be a man'. But in the end he told his mother, 'I just have to finish this. There is nothing in common.' His mother said that Adam had a duty towards his wife, since if she went back to Pakistan she would not find another husband. It was only two years since she had first come to the UK, so she needed two more years' residency before she could get a passport. So Adam agreed that they would stay married but live separately; he would support her and look after her upkeep for the next two years. He still keeps in touch with her and she has remarried and recently had a child. The experience taught Adam a lesson: he had to stand on his own two feet and take responsibility for the big decisions in his life. For a while he thought he wouldn't marry again. Then he met Fatima through his work; they hit it off; had common interests; and he asked her to marry him. Then he told his mother, who now gets on fine with her new daughter-in-law.

This shift is evident among devout Hindus, too. Ajay and Anu had not met before they married. With their children it has been different. They introduced their elder daughter to her husband – not the first husband suggested – and it took five years for their daughter to decide. With their second daughter, she looked on a website and then they looked and offered suggestions but she made the decision. Interestingly, it has gone further with their son. Ajay and Anu suggested a number of girls but he looked for himself and chose his own wife without any parental involvement.

As Ajay acknowledges, 'We have modified the approach of our parents. This is a more modern way of doing it.'

Similar trends are evident within the Sikh tradition. Mandeep met her husband through the family but it was her decision to hook up together. She had been introduced to somebody earlier and had turned him down. She is clear that the arranged marriage tradition continues in some cases, but it is different now. People go out more, it is less strict. She and her generation are happy for their children to find their own partners. Her sister-in-law's children have married out of caste completely and they haven't a problem with that. Their children are happily married. With Daljit, the tradition was beginning to loosen as she grew up. She describes her own as 'a mutually arranged marriage, not forced'. It was a traditional one in the sense that families met and recommended; she and her husband-to-be had a chat; and then decided. She thought, yes, this is the kind of person I would like to spend my life with and they were married within twelve weeks. Today, her two elder daughters are in their twenties. Socially, her kids are very active. 'They have friends from uni and work. It is up to them how they plan their social time. Who they go out with, that is up to them.'

Rehman, the newsagent, sums up the trend. He and his wife are quite clear that they are living in a new era.

'Everything has changed from when we were growing up. Only one of my brothers chose his own wife. For our children, everything is different now. If they go to university or college they may find someone they like. As long as they are happy, we are not going to force them.'

This outlook is spilling over into intermarriage, too. There has been a 'live and let live' ambience in the city for several decades. People have not necessarily been getting on like a house on fire but they have got by and learned to accept and at times respect one another. To draw a Cold War analogy, for most of the time there has been peaceful co-existence with various efforts to create a more harmonious and equal city, interrupted by the odd flare-up.

Intermarriage and mixed relationships crossing ethnic and religious boundaries are one key indication of the extent of more, far-reaching integration. It is a powerful sign at the grassroots of moving beyond passive co-existence, since nobody is forcing these relationships. Indeed, the reverse, the strength of passion, feeling and commitment, outweighs the strong community, religious and family resistance that the mixed couple often have to confront.

Survey data reveals that part of the break from traditional conservatism on social and sexual mores has been a notable shift in attitudes towards intermarriage. In the mid-1980s, a British Social Attitudes survey showed 50 per cent of the public were against marriage across ethnic lines. The figure dropped to 40 per cent in the 1990s and now stands at 15 per cent. One in four of the over-sixty-fives still say that they would be uncomfortable about a child or grandchild marrying somebody from a different race, but that falls to one in twenty of those under twenty-five.[1]

This is not just a bland answer given to opinion pollsters. These trends are evident on the streets and in the households of Birmingham. The 2011 census records nearly 25,000 households composed of whites and black Caribbeans; over 3,000 households of whites and black Africans; over 11,000 white and Asian households and 8,500 of other mixed backgrounds. In total, around 5 per cent of the city's households are of mixed heritage.

This trend is directly affecting the lives of many migrants and their families in the city.

The grip of religion and race on Irish and West Indian migrants appears to have weakened the most. Peggy says that it was not important to her whether or not her children married Catholics. Two of them have, two of them haven't. Her eldest married a girl who didn't have any religion at all.

'People from all parts of the world have married into my family. I have my grandson who has married a girl who already had a black child. He calls me granny. He loves me; I love him. I don't treat him any different from anyone else in the family. To me everybody is the same. If you're a black fella and you bleed, what colour is your blood?'

Chris was brought up as a Catholic, baptised and went to Communion but is no longer practising. His parents were aware that bringing up children in a different country meant there would be different influences on them and that they had to respect the choices that could be made by a younger generation. This was especially the case with regard to relationships. On the question of marrying a Catholic, he is adamant.

'No, no, no. It was never on the cards. There was no overt pressure whatsoever. Whoever you become friends with there was always a welcome . . . my parents would rather see and meet who me and my brother were socialising with rather than us hiding from them.'

It is happening among the new Polish migrants, too. Ewa tells me that her husband's sister, with whom they lodged when they first arrived in England, is married to an Indian Christian who works at Deutsche Bank. 'I have got no problem with that.'

Sam was brought up in a strict Pentecostal household with eight brothers and sisters. He recalls his first white girlfriend, Sarah, a wonderful woman with whom he was smitten. He remembers being terrified of telling his father that he had a white girlfriend. His dad – a minister in the Church – surprised him by asking 'do you love her?' Sam said he didn't know and his dad said, 'well, you need to figure it out. That is what is most important, son.'

In his varied life Sam has gone out with black, white and Asian women. Mo is similar. While brought up as a Methodist and attending Sunday School in his youth, Mo is not religious at all. Unmarried, he emphasises that going out with people from the same background or religion is not important to him at all.

'I'm a committed heterosexual and, let's face it, at the end of the day I have always been brought up on the idea that if you are over eighteen and consenting, you can do whatever you want – inside the law. People can settle with anybody that they want to settle with. I am not too worried about what anybody thinks. My parents are from a different generation.'

David is married to a white woman and has three children. He, too, had been brought up as a Methodist and went to Sunday School until he was fourteen. He has been married twice, both times to white women, and experienced no resistance of any kind from either his parents or relatives. He thinks the prevalence of more mixed relationships among people from the Caribbean compared to other migrant groups is historical.

'My perception is that the Caribbean upbringing, the way I behave and believe, comes more from Europe. Just the whole idea of choice . . . There is not a tradition that you just do what your parents want you to do. Not doing what your parents want you to do does not carry a Caribbean stigma. Because you have a free choice. There is far less of an African tradition to shape the structure of the family. This distinction between some African communities and the Caribbean helps to explain why there has been less resistance to intermarriage.'

Certainly, this chimes with Ben's experience, for it is the pressure of this African tradition that was a key factor in his decision to stay in Birmingham after completing his Ph.D. rather than return to Nigeria. He feels that background or religion should not be a decision as to who becomes his life partner. He goes out with people from a range of backgrounds. However, he has to carry the expectations of his family. They are more conservative. They feel they should know very well the background of the person Ben marries, which basically means Ibos.

'I don't agree with limiting people's choice of association based on religion or ethnicity. I don't approve of that. My parents know that. We had had lots of discussions on this topic which is why I know they are so conservative. So I will just have to deal with that. If I met a soulmate here right now, then I would go ahead and marry her. It is an issue that would have to be confronted. This is real life. It is one of those difficult issues.'

While there is a widening acceptance of the inevitable decline of the arranged marriage tradition, the issue of 'marrying out' arouses far greater passions, fears and traumas within Asian communities. For some it is a cultural preference; for others it is a religious diktat.

Two second-generation mothers of Sikh background clearly see it as a cultural preference. Who Daljit's daughters go out with, she says, is up to them. Within families, the children of the next generation have started to get married and generally it tends to be within the same cultural background. The kids are aware that, ideally, their parents would prefer this, purely because then the families have more in common. That is not to say that there are not interracial marriages. Her relaxed tone comes through when she says, 'Some of the children have had mixed marriages. You know, you only live once so it is whatever works out really.'

Mandeep has talked it over with her oldest daughter.

'We would prefer it if she goes out with boys from her own background. You are more likely to get on with people from a similar background but if she fell in love with someone from a different background then I'll have to accept it.'

Pam, the shopkeeper, believes in the universal values of Sikhism. His outlook is clear.

'My children are humans, they can marry any human that they choose. They will not be forced. That is an issue for them to decide, not for you to arrange.'

For the accountant Raj, it is still important that the kids his children marry are at least Asian/Indian, whether they are Hindu or Sikh.

'Me and my wife, we were brought up that we should be marrying within our caste. I am definitely relaxed about the caste business but . . . our preference is definitely that it should be Indian.'

They accept that there are more mixed relationships happening and among people he knows. He gives the example of some of his wider family and friends marrying white guys. In his relaxed, laid-back style, Raj just says, 'look, this is our preference. We would be very disappointed, but we would not disown them or anything.'

Among Muslims, while the picture is differentiated, the inhibitions and resistance are definitely stronger. There may be growing acceptance of change with regard to arranged marriage but, for many, intermarriage is a step too far.

As Kalsoom expresses it, 'To be honest with you, I wouldn't be very happy about it. I would like them to marry Muslims. Mingling or friendships OK, but ladies don't do that. I know it is happening but religiously it is wrong. That is where the religion comes in. It is *haram*. Islam is a total way of life. If you study properly you will find answers to all the issues in life. So mingling with different people as a friend – friend that is fine but when it comes to men and women, boys and girls mixing with each other for that purpose or as boyfriend and girlfriend then that is where I am still very old-fashioned. I don't agree with that because I think for one woman and one man you don't have to go through all these experiences with the different people.'

It is hard to explain, she says, as she chuckles and smiles ruefully to herself. She then admits that her eldest son is married to a non-Muslim, a Spanish Catholic, whom she gets on well with. She would have preferred that he marry a Muslim girl who is more aware of his culture, but if he chooses her as his life partner and he gets on with her, then she is prepared to go along with it.

'I was hoping that as she sees the culture and studies it, she would become a Muslim, but I don't think that she should change her religion just for the sake of marriage. That would have been just for show. Now they have two sons and I am not sure what religion they will have as they grow up. Deep inside, no matter how I try to be broad-minded, I wish that his family grow up as a Muslim, as a faith. And believing in one God.'

There is anguish and pain etched across her face as she explains the dilemma that she feels. Yet, at the same time, she has the humanity to acknowledge that her daughter-in-law is a very good mother and wife and that she couldn't hope for anyone better from the Muslim religion.

Zahida takes a harder line. Like Kalsoom, she went on a pilgrimage to Saudi Arabia in the late 1990s and returned much more devout. On intermarriage, she has explained to her children that they shouldn't be doing it but, if they do, she then asks whether the partner is happy enough to become a Muslim. This is what happened with her own daughter. The man she married was a Sikh. He converted as Zahida wanted, but she feels it was for the sake of getting married, not for the religion.

'It really hurts a lot. I do meet her but the way she has rebelled against my religion, it just hurts me. He is a good person, she is very happy with him. They have a three-year-old son. But it hasn't been done for the right reasons. The actual practice is not there.'

Yet she is quite clear what would have happened if he had not converted.

'Then I wouldn't be meeting my children. They have to separate from me. I am such a person that if I can give up everything for the religion, then why can't I leave my children behind as well?'

The contrast with Rashda, who hasn't gone on a pilgrimage to Saudi Arabia, is quite stark. To her, the question of intermarriage is not that important. Originally, when her eldest son asked her she said she would love him to marry a Muslim because there wouldn't be any complications for the children. He said 'OK, he would marry an Egyptian.' She said no, she wanted them to be Pakistani, and he said, 'so the culture is important, too'. Rashda realised from this and later conversations that she would have to change.

'I have grown up as well now. To me what is important is that they are happy, that the person is nice. It doesn't matter who the person is. He had an Indian girlfriend and he now has two children with a Chinese woman. He doesn't believe in marriage.'

Her three sons get on well with the Chinese woman and Rashda does, too. She sees the happiness of her children as the most important.

Many migrant households are grappling with these issues of tradition, religion and modernity. Ashraf's family come from rural Mirpur. He lives across the road from his mother; two brothers live in the same street; and all eight of his siblings still live locally. Yet his family's horizons are gradually widening. His sister recently got married to a Muslim from Morocco. They have moved beyond the thinking of their parents. He is very clear of the tensions between his heritage and the realities of the modern world.

'We are trying to juggle our Pakistani traditions and religion – two different things – and also trying to be part of a society where our children are happy. We have moved the acceptance level threshold so far but there are boundaries . . . I am a bit more open-minded and secular than my wife. She, as a strong believer, would like to see our children marry other Muslims, preferably Pakistanis, but there is no real rule. The key focus for us is that as long as they are happy.'

For other Muslims, these boundaries are more fluid and the rigidities of orthodox religion more open to question. Zubeda

201

comes from a Muslim household where five of her siblings have chosen to marry people from a similar background. She is not married herself and has changed her mind on the question. It has now become most important for her to find the right person, irrespective of their religion, if any, or skin colour, to marry someone who has the same values as well. She gets on well with her mum and dad and respects them, but she knows this is sensitive territory which she has still to discuss with her parents.

Ozlem had to tell her parents back in Turkey that she was going to marry an English guy. She sees herself as more of a spiritual Muslim. Her parents were not happy but her four sisters were OK with the idea. They were liberal, like Ozlem, but her mum was worried, especially about what her dad would say and what others in the community would think. They were shocked first of all, but once they met her husband and realised there was no other way, then they accepted it and have got on well with him. Ozlem is very content in her mixed marriage. She is a non-practising Muslim. She feels that the religion is a part of her at a spiritual level, helping her to believe in Allah and the goodness of humanity. Her husband is an atheist; they talk to their son about their different outlooks but make sure that they impose nothing on him.

Then there are those brought up within the Muslim faith and the Pakistani heritage community who reject the impositions of this traditional world. Samera likes the freedom that being brought up in the UK offers and she makes full use of it. Single and in her late thirties, she enjoys her work in the Bull Ring, lives at home and is happy to be part of a family, as she says, 'a bit like the Greeks and Italians do it'. She is pragmatic enough to acknowledge that it helps with her living costs. She doesn't have or want any children. She doesn't wear a headscarf in the day, only putting one on when she goes to the mosque, as a sign of respect. She likes to wear jeans and T-shirts but doesn't wear short skirts. But on men she is clear: who she goes out with is her business and no one else's.

'I like it in this country that I am free to do what I want. I go out with Italian men. That's who I like. I went out for quite some time with an Italian guy. He was a Catholic. My friend, she goes out with black men. You should be able to go out with who you like.'

She only takes boys home when it is serious, as she did with her Italian ex-partner. Otherwise, she goes round to their place. She is clear that there is a problem with many men in her community.

'You'll get a different view from Muslim men. Too many of them want to keep women in their place. They tell me if I don't marry I'll go to hell and I say, if you don't marry, will you go to hell, too?'

These shifting sexual trends are even emerging on homosexuality, as gays and lesbians slowly step out of the shadows. Sam records that it is still hard for them in the black community, but things are evolving and it is better than it was. There are more openly gay people of Caribbean extraction than when he was younger but generally for a support network they still need to look outside their immediate community.

The issue creeps into people's lives in surprising places. Rashda is telling me that it is quite common for Pakistani men to have affairs with local white women while keeping the Asian wife at home. She then recalls how her neighbour – half her age – had had an unhappy experience with her husband who kept her in the house but then had an affair with a white woman outside the home. In the end he left her. She went through a bad time and was lonely.

'One day she came round and she asked me out.'

Rashda was stunned and not quite sure how to react but just reflected that everyone has different needs and desires. This wasn't for her, but she felt, 'live and let live'.

Zahida strikes a more moralistic tone. She acknowledges that openly gay and lesbian relationships are relatively rare in her experience – unlike Asian men having affairs with other women. It still remains 'very hush hush in our community'. Children won't tell their parents as they will be shunned from the family. In a local case, where the son did admit to a gay relationship, his parents told him to leave the home. How does she relate this to her Islamic faith?

'I will have a genuine chat with them, I won't shun them. I won't hate them. I understand that it is wrong what they are doing but perhaps one day they will come back to the right path.'

Ashraf is at home in wider society, actively engaged in Labour Party politics as well as at work. He has friends from different communities, friends with different sexual preferences, people who have different views from himself. It all makes him 'more open-minded' and relaxed about these issues, although he admits that he himself knows no Pakistani gays. But he has had to stand up to some of the bigotry that he has come across.

'There are some fundamental nutters around. I'm thinking of

one person who I no longer talk to. I mean, his views on homo-sexuality had to be challenged. What he said we should do to homosexuals, views like that are unacceptable when we are living in a quite diverse, secular society.'

Adam's first experience of coming across a Muslim gay man was when he was interviewing for new special constables within the police force. He tells a story at his own expense about chairing an interview panel. He asked this Asian man what the greatest achievement of his life was. The guy answered, 'telling my parents that I am gay'. Adam was drinking a glass of water at the time and he coughed and spluttered in disbelief. He was both surprised by the answer and full of questions at the same time. The female personnel manager asked him if he had a problem with the answer and Adam said he hadn't. After the interview he walked the inter-viewee downstairs. He felt he just had to ask him about it, so he said, 'Why the hell did you tell your parents?' The guy replied, 'they were forcing me to get married and I didn't want to screw some girl's life over'. Adam asked what their reaction was, and he said, 'they kicked me out the house'. Adam and his colleague appointed the guy and he recalls that he did his job as a special constable really well.

The sexual and relationship kaleidoscope within the city is shifting, affecting all migrant as well as indigenous communities. There aren't too many like Sam or Samera, but they are not alone. Some want to hold back these tides of change but the forces making for a more open society and wider choices are winning out. A Saturday visit to the humming, mixed crowds at the Bull Ring shopping centre or the Star City cinema complex bears witness to the transitions underway. Wing Yip, the global businessman, sees the inevitability of mixing and intercultural relationships. He has one daughter who has married an Englishman from a Warwickshire farming family; he also has two nieces who married locally.

'That is inevitable. Put it this way. In America they are called "banana" – outside yellow, inside white. It is not an abusive term. Born here they have more in common with local people as they are. In a globalising world this is just a matter of time.'

How long is a question of politics, culture and religion. This will not be a smooth linear process, an upward curve of gradual, molecular integration as the power of sexual attraction overcomes the fear of 'the other' and the pull of tradition and religion.

The growing social split with regard to religion will be a key factor. In the three decades since the British Social Attitudes survey started in 1983 the proportion of those surveyed in the general population claiming no religion had risen from less than one-third to more than a half.[2] Regular religious attendance continues to fall. The influence of religion is declining in a number of migrant communities such as the Catholic Irish and Afro-Caribbean but, in stark contrast, its hold is growing among Muslims, for reasons explained in the previous chapter. This combination of the Muslim faith with personal identity and world politics is a powerful one, which the government and religious organisations within Saudi Arabia actively promote within Sunni Muslim communities in Europe. The mass pilgrimages to Mecca serve as a strong reinforcement of the most fundamentalist sentiments within Islam, as a number of the interviewees have shown. The stricter the religious interpretation of Islam, the harder it is to intermarry. The injunction that in a mixed marriage the non-Muslim has to convert is a particular barrier which cuts across a 'live and let live' philosophy and helps to explain why white Britons have much stronger concerns about intermarriage with Muslims than with other blacks or Asians. This is a touchy topic for others, too. Pam, as a Sikh, recalls that he explained to his daughter that if she wanted to marry a Muslim and he wanted to marry her for what she is, that is fine. But if he wants to marry in order to convert her, it means he doesn't love her for what she is. Forcing you to change your religion is what he sees as dangerous.

This is an ongoing tussle within Islam. The cross-section of views outlined here shows the diversity of opinion that exists on the ground in Birmingham between fundamentalist and more liberal strands of opinion. That tension exists within all religions, as illustrated by the experiences of the Catholic Church over the last three decades. The extent to which those strands of opinion most prepared to accommodate the realities of a twenty-first-century world – above all in respect of recognising other faiths, women's rights and sexuality – come to predominate within all religions will be crucial in determining the pace of integration within our societies. Here, the big cities are the harbingers of the future. In Birmingham, the dominant temperament remains one of 'live and let live'. There are those of a fundamentalist disposition on social and religious as well as political issues, but Raj captures the prevailing mood with his cryptic observation, 'Of course, intermarriage is happening. Like I said, our preference is for our kids to marry within the Indian community. But where inter-marriage does happen, we are not going to be Taliban about it.'

# 11

## *The Political Kaleidoscope*

Paul Tilsley is a tall man with a gangling gait who has never been known to be short of a word or three. A Brummie born and bred, he joined the Liberal Party at the age of sixteen in 1961, as it was the only pro-European party. He contested the inner-city Aston ward in 1967 and the following May, with the Labour government at the height of its unpopularity, he was one of three Liberal victors in the inner city, with the other thirty-six seats going to the Conservatives. The councillors were elected in a three-yearly cycle and met monthly in the august surroundings of the ornate Victorian Council House.

When the newcomer attended his first full council meeting in June 1968 the racist bandwagon unleashed by Enoch Powell was rolling. The meeting discussed a report from the General Purposes Committee proposing to ban all immigration into the city due to its adverse effect on public services. Paul thought this was stupid.

'The people coming over were pioneers, mainly single men coming to look for work. I was the lone voice who spoke against the motion and then voted against it.'

His Liberal colleagues and the Labour opposition both supported the motion. Then within the Liberal group he was told to 'shut up', with the national Chief Whip, David Steel MP, getting involved. There was discussion about whether immigrants should have different-coloured national insurance cards.

'I said that sounded like the Pass Laws in South Africa and do we want to be associated with that? I was expelled from the party. It was a pretty torrid time, being a lone voice in the Council. Counting the Aldermanic bench it was one councillor against one hundred and fifty-five. I felt like a pariah.'

Standing out from the crowd is never easy. Combating discrimination and prejudice has depended on countless brave individual and collective actions, which have shifted the agenda and changed the political boundaries. Tilsley survived with support from a couple of Labour councillors and within two years he was back in the Liberal group. By 1971 his Young Liberal Turks had wrested control from the racist old guard.

This ebb and flow continued through the 1970s. The introduction of the Race Relations Act in 1976 created more favourable conditions to challenge racism and discrimination. Yet while the outside world showed signs of change, until 1979 the 117 councillors representing the city's thirty-nine wards – each with three councillors – were entirely white. A handful of councillors drawn from the Irish community had been elected but it was only in 1979 that the first two black councillors were elected for Labour in inner-city wards. Three more black and Asian councillors followed in 1982. From then on, the number of black and Asian councillors within Labour ranks grew steadily. A range of factors were at play here.

On the one hand, the economic crisis of the late 1970s and the election of the Thatcher government of 1979 broke the post-war consensus on full employment and the welfare state. Thatcher accompanied her monetarist economics with a harder edge to welfare and social policy and a harsher tone to the issues of race and immigration. At the same time, a more radical municipal left began to emerge in many metropolitan areas. Their calls for militancy often threatened to overturn the established patterns of local Labour Party business, a danger exacerbated when the left began to stress the importance of the re-selection of sitting MPs. In inner-city areas, many local Labour parties had become moribund, the active working-class base of the post-war years having long been eroded. The response of established figures in these situations was to look for new sources of support. In Birmingham, traditional right-wing Labour politicians sought to recruit ethnic minorities to reinforce support for their local leadership. This was an instrumental form of political mobilisation: white, right-wing MPs bolstered their support; in return black power brokers achieved specific promises. By 1991 there were eighteen black and Asian councillors and by 1994 a third of the Labour group were from black and Asian communities.

This instrumental form of mobilisation began with the Irish migration and the way that the Irish community was engaged in local politics in the 1960s and 1970s. The Labour Club on the Stratford Road was run by the Irish community and Roy Hattersley, the local Labour MP – and over the period Cabinet Minister and Deputy Labour Leader – used that location as his base in the Sparkbrook constituency. As former Labour leader Albert Bore recalls, 'you had to be part of that community to have any influence in Sparkbrook. What happened with Roy Hattersley and Dick Knowles was that they had strong contacts with individuals. Certain people and certain families were identified with certain politicians. This was the case with certain Irish people; it wasn't long before certain Pakistani heritage families became identified with certain politicians in Sparkbrook in the same way. It was based on trust and long-term understandings. These arrangements were all personal. They were not political, so politics began to have a personalised basis to it, rather than the traditional political and ideological underpinning.'

That has been the basis on which the Labour Party's relationship with the newer ethnic minority communities in the city has grown. It is very reminiscent of the experience of Jews in pre-war Stepney. When I told my dad about these patronage relationships he just said, 'oh, you've got communal crooks, too' and recounted how Jewish community leaders in the 1930s had made sweetheart deals with the anti-Semitic Catholic leadership of the Labour Party within the East End of London. This communalist politics – rallying around a local figure from your own ethnic community – has long been a feature of US Democrat politics and of Irish Catholic engagement within UK Labour politics. Jeremy Corbyn's predecessor as the MP for Islington North was Michael O'Halloran, a Tammany Hall-style wheeler-dealer who won his nomination and retained his position for more than a decade in this way.

The Pakistani link to Labour was sustained by the 'bradthery' (brotherhood) system. The emergence of Pakistani heritage engagement in local politics undermined Paul Tilsley's position in the Aston ward. He had a strong following. He supported the Bangladeshis in their war of independence in 1971, but he also gave support to those Pakistani/Kashmiri soldiers who were captured and detained in Bangladesh during that war. He did this even though he had supported Bangladeshi independence. However, in the full set of elections that were held in 1982, when all three seats were contested in one go he lost out to a Labour candidate of Pakistani origin.

'I came across the "bradthery" (which roughly translates as brotherhood). I was told from within the Pakistani community that although I had a great reputation, the "bradthery" wanted to elect one of their own, i.e. a Pakistani Muslim. By then, the Sikhs and Hindus had largely moved on; those left were largely Muslim, in a closed community, like a village. There were claims that local leaders would threaten people if they didn't vote Labour.'

Tilsley had to look for electoral success elsewhere and found it several years later in the eastern suburbs.

The 'bradthery' clan system has undoubtedly acted as a strong glue between Pakistani heritage communities and Labour. It only broke down in 2003 following Tony Blair's fulsome backing for the Iraq War. Tilsley recalls, 'We [Liberal Democrats] had a surge of ethnic minority support but it was a one issue surge on the back of the Iraq War. We were unable to maintain it. We held some of the seats over a couple of electoral cycles but Labour chipped away. And in the end they were too strong for us.'

Today, in some areas of the city, the Labour Party membership is almost entirely composed of people of Pakistani or Bangladeshi heritage. Albert Bore acknowledges that in those areas membership is 'controlled' by one or two key individuals or families. So what you have is a very different political environment from the 1970s. Compared to then, there is now a situation where a great deal of the Party machinery is influenced by personal rather than political positions. There are wards in Birmingham where all three councillors are of Pakistani heritage and come from that extended family. As Bore notes, 'It means there is less focus on the policy and political issues.'

The growing presence of black and Asian councillors alongside those of Irish background within Labour's council ranks was accompanied by demands to tackle the shortcomings and discrimination experienced among these communities. These included tackling the external issue of family resettlement that was a major concern for many South Asian communities along with issues of employment and improved service delivery. Key demands included the collection of accurate data to show how ethnic minority communities were accessing council services; adjusting services to meet the diverse needs of the city's multi-ethnic population; improving the examination results and general school performance of black and Asian children; and for the council itself to achieve a balanced workforce so that its ethnic characteristics reflected the population of the city.

Gradually, but not without difficulty, significant changes started to take place. Extensive consultative mechanisms with a wide range of BME voluntary groups and civil society organisations were established. This helped to improve service access and to address specific needs of migrant communities, for example with regard to elderly care and meals on wheels services, while there was a substantial improvement in the GCSE results of the city's pupils. Fully accurate figures for the ethnic composition of the council workforce are not available since a fifth of the workforce does not declare its ethnicity, but by mid-2016, 30 per cent of the

Council's workforce were from black and ethnic minority communities.

There has been some improvement in upper echelons of the pay scales, too, but at a significantly slower rate. This picture is reflected across other public organisations in the city and beyond. Connect Justice's report, 'A Tale of Three Cities', written by Zubeda Limbada (see Chapter 3), looks at police, hospital, university and council bodies in Birmingham, Bristol and Manchester. It shows a common picture of public organisations making progress in the lower ranks but failing to promote black and minority ethnic people into the managerial and senior ranks of their organisations. The report calls for these organisations to set three specific and long-term targets which are then reinforced by regular staff training. At the launch of the report a hospital personnel manager told how, in a brief to consultants, she had specified that for vacancies to their trust board they wanted a shortlist that included black and minority ethnic candidates. 'If you present us with an all-white list, then you won't win the next contract. In some areas there is no excuse.' A mixed list was provided and suitable BME candidates chosen. Changes are occurring but at a very slow pace. As Zubeda says, 'Among the big institutions in the city, diversity is not reflected in their organisation. We haven't changed the hierarchies of the city, in the universities, local government, the police and the NHS. They are predominantly white. Gender has made great strides but elsewhere no.'

Despite the various improvements that have occurred and the breakthroughs that have been achieved, there remains a grimmer side to Birmingham. Inequality continues to scar the city. Unemployment levels within the inner-city wards where the black and Asian population is concentrated continue to run at double the rate for the city as a whole. Along with some of the mainly white working-class outer estates, these are the places where multiple deprivation is at its worst. With poverty comes alienation and a high use of drugs.

Fatima grew up in a very enclosed community in Lozells and it was hard going. She was very affected by what she saw when she was a child there, especially with drugs. In her area, it was Asians who were running the drugs trade. There were people in her street selling drugs and getting addicted. Her mum's nephew was involved. He has got through it now with the help of his family. She had it at school, with the thug of her year and his little minions that followed him. The thug ended up in prison. She remembers one boy in her year, who in Year 11 was so intelligent, top of the class, everything, but one day he came in and his face was blue. She just thought, 'I don't like what drugs are doing to people in my area. He wanted to be cool and got involved with the wrong people. That boy, he hasn't done much with his life. So many young people lose it all, they have loads of ability but they just waste it. Lots of inner-city youth have a lack of confidence. They just don't reach their potential.'

Fatima was fortunate. She got help and support from her dad.

'He helped me want to explore the world and made me realise there is so much more to life than Lozells. The school also helped me. The teachers encouraged and motivated me.'

She didn't want her nieces to grow up in situations like this, so she went to study social policy at university.

These dangers affect youngsters in all the poor parts of the city. However, since the turn of the century for those within Muslim communities there has been the additional allure of radicalisation and the attractions of war, adventure and terrorism. A small but significant number of Birmingham people have gone over to Syria. In 2012, Kashan and a small team of embedded local researchers engaged with 400 Sparkbrook men and collated data through group interviews and discussions on the streets, in restaurants, gyms and shops over the course of sixteen weeks. The majority of those in the Birmingham 400 report[1] did not see themselves as British but, rather, as Muslim or Pakistani. Among the key findings were that: they were not particularly religious or well informed about the Koran; 'substance misuse amongst the sample group was widespread and normalised'; the group 'had a lack of regular and sustained interaction with other ethnic or religious groups'; the group was highly politicised about British foreign policy and its complicity in torture abroad; and they were competent internet and social media users. The Birmingham 400 report was clear that a very enclosed geographical upbringing is one of the key factors that increase the likelihood of radicalisation. Kashan contrasts that experience with his own.

'I suppose the noticeable thing about growing up is that we lived outside the "hood". That was a noticeable difference from others who grew up within the ghetto, who didn't widen their footprint. That made a difference.'

Adam knows that feeling.

'You socialise with the same circle of friends; everything revolves around the same circle, so you are stuck in that bubble. So when you hit the big, bad world you struggle. In my class at school there were very few non-Pakistanis.'

He is aware of the potential attractions of Islamist fundamentalism.

'I don't think radicalisation is on the rise but it has a presence. Partly young people are brainwashing themselves on the internet. I don't think it is so much the official mosques and religious leaders any more. Anybody can become radicalised. There are three main routes to fundamentalism: people who oppose Western military intervention in the Middle East; secondly, those attracted to a state run on religious lines as interpreted in the Koran; and thirdly, released prisoners.'

Adam attempts to mentor those who come out of prison.

'They are directed to our mosque. They were just young kids. They were sold this adventurous story about fighting Americans, but when they get there it is a lot more sinister, about suicide vests and targets in London. And they call up their parents, and say "get us out of here". They didn't do it because they wanted an Islamic State. They were kids who were influenced. There are various different actors now, different factors radicalising. I want to pull young people away from that sort of discourse.'

This gives a flavour of Birmingham's shifting political kaleidoscope as it tries to adjust to substantial economic, cultural and social change. The fact that Birmingham is one of the youngest cities in Europe adds further to the mix. The challenges confronting the city are similar to those facing all big cities, from Barcelona to Berlin, Munich to Malmö: how to integrate newcomers and migrants while supporting existing residents; how to ensure there are fulfilling opportunities for both; and how to establish open, dynamic cities which draw on all their talents and so create new hybrids. What model is best suited to achieve this type of integration?

Of course, there are those who want no integration and would prefer to 'send them back' or expect migrants to 'shut up and be grateful'. The sheer number and the extent of economic integration of migrants in almost all the major European cities (outside Eastern Europe) makes this option politically implausible as well as morally reprehensible.

The most common call is for an assimilationist form of integration. Basically, you become like us. This varies between European countries but is a common refrain. Even Angela Merkel, who risked her political standing with the brave decision to open Germany's borders to one million refugees from the Syrian civil war in 2015, sees integration in this light: 'The opposite of that [multiculturalism] is integration. Integration that demands openness to those who come to us, as well as the readiness of those who come to us to adhere to our values and traditions.'[2]

Merkel's policy is to extend a welcome to newcomers and in that she differs markedly from the Cameron and May governments and their supporters in the UK media. But there is no sense in her speeches that Germany has to change at all. A more recent convert to this approach is Trevor Phillips, the former head of the Equality and Human Rights Commission, who has become more apocalyptic in his warnings against multiculturalism ever since leaving his post.[3] With a particular concern about Muslim communities, Phillips claims that the multicultural 'live and let live' philosophy has paved the way to separatism and encouraged more sympathy in the Muslim community for terrorism. Instead of a French model of forced integration, Phillips calls for 'active integration'. Proposals to encourage the learning of English are broadly non-controversial although many courses have fallen victim to central government's austerity programme. Once he strays beyond this, the practicality of his proposals becomes open to question. He suggests no more than 50 per cent of the pupil population of any one school should be drawn from one particular ethnic minority but does not indicate how he would impose the bussing of pupils that this would entail. His call for 'a much more muscular approach' wins applause from right-wing commentators but offers little by way of practical solutions.

A traditional response to the assimilationists is to defend the achievements of multiculturalism, many of which are evident in the preceding pages. However, there is a sense that the multicultural movement has got stuck and entrenched with too many communities defending their own silos. As Kashan puts it, 'too much focus on ethnicity, giving money to people because of who they are rather than what they do or the issues they are tackling'.

That is why Amartya Sen's warning of the dangers of plural mono-culturalism has such weight. It is reinforced when one reads the arguments presented by those who disparage the efforts of the past four decades and seek to minimise the shifts that have occurred. Karamat Iqbal, a Birmingham educational practitioner, is one such example.[4] His book is a sustained complaint about the failures of Birmingham to meet the needs of its Pakistani heritage community. The book has significant omissions: no mention of the high number of Asian GPs or the very significant number of Pakistani heritage councillors. But more significantly it gives a new and dangerous twist to communal 'interest group' politics by asserting that Pakistanis are the most disadvantaged group within the city. The book is seriously divisive in that it sets one ethnic minority against the rest. It claims Pakistanis have 'lost out to Indians . . . and also lost out to black Caribbeans who, unlike earlier times [are] now seen to be both more suitable and acceptable given their cultural and religious background'.[5] The book panders to the most socially conservative elements within the Pakistani heritage community supporting faith healing, restrictions on sex education in schools and assuming that these are the views of the entire community. Further, by presenting the Pakistani community as a 'victim', it fails to see the need for common cause with all low-income citizens – white as well as black – in challenging inequality across the city. By formulating his arguments in such a narrow frame, Iqbal inevitably makes it harder, if not impossible, to forge the alliances that are necessary to challenge this deep-rooted inequality.

That requires the pursuit of an intercultural approach that does not seek to privilege one ethnic minority or, indeed, a group of them but, rather, seeks to bring all disadvantaged communities together. The development of an open, mixed city breaks down enclosed communities and frees up opportunities for all – from its inner city to its outer estates. In the process, all aspects of the city are opened to change, just as the city's eating habits have been transformed over the last few decades. In a diverse and increasingly fragmented city, there needs to be an overarching narrative that defines Birmingham's direction and purpose. That spirit of an open city drawing on the talents and skills of all its citizens is well captured by the Berlin slogan, 'No one asks where you come from, but each asks, where do you want to go?'

Some in the city such as BRAP (Birmingham Race Action Partnership)[6] – a multiracial social enterprise devoted to promoting equality – are seeking to pursue this approach. Joy Warmington, the BRAP chief executive, and Ghiyas Somra, their research manager, think that Iqbal and others are pursuing an old way of thinking that has had its day. BRAP argues against specific aspects of the ethnic identity approach. They stress that people have multiple identities; that no one identity should be imposed on a community from above; and that individuals have the right to self-determination rather than being frozen within an assumed straitjacket. Furthermore, there are around thirty nationalities of some size in the city. How practical is it for them all to compete with each other for limited resources? Ghiyas believes that 'Iqbal's position is more like that of a trade union defending its sectional interest; rather than the needs of a community as a whole'.

It is increasingly clear that to tackle inequality and disadvantage, race and class have to be tackled together. Looking at the city's GCSE educational results shows why. The chart below shows the 2015 results for those gaining five or more A*–C grades including English and maths by ethnic group and gender. The chart highlights which ethnic groups were performing above the local authority average and which were under-performing.

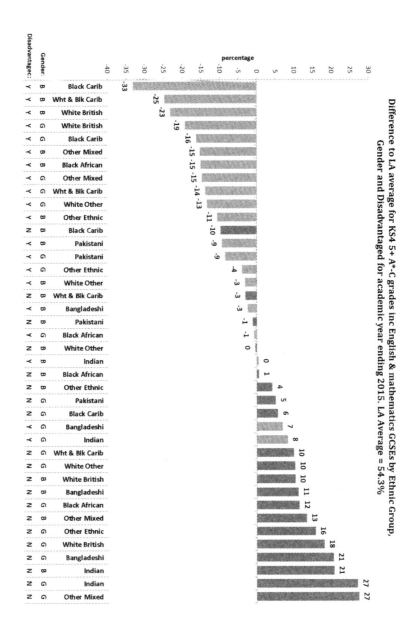

Difference to LA average for KS4 5+ A*-C grades inc English & mathematics GCSEs by Ethnic Group, Gender and Disadvantaged for academic year ending 2015. LA Average = 54.3%

What stands out is that the key determinant is parental income. For both white British and ethnic minority households the figures show that those on low incomes suffer a huge disadvantage when it comes to GCSE results. For white British boys there is a 33 per cent gap between the achievements of those from disadvantaged households and those who are not. There is a similar if smaller and more varied gap between poorer and better-off ethnic minority households. Contrary to Iqbal's assertions, it is black Caribbean and mixed-race pupils who perform worst among ethnic minorities.

For the last three decades talking about class has gone out of fashion. It was so 'old Labour'. Progressives have addressed issues of gender, race and disability but in the process forgotten about inequality and poverty. A simple reversion to old class-based mantras is not plausible at a time when the traditional working class based in large manufacturing plants is swiftly disappearing. Yet there are approaches that recognise the plurality of difference and the ways to tackle them together. The response to the huge discrepancies in attainment should be for educational interventions that bring additional resources and teaching staff into schools in both the inner city and on the outer estates. A politics that simply argues for resources for one ethnic minority cannot unite all those who are being disadvantaged.

Predominantly white working-class communities, especially those on the edge of the city or in the older industrial centres of the Black Country, face issues about heritage and globalisation, too. The free market model of globalisation has deprived them of steady, reliable jobs and instead obliged them to compete with migrants within a casualised labour market. The influx of new-comers has changed the nature and face of their towns and workplaces, in the process disrupting much of the heritage that they once knew. These issues exploded onto the political arena in the Brexit Referendum. Their consequences will remain with us for decades to come. The progressive response is to indicate how these concerns can be welded together.

BRAP believes, following the arguments of Richard Wilkinson and Kate Pickett, that all citizens will benefit if the city is fairer. They see human rights and citizen entitlements as the crucial focus. As Joy Warmington says, 'we are not fixed and rigid' so we look to apply this concept in the housing association sector and use the concept of human rights and entitlement to win a broader position. It is similar on employment.

'We turn the issue on its head and look at employers, rather than the community. We look at discrimination done by employers. Previously, it was easier to have an outreach worker post for a particular community, rather than tackle the employers.'

They intend to develop a City Plan on diversity and equality to consider how a city can successfully meet the demands and ambitions of all its citizens. They see this as an intercultural cities project.

'If we understand that people have entitlements then we can tackle systemic inequality as a whole. You can't do it by separate banners representing each separate ethnic community.'

This thinking echoes that of the Council of Europe and that being adopted by trailblazers such as Munich and Barcelona. Munich is promoting interaction between neighbourhoods, while encouraging intercultural mixing in its public spaces such as libraries, museums, playgrounds and squares. The municipality organises events and activities in the fields of arts, culture and sport to encourage inhabitants from different ethnic groups to mix, while as part of its support for cultural openness and exchange the city brings a regular stream of cultural artists from across Europe to Munich on three-month placements to showcase their work. These are practical examples of an open, mixed city at work.

Barcelona is on a similar trajectory. In the last two decades its foreign population has risen fast. From just 2 per cent in 1997, it rose to 17 per cent by 2014, drawn from Latin America, North Africa, the EU and Asia. In response interculturalism has become a mainstay of the city's policy. The Interculturality Plan in 2010 defined the Council's policy and the principal lines of action.[7] It clearly sets out the contrast with multiculturalism. For interculturalism the issue is not to extol the virtues of each culture but, rather, their relationships, the co-existence of people from different cultures and what is shared among them all. Relationships and interaction are seen as crucial. Thus diversity is recognised as an asset but within a context where it goes alongside equality and positive interaction.[8]

BRAP is moving cautiously into this new political terrain. There is some interest in the upper echelons of the council but how much impact the approach will have is unclear. The city has proved unable so far to develop an interculturalist narrative and maximise its diversity advantage. The contrast with Sadiq Khan, the Mayor of London, is noticeable.[9] He is a Muslim and proud of it, but he is not a product of the clan. He is a recognisably soft-left politician. In his campaign to be the Mayor of London he was sponsored by the LGBT community.

'I can't think of another city in the world where the LGBT community would happily organise a fundraiser for me, a Muslim candidate. That is the joy of this city. The rest of the world looks on us with envy.'

It is certainly not a position that would currently be repeated in Birmingham. For the dominant ethnic minority community, politics remains stuck within the clan system. This has negative, socially conservative consequences. When the teaching of sexuality to children was raised all the Pakistani heritage members of the Labour Group demanded a meeting with the Cabinet member Brigid Jones to try to force her to abandon the CHIPS programme (Challenging Homophobia in Primary Schools). They wanted no sex education for children in primary schools; they objected to the teaching materials. They were adamant that this had to be abandoned. It was only because she stood her ground that they backed off and the issue did not come into the public domain.

The shortcomings of this system are evident more widely. The most well-known and widely respected progressive Asian figure in the region – and indeed beyond – is Salma Yaqoob. She is not a product of the clan system. She has made her way in life independently and made her impact outside of the Labour Party. Within it, the clan system has been unable to produce a politician of equivalent calibre.

The London example offers hope to Birmingham. Of all the major cities outside London, Birmingham is the one with the most potential to maximise its diversity advantage. It is one of the youngest cities in Europe and there are plenty of rising talents emerging. The dead hand of the 'bradthery' system cannot last for ever. Ashraf is optimistic about the future.

'We have a lot of young, aspiring individuals keen to change. In last twenty-five years we have come a long way. The racism today is a bit more hidden. It is hidden because people know it's wrong, which I think is progress. In some parts of Birmingham we are starting to get places mixing as people move out into other parts of the city. We are optimists. I see it in politics.'

# 12

## *Creating the Open City*

Stepney, where I was born and spent my early years, was a mixed community with a large Jewish population. My infants' school closed early on Fridays in the winter so that pupils and parents could observe the Jewish Sabbath. Today, the main migrant population there comes from Bangladesh. When we moved to Walthamstow there were a handful of Jewish kids at my school, a few Catholics, the occasional Greek Cypriot, but the rest of the pupils were white, British and Protestant. Today, in a borough of over a quarter of a million, almost half the residents are of a minority ethnic background with Pakistan, Jamaica, Poland, India and Romania being the five top countries of origin for residents born overseas.[1]

That broad story of demographic change and migrants coming to settle has been repeated in every major city across Europe. The origin of the migrants has varied. While Germany drew its new labour supply from the rural hinterland across southern Europe extending into Turkey, the ties of old empires influenced migratory flows elsewhere. The French drew from North Africa, the Dutch from Indonesia and the British from the Commonwealth. Initially, the health service recruited nurses from Ireland and the

West Indies. Later, it was Enoch Powell, no less, who in 1963 as Conservative Health Minister launched a campaign to recruit trained doctors from overseas to fill the staff shortages caused by NHS expansion. Some 18,000 were recruited from India and Pakistan.[2]

Language, culture and religion have been further reinforcing factors: in the last two decades many young Latin Americans have flocked to Spain, while the emergence of English as the world language of the computer age has reinforced the attractiveness of the UK and Ireland as destinations. And then there is serendipity: an initial group of migrants establish themselves in a town and this becomes the place where others from the same area have family or friendship connections, which turns into a reinforcing cycle. Just as was the case with the Irish in New York, Boston or Liverpool, or the Jews in London's East End or Leeds, so it has been with the Mirpuris in Birmingham and Bradford, the Afro-Caribbeans in Brixton and the East African Asians in Leicester.

This has been Europe's urban story for more than half a century. Only the closed societies of Stalinist Eastern Europe were immune from this phenomenon. As these countries open up to the world, they are likely to find more newcomers in their midst. Leipzig is the shape of things to come. East Germany's second largest city was depopulated after German reunification but over the last seven years it has grown by more than 100,000 and today has a migrant population of 9 per cent.

Future numbers will need to be managed but the reality is clear. Twenty-first-century European cities are multi-ethnic and they will continue to be so. There is no going back to the 1950s.

Politicians, policy-makers and citizens need to start from that basis and develop policies and approaches that accept Europe's multicultural urban reality.

When my grandparents arrived more than a century ago, they were met by fear and loathing in the popular press. Ignorance and the fomenting of prejudice have been standard practice in parts of the tabloid press throughout the last century and into the present one. One regular claim has been that migrants are 'spongers', who 'come here to live off our welfare state'. The working stories that form the first half of this book show that claim to be false. Peggy, Mashood, Ajay and Wing Yip came here to graft, and their sons and daughters have been brought up in the same spirit. It has been the same for more recent newcomers like Anita, Christo and Jakub. Their voices show how migrants have contributed to the wealth and health of the city, its economic and educational dynamism, while also undertaking a large share of the dull and difficult 'donkey work', the often unnoticed or ignored underbelly of a society which is so crucial to its smooth functioning.

These people are not a statistical quirk. Detailed government data confirms the picture: migrants come here to work. Figures from the Department of Work and Pensions reveal that migrants to Birmingham are far less likely to claim benefit than those people born in the UK. In Birmingham, 15.7 per cent of all working age benefit claimants were from overseas as against the estimated 21.7 per cent of the population that were born overseas. Across the whole of the West Midlands, the figures showed a similar pattern. In neighbouring Sandwell 10.5 per cent of claimants came from overseas yet accounted for 16.4 per cent of the population; in Coventry 12.2 per cent of claimants were born overseas, but they accounted for 26.9 per cent of the population. These trends were repeated nationally where 8.5 per cent of the claimants were born overseas while the total number of people born overseas constituted 14.7 per cent of the UK population. The findings were so stark that only five of the 369 local authority areas for which there were figures showed a larger proportion of migrants claiming benefits than migrants in the local population. In each of these cases the margin was half a percentage point or less.[3]

Not all migrants and their offspring are angels and there is no suggestion here that they are. However, the testimonies in this book show how closely they correspond to the cliché of 'hard-working people' spoken of so frequently by politicians and newspapers. That is not surprising when one considers where they have come from. Migrants leave their homes and familiar surroundings; travel hundreds – or in many cases thousands – of miles; arrive in a strange land, where they often do not speak the language; and sometimes meet with suspicion and hostility from the locals. People only do this if they are driven by the hope of a better life and are committed to work for it. That is why they are often prepared to work for longer hours and lower pay than locals and at times take jobs that do not match their qualifications. A consistent thread running through these interviews is how positively migrants view Britain and the life they have made here, despite the hardships. A certain ease and pride in the country comes through in their responses. For some this relates basically to where they have lived and put down roots. When asked what he likes and values about Britain, Zahoor the shopkeeper replies,

'It's my home country. I am part of this country. The place you live is the place you have to love.'

So you see yourself as a British citizen? 'Of course.'

For Kalsoom who came here in an arranged marriage there is an appreciation of what the country offers.

'I feel England is a nice place to live. You should appreciate it, I certainly do. Opportunities we have in this country, you won't find them anywhere else. There are opportunities for progression. You have the chance to get the best out of yourself.'

Samera, the shop assistant, values the freedom.

'I was born here. I'm English. I feel British. I like the freedom here. You can go to the mosque or the church or whatever. I've got lots of different friends. One of them is Christian. She wears a cross. It doesn't offend me . . . I like it in this country that I am free to do what I want.'

David, the car engineer, also emphasises freedom.

'I like the freedom to criticise. You can make your own bed and do something that other people don't like and you are not break-ing any laws. Then you can do it and no one stops you.'

Underpinning this is also a pride and a fierce belief that he has contributed to the country.

'I am a British citizen. I have contributed to what the country is. In that sense I don't feel like I owe it something.' His voice rises as he emphasises, 'I feel like I have given to it. I have given it wealth. I have been part of the wealth creation. And my dad. He worked hard, too. And my mother.'

Another positive feature is support for the social, health and educational institutions that the country has built, with migrants

232

acknowledging the role of the welfare state. As the newsagent Rehman puts it: 'I have been born and spent all my life here. If something goes wrong they look after you. If you are not working there is a benefits system, if there is something wrong with your health and you are ill there's the NHS. It's good. The only bad thing is the weather. When you realise how bad other countries are, it's good. When I hear some Asian people criticise, I say to myself what are you doing here then? I see myself as a British citizen. I am proud of the country.'

Hasan sees it the same way.

'The moral outlook that we have here. Like the NHS. That's amazing. The fact that here we will treat somebody first and then find out who they are and what their background is afterwards. The most important thing is that we see them as a human being first. And with education. We give everybody that free till they are sixteen or eighteen.'

The optimism is not universal. Mandeep is concerned about emerging social and political tensions.

'I felt we were making really good progress with integration but the last period we seem to have gone backwards: all the stuff in the press and with the refugees. Definitely I feel it's a worse atmosphere.'

Adam feels that young people of migrant descent are not taught about their own history in this country.

'They are never taught about the Muslim, Asian, African, Afro-Caribbean contribution to make us feel a sense of achievement. I learned about the American West; we learned about castles. It meant nothing to me. It was only when I went to Woking and visited the oldest British Muslim cemetery and I saw the graves from the eighteenth century or that there were Asian privy counsellors and knights. We have a history here from before the economic migration and we are not taught about it.'

When probed as to whether he feels British, he replies, 'I feel more comfortable here than there. This is where my friends are, this is home. Most young people feel the same but they are not made to feel welcome. Frustration towards the government is on the rise. It doesn't help to tell them they are not integrating.'

Kashan found these sentiments more strongly expressed in his study on inner-city Sparkbrook young men mainly out of work and on the margins of society. Here the disaffection with mainstream society is strongest in ways not dissimilar to sentiments often expressed by disaffected young white working-class men on outer-city housing estates.[4]

Yet the general tenor of the conversations is optimistic. Ewa highlights the toleration that she finds in the country: 'I find it really easy to live here. Compared to Poland, people are a lot more open-minded and tolerant. Polish society is closed.'

She cites the example of homosexuality. Her son is at a Catholic school.

'There are teachers who are homosexual, but they teach there and they are part of a Catholic community and are free to teach. These teachers are gay, the staff know and it is absolutely fine. That's a big contrast with Poland.'

Ozlem is similarly positive about Britain.

'What I like is that it is a very tolerant society. It is quite open. I didn't feel discriminated about here because of the way I talk or who I am. It is less hierarchical at the institutional level compared to Turkey. They have a hierarchical way of doing things.'

As a second-generation Irish migrant who grew up during the Troubles of the 1970s Chris is optimistic. He also suggests why Birmingham has perhaps been more open to migrants than other cities.

'I don't look at race relations with rose-tinted spectacles but Birmingham is an incredibly tolerant city. This partly arises from the nature of its history, the city of a thousand trades. It broke the guilds and crafts when it began doing a bit of copying and jiggery-pokery so it always had a bit of an edge to it. This has made it more welcoming to "the other" than elsewhere and this tolerance is something that we should all be proud of and see as an asset for all of us . . . I have plenty of worries about issues such as air pollution but no worries about the people of Birmingham.'

The interviewees here defy the pessimistic musings of the tabloid press and of authors like David Goodhart.[5] The migrant presence has reshaped this city, other cities and the country as a whole. From its football teams and terraces to its food culture; from its workplaces to its TV screens; from its bedrooms to its popular music, Britain above all in its cities has adapted and changed. And in many schools, too, where multicultural assemblies have replaced a formal act of Christian worship. They show that migrants have a sense of place, that they put down roots, see Birmingham as their home and have an affection for and affinity with the city and the country. Their integration has been a positive story that is all too rarely told.

This is not to say that Birmingham, like other cities, faces no challenges arising from migration. Chris may be optimistic about the toleration of 'the other' within the city's population but undoubtedly the passions and emotions stirred by Brexit are testing the strength of the city's – and the country's – commitment to peaceful co-existence. There has always been a racist element across all layers of British society. However, the British Attitudes Survey data has shown how this has been steadily declining.[6] The last quarter of the twentieth century showed that Britain was able to adapt to significant shifts in its population make-up, integrating large numbers of people often from significantly different language, religious and cultural backgrounds. The country's political leadership and wider social and cultural movements countered the Powellite challenge. It was a difficult and protracted process but Conservative leader Ted Heath sacked Powell from his Shadow Cabinet and he never returned to high office; Labour passed race relations legislation countering discrimination in 1965, 1968 and 1976; and as Chapter 7 shows both grassroots campaigning and wider cultural movements from popular music to football enabled a multicultural country to emerge. However, the initially slow and complacent response to the new waves of East European migration after 2004 allied to the insecurities provoked by the 2008 financial crisis and subsequent austerity politics has thrown the country's support for its multi-ethnic settlement into doubt.

Furthermore, the inevitable concentrations of specific migrant communities that occur when newcomers first settle in a city can ossify over time as indigenous white households move out to be replaced by additional newcomers. Birmingham has this danger of closed neighbourhoods, particularly where there are dense clusters of Pakistani heritage populations. The development of a more powerful Muslim religious identity can reinforce this tendency, while the re-emergence of overt racism pushes vulnerable communities to close ranks and cut themselves off from others within the city. That is why the assertion of religious freedom is so vital to ensuring that migrants feel comfortable within the city. As Abdul, the Somalian taxi driver puts it, 'one of the reasons we come here is because of the religious freedom'.

That includes the right to disagree too. As Ozlem expresses it: 'As long as everyone is respectful of others' beliefs and are tolerant, then there is no problem. I know there are people who would not count me as Muslim. That is their problem, their judgement. I used to meet people like that at university. There is a very small group of people who would see me as a heretic, who are very extremist in their interpretation of Islam but 90 per cent would not say that.'

There is a slow dispersal of ethnic minorities out across the city but the pace of movement along with the degree of intermarriage will be indicators of whether the city's integration is gathering momentum.

A less immediately obvious challenge arises from dangerous trends in global politics. Across the world there is a rise in authoritarian nationalism with political leaders mobilising support around ethnic and/or religious identity. For Birmingham with its large Mirpuri heritage population the potential tinderbox is Kashmir. Indian Prime Minister Narendra Modi with his strident assertion of Hindu nationalism risks war with his desire to impose a military solution to this long-standing national dispute – a legacy of Britain's botched partition and withdrawal from India in 1947. As events in the Middle East have shown, in an interconnected world wars in faraway places have significant blowback potential. Protracted martial law in Kashmir leading to skirmishes and military clashes could easily spill over into UK cities. At the same time there are signs of a resurgence of Sikh fundamentalism. This currently has a largely purist religious character but, as the events at the Golden Temple in Amritsar in 1984 showed, this can quickly turn into sectarian bloodshed between Sikhs and Hindus. As the old world order crumbles and autocratic nationalists take the stage, attempts to resolve territorial disputes by force could have unexpected consequences within many European cities.

A more mundane challenge arises from the dramatic reduction in overall local authority funding since the onset of the financial crisis. This is the fundamental common feature affecting local government across the UK. In autumn 2016 the Institute for Fiscal Studies calculated that English councils had seen an average real-terms funding cut of more than 25 per cent since 2009–10.[7] For Birmingham the reductions have been sharper with the city losing 34 per cent of its budget. Central government has skewed the funding reductions so that they fall heaviest on urban areas. The local authority sector has borne the brunt of the austerity policies which central government has pursued. This is fundamentally transforming the role and functions of local government. Many previous activities are no longer being undertaken, for example youth and community work, while mandatory functions are being severely pruned, especially in the adult social care sector. This creates substantial significant additional pressures on citizens and services in many parts of the city and makes the development of a prosperous, socially balanced city all the more difficult.

*

Large-scale people movement is one of the great challenges of the twenty-first century, not just in Europe but across the world. As the vast bulk of these shifts are from rural to urban, it is cities that have to respond immediately to the challenges that arise. These vary in scale and intensity from the mega-cities of Istanbul, São Paulo and London to the small market towns with a rural hinterland such as Wisbech or Boston. But the issues of the pace of change; access to employment; cultural adjustment; and the impact on existing low-income urban citizens are common.

Over the last half-century the UK has sought to resolve these challenges within a multicultural framework and shown the fallacy of the doomsday scenarios painted by Enoch Powell and other far-right Conservatives and nativist commentators. Today, similar voices are using the dangers of Islamicist extremism and the UK vote to leave the EU as reasons to reassert an assimilationist British identity. This finds 'on the street' expression in the sharp rise in incidents of verbal and physical abuse against all sorts of 'foreigners'. But the argument is found in liberal circles, too. At times it is delivered with a 'radical centre' gloss, as with David Goodhart, or a Blue Labour sheen, as with Jonathan Rutherford.[8] The inward-looking debates of those multiculturalists who argue for special rights for ethnic or religious minorities serve to leave the field free to these assimilationists and give succour to them. As Sadiq Khan warns, 'we should not . . . seek to recreate ethnic and isolated islands of mono-communities'.[9]

Instead, the response should be a firm defence of the principles of racial equality with a confident assertion of why mixed, open societies are the way forward for modern twenty-first-century cities with a focus on the practical policies to show how they can be fostered.

Cities cannot fence themselves off from the wider world and inoculate themselves against its dangers. However, they do have the potential to create liveable, open cities reflecting their ethnic diversity. They do have significant autonomy to shape and steer their direction of travel. Elements of the vibrant, mixed city story are already present in Birmingham. They are dotted around the city and appear at different places in this book. An open-city strategy has to weave together the economic and the cultural and pull them together into a consistent narrative.

The starting point has to be economic. If a city cannot offer a decent range of jobs at reasonable pay to its residents then it is storing up trouble for the future. Birmingham's low-income households, whatever their ethnic origin, have faced similar difficulties – unemployment; short-term, casual contracts; long hours and low wages – as the city has tried to move on from its traditional manufacturing past. In an interdependent age where economies have escaped the confines of the nation state, cities have to be open to the world and able to attract external investment. Here Birmingham's record has been impressive. The economic regeneration of the city region means that the last two decades have seen an influx of European companies into the Greater Birmingham area. Since 1991 the West Midlands has attracted over 230 investments from Germany, while currently there are more than 300 German-owned companies across the Birmingham–Solihull area including in the engineering, clean tech and financial services sectors. This helps to boost the high-skilled, more modern elements within the economy able to offer decent wages to local people.

As well as sustaining an internationalist outlook, cities need to develop indigenous talent and respond to the new employment opportunities thrown up by the ICT revolution. Here, the development of spaces like the Impact Hub is crucial: modern, IT-savvy and palpably intercultural. Clustered around Digbeth there is a set of these venues which are low-cost entry points for new social enterprises, micro-businesses and start-ups, where people can begin their working lives.

Immy, the director of the Impact Hub, is clear about the potential.

'Birmingham is still a place where you can do anything. You can come here and make your idea real. But not enough is happening, especially compared to London. Birmingham needs to get crowded, full of initiatives like this. The city is affordable, it is vibrant, it has good connectivity. I am looking for lots more spaces like this to spring up, not just in the city centre. And new businesses.'

This is not the traditional, corporate image of economic development. It is a more innovative, bottom-up process, which goes with the grain of the emerging ICT economy, where many of the new jobs will be created. Initiatives like this, utilising redundant factories and derelict sites and premises, require the active encouragement of both the City Council and business organisations. There is plenty to learn from other cities here, too. Birmingham's Italian sister city of Milan has its own smart city initiative which promotes civic crowdfunding along these lines with a strong focus on the renovation of older industrial buildings.[10]

One element of this indigenous development has to be a concerted drive to boost employment opportunities in deprived areas. While there has been an improvement in the wellbeing of Asian communities, both the census and local economic development data show that many women from the Pakistani and Bangladeshi communities are not getting into work, even when educated to degree level. There remains a marked discrepancy compared to other communities in the ratio of female to male employment rates. As one of his last acts as Council leader, in autumn 2015 Albert Bore opened a women's enterprise Hub in Sparkbrook.

'It's a very specific measure open to all women. The Hubs are to encourage new business, workshops and link to nearby retail outlets. For example, there is real potential in the bridal industry. At the moment this is all done via India and Pakistan. There is a real marketplace for this to be done in Birmingham. The Hub will work with South Birmingham College and open up opportunities for women in the textile and clothing sector.'

This is an attempt to identify a specific economic niche where there is genuine commercial potential. Two other women's enterprise Hubs are planned to follow.

The success of these initiatives will rest on the city's ability to give detailed attention to all aspects of the education and skills agenda. The drive to lift educational achievement levels in the city's schools has made significant progress yet plenty remains to be done. Higher education institutions will play a pivotal role in the emergence of flourishing twenty-first-century cities. The last decade has seen the development of the city's universities with stronger links to the growth sectors within the city region economy; their growing international reach with significant increases in the numbers of overseas students and staff; and at the same time their increased capacity to attract second- and third-generation students from local ethnic minority communities. This both gives Birmingham significant economic benefits and offers ladders of opportunity to local black and Asian youth. The continuation of both of these trends is crucial to the ongoing development of a flourishing, open city.

For too long, those broadly supportive of immigration have overlooked the economy and class and focused just on cultural diversity. Yet an intercultural city can only thrive if it has a sound economic basis and offers opportunities for all those from low-income backgrounds. Both these elements of Birmingham's future are jeopardised by Britain's departure from the EU, especially if this entails leaving the Single Market and Europe's research and development programmes. Hence the city's vital interest in ensuring that the UK seeks to negotiate a new relationship with its European partners that retains access to both.

This economic and educational openness has to be complemented in the cultural arena. Again, a combination of elements has to be woven together. One crucial component to the successful open city is to nurture and value a transformed food culture. Migrant communities and their restaurants, curry houses and takeaways have become embedded in the everyday life and eating habits of Birmingham. I still like the occasional fish and chips but there is no going back to the days when it, along with roast beef and two veg, represented the culinary choice to local people. Today Birmingham's food offer in its suburbs as well as its city centre is increasingly diverse and not just restricted to the well off.

It gives visible expression to the welcoming international character of the city. Here, the Council's initiative with the six-week annual Frankfurt German Christmas market and its huge popularity across – and beyond – the city is emblematic of its transformation to an open city, prepared to embrace another cultural tradition and recognise how it helps Birmingham's overall cultural and commercial profile.

A further cultural element is to assert that the city sees religious freedom as a core value but also openly acknowledges that the essential corollary to the right to pray is the right to dissent. The City Council and police failed to uphold these values in the *Behzti* affair. It has done better in addressing the conundrum arising from the obligation to provide a daily act of Christian worship to school pupils, who are either increasingly agnostic or come from different religious backgrounds. The emergence of general assemblies is a genuine innovation responding to the multicultural reality of Birmingham and other conurbation schools. This should be consolidated, extended and given proper legal recognition.

Open cities have to have a whole range of public spaces and venues where people meet, socialise and relax. The revamped Bull Ring shopping centre is one conspicuous example. As Samera, who works there, says, 'I like the mix of people who come to the city centre to shop. It is cosmopolitan.'

The new Central Library is another intercultural meeting point, full of youngsters reflecting the ethnic diversity of the city. Then there is the Midlands Arts Centre (MAC) based in Cannon Hill Park, neighbouring a largely Asian part of the city where both the park and the venue serve as a different type of crossover point. MAC hosts a diverse range of music, dance, theatre and film, as well as exhibitions and an extensive array of adult education and children's arts activities. The night I am there African Cultural Exchange (ACE) are performing to more than 300 people. ACE is a national touring dance company based in Birmingham, which is an internationally recognised leader in the field of contemporary African and Caribbean dance. Their signature style is Afro-fusion, which they describe as dance 'rooted in traditional forms yet expressed through a purely contemporary lens'. They have been going for two decades. Iona, a vivacious member of the troupe, tells me that they are a black-led cultural organisation that has a mixed membership with a German, a Japanese, a couple of white as well as black dancers. Iona enthuses about the diversity agenda and how they work together with counterparts from across Europe. Twenty Dutch youngsters have come over as part of an EU exchange programme. She has been with the group for seventeen years, starting off as a school kid with their youth group.

Then there are more recent initiatives where people are 'doing it for themselves'. Gap Arts fits into this category. The project is based in unused warehouse space on the edge of the city centre. It is a venue for young people to perform drama, music, dance, show video and films, develop their video and digital skills and exhibit their photography and art. There are over a hundred people – white, black, Asian and mixed race – at a boisterous launch in the austere setting of a third-floor warehouse where iron girders stretch across the ceiling but the scene is enlivened by art and photo exhibits on the walls. Second-hand chairs and cupboards are scattered across the two rooms; bits of coloured carpet cover the lino floor. Cast-off settees and metal filing cabinets, a few shelves and cups for tea and coffee give it a lived-in feel. Arron is a twenty-two-year-old third-generation man of East African/ Indian origin and is one of the mainsprings behind the initiative. He explains the purpose of the initiative: 'This is a space to open up opportunities for young people and to develop projects. Where young people can work and share together, develop the creative activities that they want to do.'

The project uses the concept of the 'salad bowl' in contrast to the traditional American model of the 'melting pot'. As Arron describes it, 'Rather than there being one homogenised culture we are looking for a culture where each brings their own flavour to the dish. Each contributes to the dish without losing its own distinctive contribution.'

This is one of the ways to describe the intercultural city. Here, with ACE, at the Impact Hub and the Library is the throbbing heart of Birmingham's youthful, mixed future. Yet Gap Arts has to scramble and hassle for temporary premises, while youth provision across the city has been decimated by government-imposed cuts to services. A mixed city has to be lived and experienced through its everyday interactions. That is why architects, urban planners and designers of public spaces are so crucial. There have to be safe, accessible places where the city's multiple cultures and ethnicities can go and meet, whether on the football or cricket pitch; the bar or dance club; the shopping centre or community venue. It is from the interactions that take place here – as well as in the office, workplace and classroom – that the mixed, open city will be made.

These are examples of the way commercial, educational, civic and cultural forces within Birmingham are looking to the future and constructing a city that is open, happily mixes different cultures together and provides opportunities for people from all backgrounds. It is the route for all municipalities to follow if they are to create genuinely intercultural cities, places which recognise that people come from different backgrounds but do not try to 'freeze' them there or restrict them into ghetto neighbourhoods but, rather, seek to develop interculturally and look to promote actively places and spaces for mixing and integration.

However, this optimism about the city has still to find coherent political expression. As yet, there is no confident narrative about how Birmingham will develop as a mixed, open city over the coming decades. The examples cited above are largely sectional initiatives that remain to be welded into an overall strategy of reform. The emerging hybridity needs a new type of politics, which can bring it together and tackle inequality in the process.[11]

All major cities are trying to adapt to this challenge. These issues reach across Europe. There are no glib answers, but the big cities are making a better fist of the challenge than most national governments. This book has indicated some of the steps that cities such as Barcelona, Milan and Munich are taking to open up their cities to these multi-ethnic realities. The election of Sadiq Khan, a second-generation Asian with an openly Muslim background, as London's Mayor in May 2016 shows that prejudice can be overcome. In its choice of mayor, London adopted the spirit of Berlin with its call to focus not on where you come from but what you have to offer. That is a framework that can be applied across Europe's cities alongside Arron's metaphor of the 'salad bowl'.

However, cities are not islands. They need a wider supportive context, especially because many of the most intractable issues are interrelated and link to broader global processes. Ultimately progress has to combine racial equality with economic and social equality. That is why Joy Warmington, chief executive at BRAP, stresses that 'A framework based on a firm commitment to universal human and civil rights is the way forward.'

The successful open city has to combine economic prosperity with relative social equality. Immy warns that 'Birmingham is now entering a really critical phase. There is loads of inward investment happening at the moment. The city needs to think what creative policies to put in place to make sure that this investment creates a place we can all support in ten years' time and how they don't drive further inequality by these developments.'

Wing Yip is the most economically successful migrant interviewed for this book. Yet, instinctively he understands the economic and social dimensions to race relations.

'It depends which layer you are in. It is more easy for people to get on if you live in wealthy St John's Wood or Edgbaston. When you have conflict for jobs, for survival, then it's much harder. It depends what level you are at. If you are facing poverty, good race relations are much harder.'

The overwhelming majority of migrants interviewed for this book are optimistic about the future in ways that defy the tabloid press and the pessimists. There is plenty of achievement to build on, but as Zubeda warns the visibility of migrant representation is lacking within the hierarchy of local institutions, as are those able to give it clear political direction. The building blocks for Birmingham's emergence as a dynamic intercultural city are there. They are laid out in these pages. They urgently need to be woven together into a cogent narrative. To be successful, the twenty-first-century city has to be modern, mixed and open. As Immy states simply, 'We need to bring new voices into the Birmingham story.'

# *Notes*

*Introduction*

1. http://citiesofmigration.ca/good_idea/diversity-moves-frankfurt/
2. http://www.comune.milano.it/wps/portal/ist/it
3. http://www.insee.fr/fr/themes/tableau_local.asp?ref_id=IMG1A& millesime=2012&niveau=1&typgeo=UU2010&codgeo=00758
4. This is stated very clearly in the Barcelona Plan 2012–2015, Pla de Treball d'Immigracio 2012–2015. 'Diversity is now an inherent feature of all the world's big cities and Barcelona is no exception', p. 8.
5. http://www.liberation.fr/france/2016/04/13/voile-a-l-universite-valls-pas-suivi-par-ses-ministres_1445881
6. See *Sun*, 15 August 2017. A third of Premiership players at the start of the 2017–18 season had a black or mixed-race background.
7. Interview in *Guardian*, 9 April 2016.
8. Richard Littlejohn, *Daily Mail*, 12 April 2016.
9. *Daily Mail*, 11 April 2016.
10. David Goodhart, *The British Dream: Successes and Failures of Post-War Immigration* (London: Atlantic Books, 2013), p. 70. See the pungent critiques from David Edgar, *Guardian*, 3 April 2013, and Jonathan Portes, *London Review of Books*, Vol. 35, No. 12, 20 June 2013.
11. Tariq Modood, *Multiculturalism. A Civic Idea* (London: Polity Press,

251

2007), pp. 72–86; and Tariq Modood, *Multicultural Politics: Racism, Ethnicity and Muslims in Britain* (Edinburgh: Edinburgh University Press, 2005).

12. Amartya Sen, *Identity and Violence: The Illusion of Destiny* (London: W. W. Norton and Co., 2006), pp. 156–60; and an interview with *Financial Times*, 21 August 2006.

13. On this see Robin Wilson and Jon Bloomfield, *Building the Good Society* (Compass, 2011). http://www.compassonline.org.uk/wp-content/uploads/2013/05/Compass_good_society_report_WEB.pdf

14. Otto Bauer, *The Question of Nationalities and Social Democracy* (Minneapolis, MN: University of Minnesota Press, 2000 [1906]).

15. David Robinson, 'Community cohesion and the politics of communitarianism', in John Flint and David Robinson (eds), *Community Cohesion in Crisis? New Dimensions of Diversity and Difference* (Bristol: Policy Press, 2008), p. 15.

16. Council of Europe, *White Paper on Intercultural Dialogue: 'Living Together as Equals in Dignity'* (Strasbourg: Council of Europe, 2008, www.coe.int/t/dg4/intercultural/source/white%20paper_final_revised_en.pdf).

17. For one example see Ajuntament de Barcelona, *Barcelona Interculturality Plan* (Barcelona: Ajuntament de Barcelona, 2010, http://ec.europa.eu/ewsi/UDRW/images/items/docl_18310_856665954.pdf.

18. Here there is common ground with Modood. 'Assimilation is something immigrants or minorities must do or have done to them, whereas integration is interactive, a two-way process: both parties are an active ingredient and so something new is created.' Modood, *Multicultural Politics*, p. 141.

19. http://www.telegraph.co.uk/comment/3643823/Enoch-Powells-Rivers-of-Blood-speech.html

20. Kenneth Newton, *Second City Politics* (Oxford: Oxford University Press, 1976), p. 211. See more generally pp. 208–22 for the attitudes on race relations and Appendix 1 on the interviewing sample.

## Chapter 1: At the Heart of Britain

1. See *The Pakistani Muslim Community in England. Understanding Muslim Ethnic Communities*, p. 25 (March 2009), Department for Communities and Local Government.
2. Abstract of Birmingham Statistics, No. 24, 1981–2, Alan B. Neale and Gillian V. Haine (eds), Table 63, p. 89.
3. World Trade Organization, Statistics Database. http://stat.wto.org/ CountryProfile/WSDBCountryPFView.aspx?Country=GB&Language=S

## Chapter 2: From the Cradle to the Grave

1. http://www.historyandpolicy.org/policy-papers/papers/immigration-and-the-national-health-service-putting-history-to-the-forefront
2. Birmingham CCG Annual Equality Report 2016.
3. See *Guardian*, 11 March 2017.

## Chapter 3: Moving On Up

1. For more on this see Adrian Campbell, *Decentralisation and Localism: Beyond Saxons and Normans*, pp. 5–12, *Regional Innovations*, No. 1, 2016.

2.  http://www.connectjustice.org/admin/data/files/A%20tale%20of%20
    three%20cities.pdf

3.  See Aster van Tilburg, 'Civic Crowdfunding is not about money',
    pp. 53–7, in a set of essays, *Making Cities: Visions for an Urban Future*.
    http://eurocities.eu/30visionsforcities

## Chapter 4: *The New Entrepreneurs*

1.  http://news.bbc.co.uk/onthisday/hi/dates/stories/april/1/
    newsid_2819000/2819261.stm

2.  Andy Munro, *Going for a Balti: The Story of Birmingham's Signature
    Dish* (Studley: Brewin Books, 2015).

3.  *Birmingham Post*, 18 August 2004.

4.  Ibid., editorial, 18 August 2004.

5.  All data from information provided by Jim Kelly, former Head of
    Events, Birmingham City Council.

## Chapter 5: *The Global University*

1.  https://www.timeshighereducation.com/world-university-rank-
    ings/2016/world-ranking#!/page/0/length/25/sort_by/rank/sort_order/
    asc/cols/stats

2.  The breakdown of student numbers is broadly as follows: Birmingham
    University 30,000; Birmingham City University 23,500; Aston
    University 10,000; University College Birmingham 8,000; Newman
    University 2,895.

3.  University of Birmingham Equality Information Report, January 2015.

4.  Aston University Student Equalities Report, April 2014.

5.  Aston University Equality, Diversity & Inclusion Annual Report, March 2014.

## Chapter 6: Doing the Work that Nobody Else Wants to Do

1.  For an insightful account see James Bloodworth, *Hired: Six Months Undercover in Low-Wage Britain* (London: Atlantic Books, 2018).

2.  GB Resourcing continues to operate and has a Polish website http://job.bham.pl/details/company/731/

3.  See *Guardian*, 1 June 2016. http://www.theguardian.com/politics/2016/jun/01/british-asians-views-eu-referendum-figures-brexit; *Los Angeles Times*, 3 July 2016. http://www.latimes.com/world/la-fg-britain-birmingham-brexit-snap-story.html. Ozlem (see previous chapter) reports similar sentiments among Asians in interviews she undertook during this period for a separate piece of research in northwest Birmingham.

4.  Robin Cook, *Point of Departure: Diaries from the Front Bench* (London: Pocket Books, 2004), p. 226, records an exchange between Pascal Lamy, former French Finance Minister and then head of the World Trade Organization, and Peter Mandelson, former UK Cabinet Minister and then EU Commissioner for Trade, where Mandelson declares that 'Globalisation offers all the best the world can offer. We must not sound as if we believe there is a tension between labour and capital, or competition and solidarity.'

5.  Dustmann, C., Casanova, M., Fertig, M., Preston, I. and Schmidt, C. M. (2003), 'The impact of EU enlargement on migration flows'

(Home Office Online Report 25/03), Research Development and Statistics Directorate (Home Office: London, UK). http://www.ucl.ac.uk/~uctpb21/reports/HomeOffice25_03.pdf

6. At a speech to business leaders in Yorkshire reported in the *Daily Telegraph*, 14 June 2005, under the heading 'Governor: immigrants keep down inflation.' https://www.telegraph.co.uk/finance/2917335/Governor-immigrants-keep-down-inflation.html

7. A welcome, if belated, recognition of the need to manage and tame globalisation came from Gordon Brown in a post-EU Referendum article. See *Guardian*, 29 June 2016.

8. For the relevant EU Parliament and Council Directive see http://eur-lex.europa.eu/LexUriServ/LexUriServ.do?uri=O-J:L:2004:158:0077:0123:en:PDF

9. See cross-bench peer Karan Bilimoria, https://www.theguardian.com/commentisfree/2017/jul/31/britain-take-back-control-immigration-eu-directive-brexit

10. I proposed how this could be done back in 2010. https://www.social-europe.eu/responding-to-eu-migration-a-progressive-policy-response

## Chapter 7: The Changing Face of Racism

1. *Birmingham Post*, 15 May 1968.

2. *Birmingham Post*, 15 July 1968

3. See David Clark, *Immigrant Responses to the British Housing Market: A Case Study in the West Midlands*, Working Papers on Ethnic Relations, No. 7, SSRC University of Bristol 1977, for a detailed discussion.

4. *Birmingham Mail*, 7 August 2015.

5. *Birmingham Post*, 9 April 2015.

6. *Birmingham Mail*, 12 March 2014. See article entitled 'Birmingham St Patrick's Day history to be revealed in city exhibition'.

7. See Anthony Clavane, *Does Your Rabbi Know You're Here? The Story of English Football's Forgotten Tribe* (London: Quercus, 2012).

8. *Birmingham Evening Mail*, 3 May 2000.

9. *Observer*, 3 July 2016.

## Chapter 8: Educating the Kids

1. Local Economic Assessment 2014.

2. See Examination and Assessment Results Secondary 2015; Report to Overview and Scrutiny Committee, 16 March 2016; *From Benign Neglect to Citizen Khan: 30 Years of Equalities Practice in Birmingham* (BRAP, 2015), pp. 36–7. This issue and its linkages to poverty, class and disadvantage are discussed further in Chapter 11.

3. Between 2006 and 2011 the percentage of Bangladeshi boys achieving 5+ A–C grades rose from 36 to 63 per cent; in the same period the results of Bangladeshi girls rose from 40 to 61 per cent.

4. An example of its theocratic outlook is evident in the following. 'It [the Caliphate] is established on divine law, not the human mind, so is immune from forever-changing norms.' http://www.hizb.org.uk/current-affairs/muslims-will-not-compromise-on-the-khilafah

5. 'Towards Greater Understanding – Meeting the Needs of Muslim Pupils in State Schools' (Muslim Council of Britain, 2007).

6. Ibid., p. 20.

7. Ibid., p. 26.

8. Ibid., pp. 52–3.

9. Ibid., p. 47.

*Chapter 9: God and the City*

1. See in particular 34th British Social Attitudes survey, June 2017. This showed that half the UK population do not regard themselves as belonging to a particular religion, a sharp increase from less than a third thirty years earlier with the shift most marked among younger adults. www.bsa.natcen.ac.uk

2. For more on these issues see Omid Safi (ed.), *Progressive Muslims: On Justice, Gender and Pluralism* (Oxford: Oneworld, 2005). Written by a group of scholars who see themselves as progressive Muslims committed to justice and pluralism, the authors embrace a different vision of Islam from that offered by communitarians or fundamentalist Wahhabism but also offer a critique of Western structures that perpetuate an unequal distribution of resources around the world. Hence they do not seek to imitate prevalent notions of Western modernity.

3. http://www.ohchr.org/EN/UDHR/Documents/UDHR_Translations/eng.pdf, The Universal Declaration of Human Rights. For the purposes of this discussion key elements include Article 18, 'everyone has the right to freedom of thought, conscience and religion; this right includes **freedom to change** his religion or belief . . . and to manifest his religion or belief in teaching, practice, worship and observance' (my emphasis). Article 19 states that 'everyone has the right to freedom of opinion and expression, this right includes freedom to hold opinions without interference'. Article 21 declares that 'everyone has the right of equal access to public service'.

4. John Gray, *Two Faces of Liberalism* (London: New Press, 2000), p. 21.

5. For a full discussion of the circumstances and surrounding issues see Jane Woddis (2011), 'Religious protest and its impact on

cultural policy', *International Journal of Cultural Policy*, 17:2, 209–224.

6. See *Birmingham Post*, 20 December and 21 December 2004.

7. Ibid., 20 December 2004.

8. For example, 'Towards Greater Understanding', MCB (2007), p. 44, claims that this makes 'worship meaningless and inappropriate for pupils'.

9. See J. Baggini (2006), 'The rise, fall and rise again of secularism', Public Policy Research, 12 (4), p. 209. See also the discussion in J. Bloomfield and F. Bianchini, *The Intercultural City* (Comedia, 2004), pp. 24–5.


## Chapter 10: Sex, Love and Marriage

1. British Social Attitudes survey 2013; Professor Rob Ford, University of Manchester http://blog.policy.manchester.ac.uk/featured/2014/08/the-decline-of-racial-prejudice-in-britain/; and *Daily Telegraph*, 28 November 2017 https://www.telegraph.co.uk/women/life/mixed-race-relationships-no-longer-exotic-rarity-new-normal/

2. http://www.natcen.ac.uk/news-media/press-releases/2017/september/british-social-attitudes-record-number-of-brits-with-no-religion/


## Chapter 11: The Political Kaleidoscope

1. The Birmingham 400. A Community Conversation (Radical Thinking Group, 2014).

2. Speech at her Christian Democratic Union conference, 14 December 2015.

3. See *Daily Mail*, 10 May 2016.

4. Karamat Iqbal, *Dear Birmingham: A Conversation with My Hometown* (Dartford: Xlibris, 2013).

5. Ibid., p. 104.

6. BRAP. Initially the Birmingham Race Action Partnership, it has broadened its approach over the last decade and now brands itself as BRAP with the strapline 'Making Equality Work for Everyone'.

7. Barcelona Interculturality Plan, March 2010. https://ec.europa.eu/migrant-integration/index.cfm?action=media.download&uuid=2A1FF3D8-E3AC-3F23-5F6391266C483D6F

8. Their thinking has been shaped by Carlos Gimenez, Professor of Anthropology at the Autonomous University of Madrid. For more on this see Blanca Garcés-Mascareñas, 'Local Integration Policies in Barcelona – KING Project Research Paper' (Fondazione ISMU).

9. See *Evening Standard* interview, 14 April 2016.

## Chapter 12: Creating the Open City

1. https://www.walthamforest.gov.uk/content/statistics-about-borough

2. http://www.historyandpolicy.org/policy-papers/papers/immigration-and-the-national-health-service-putting-history-to-the-forefront. Powell praised these doctors, who, he said, 'provide a useful and substantial reinforcement of the staffing of our hospitals and who are an advertisement to the world of British medicine and British hospitals'.

3. *Birmingham Post*, 1 September 2016.

4. The Birmingham 400. A Community Conversation (Radical Thinking Group, 2014).

5. David Goodhart. See *The British Dream*, and *The Road to Somewhere. The Populist Revolt and the Future of Politics* (London: Penguin, 2017).

6. http://www.democraticaudit.com/2014/08/27/a-close-inspection-of-the-british-social-attitudes-survey-shows-that-racial-prejudice-is-in-long-term-decline/

7. https://www.ifs.org.uk/publications/8705 See also Tom Crewe, 'The Strange Death of Municipal England': https://www.lrb.co.uk/v38/n24/tom-crewe/the-strange-death-of-municipal-england

8. Jonathan Rutherford, *New Statesman*, 3 February 2017.

9. Sadiq Khan, 'Fairness not Favours. How to Reconnect with British Muslims', Fabian Society (2008), p. 14.

10. See www.Milanosmartcity.org for examples on the sharing economy and civic crowdfunding.

11. This linking of race to class unified by the thread of tackling inequality is part of a wider reassessment underway in the light of events following the Brexit Referendum. See Owen Jones, *Guardian*, 17 August 2016, and Kenan Malik, *Observer*, 11 March 2018.

# List of Interviewees

| Name | Place of birth | Job |
| --- | --- | --- |
| Abdul | Mogadishu, Somalia | Taxi driver |
| Adam | *Karachi, Pakistan | Special constable, project officer, NGO |
| Ajay | Gujarat, India | Tailor, manual worker |
| Akram | *Mirpur, Pakistan | Taxi driver |
| Anita | Gdynia, Poland | Care worker |
| Anu | Gujarat, India | Housewife |
| Arron | *Asian East Africa | Cultural worker |
| Ashraf | *Mirpur, Azad Kashmir | Delivery driver |
| Ben | Lagos, Nigeria | Postgraduate student |
| Chris | *Co. Mayo, Ireland | Officer, Friends of the Earth |
| Christo | Veliko Tarnovo, Bulgaria | Fruit and veg picker |
| Daljit | *Punjab, India | Administrator |
| Dariusz | Olsztyn, Poland | Warehouseman |
| David | *St Kitts, West Indies | Car engineer |
| Ewa | Koszalin, Poland | Teaching assistant |
| Fatima | *Mirpur, Pakistan | Officer, NGO |

* Signifies place of birth of parents.

| Name | Place of birth | Job |
| --- | --- | --- |
| Hasan | *Gujarat, India | Project officer |
| Hies | Harissa, Somaliland | Cleaner |
| Immy | *Punjab, India | Social entrepreneur |
| Jakub | Torún, Poland | Orthopaedic registrar |
| Kalsoom | Punjab, Pakistan | Mother, teacher |
| Kashan | *Punjab, Pakistan | Prison officer |
| Magda | Olsztyn, Poland | Hotel cleaner |
| Mandeep | *Jalandhar, Punjab, India | Administrator |
| Mashood | Bihar, India | Engineering worker, factory owner |
| Mo | *West Indies | Market trader |
| Nazir | Mirpur, Azad Kashmir | Factory worker, then teacher |
| Nikos | Thessaloniki, Greece | Professor of engineering |
| Ozlem | Istanbul, Turkey | Research assistant |
| Pam | Chandigarh, Punjab, northern India | Shop owner |
| Peggy | Co. Cavan, Ireland | Nurse, barmaid |
| Raj | *Punjab, India | Accountant |
| Rashda | Punjab, Pakistan | Interpreter, mother |
| Rehman | *Mirpur, Pakistan | Newsagent |
| Salma | *Punjab, Pakistan | Nurse, health manager |
| Sam | *Huntspen, Jamaica | IT specialist, health professional |
| Samera | *Pakistan | Shop sales assistant |
| Simona | Veliko Tarnovo, Bulgaria | Fruit and veg picker |
| Tomasz | Wrocław, Poland | Factory worker |

| Name | Place of birth | Job |
|------|----------------|-----|
| Wing Yip | Hong Kong | Owner, major grocery business |
| Xavier | La Vendée, France | Project and policy officer |
| Yasin | *Mirpur, Pakistan | Bus driver, taxi driver |
| Zahida | *Lahore, Pakistan | Teacher |
| Zahoor | Islamabad, Pakistan | Shopkeeper |
| Zainab | *Pakistan | Teacher |
| Zubeda | *Gujarat, India | Social enterprise director |

46 interviewees: 28 men, 18 women; 13 countries; 23 second-generation.

Country of origin: Pakistan 14, India 11, Poland 6, West Indies 3, Ireland 2, Somalia 2, Bulgaria 2, Greece, China, Turkey, Nigeria, France, Kenya/Uganda 1.

Additional interviews with councillors Albert Bore and Paul Tilsley; Ghiyas Somra and Joy Warmington from Birmingham Race Action Partnership; Chris, a head teacher; and Roger, a fruit and vegetable grower.

# *Acknowledgements*

In any collective endeavour there are many people who make it possible. This book is no exception. My main debt of gratitude is to the generosity, openness and honesty of all my interviewees. They were warm, thoughtful and informative; I learned a lot from them; and I hope that I have communicated their humanity and commitment in these pages. Finding them was no easy task, so I owe special thanks to Cynthia Bower, Chris Cooper, Pat Killarney, Jo Klaces, Kishor Pala, Joanna Pierożyńska, Victoria Quinn and Polly Wright, who helped me find a number of the interviewees.

The assessments and judgements in the book are my own, but I have been aided by the scrupulous attention of my editor Phil Connor at Unbound. Bob Carter, Martin Jacques, Jason Lowther and Fred Steward read all or part of the script and offered invaluable advice which helped to strengthen the book. Equally, I owe thanks to all my close family, my two sisters Rachelle and Jude, my two children Steve and Jenny and my partner Jane, who all made insightful and useful suggestions on how to improve the script, while Jane gave me the emotional support and backing that an author always needs at times during a long project.

The crowdfunding route was a new venture for me. Its success was undoubtedly aided by Unbound staff and the social media skills of younger friends, in particular Stuart Bowles, Tony Smith, Claire Spencer and Patrick Willcocks, who both gave me advice and helped to spread news about the book on Twitter, Facebook and LinkedIn. I hope that all enjoy the finished product.

# *Index*

# Index

# Index

**Unbound**
Liberating ideas

Unbound is the world's first crowdfunding publisher, established in 2011.

We believe that wonderful things can happen when you clear a path for people who share a passion. That's why we've built a platform that brings together readers and authors to crowdfund books they believe in – and give fresh ideas that don't fit the traditional mould the chance they deserve.

This book is in your hands because readers made it possible. Everyone who pledged their support is listed below. Join them by visiting unbound.com and supporting a book today.

John Adams

Julie Allder

Lynne Amery

Lucy Baines

Steve Ball

Karin Barber

John Beavan

Rosemary Bechler

Iris Bertz

Philip Beyer

Franco Bianchini

Anna Biley

Egil Bjornsen

Jude Bloomfield

Steve Bloomfield

Jenny Bloomfield and Frank
  Davies

Arthur Blue

Helen Bocarro

Sophia Bokhari

Albert Bore

Tony Bovaird

Gareth Bowden

Cynthia Bower

Daniel Bower

Ric Bowl

Emma Bridger

Elizabeth Briggs

Anne Britton-Munoz

Lloyd Broad

Chris Bruce

David Bryan

Richard Bubb

Keith Budden

Andrew Burns

Sally Burton

John Cade

Adrian Campbell

Greg Campbell

David Carroll

Douglas Carroll

Abi Carter

Erica Carter

Michael Carter

Robert Carter

Arianna Cecchi

Sarah Chant

Paul Chapman

Jacob Clark

John Clark

Eddie Clarke

John Clarke

Radley Cleavers

Bernadette Collins

Myra Connell

Barry Connolly

Valerie Cooke

Angela Cooper

Chris Cooper

Julian Cooper

Martin Cooper

Andrew Coulson

Brian Cox

David Cox

David Crabbe

Maria Elisabetta Cremaschi

Daniel Cremin

Jennifer Crisp

Gill Cummings

Tom Cutterham

Mary Davis

Julien De Ridder

Hazel Dempster

Jan Dictus

Gijs Diercks

Jitka Dolezalova

Bianca Dragomir

Jean Elledge

Alan Emery

Peter Faulkner

Kamran Fazil

Rayah Feldman

Kirsten Forkert

Steve Freer

Katharine Fuller

Chris Game

The GAP Arts Project

Jean Gardiner

Maria Gee

Pauline Geoghegan

Julie Gibbon

Tim Gibbons

JT Gibney

Alison Gilchrist

Alan Goldberg

Paul J Goodison

John Goodman

Neil Grant

Sally Gray

Dave Green

Vivien Griffiths

Irena Guidikova

Jacky Guter

John Haldon

Catherine Hall

Lisa Hamilton

Malcolm Harbour CBE

David Hardman

Christine Hardy

Sue Hastings

Liz Haydon

John Hibbard

Jessica Higgs

Joe Holyoak

Jacqueline Homan

Richard Honey

Chris Hornby

Matthieu Hornung

Lynne Howells

Leslie Huckfield

John Hudson

Kate Huggins

John Husband

Belinda Hutchings

Sonja-Maria Ignatius

Bill Innes

Sharon Jacobs

Martin Jacques

Trisha Jaffe

Diana James

Rebecca Janowitz

Rohan Jassal

Stephen Jeffares

Charlie Jeffery

Charles Jones

Harrison Jordi

Andrew Kelly

Cathy Kennedy

Martin Kettle

Dan Kieran

Tricia Killarney-Foreman

Paul R. Kimber

Kings Heath Library

Paula and Eoin Kingston and McCarthy

Rix Kloss

Esther Knight

Ray Kohn

Robert Kornreich

Nick Lampert

Charles Landry

Patricia Langton

Philippa Langton

Neal Lawson

Peter Laybourn

Robert Lentell

Sonia Liff

Helen Lloyd

Vic Lloyd

Michael Loftus

Maria Loloni

Rachel Lombardi

Derk Loorbach

Robert Luck

Michael & Jane Lyons

Henriette Lyttle-Breukelaar

Stuart Macintyre

Ilse Mackinnon

Chiara Malagodi

Francis Mallon

Paul Marginson

Bev Marks

Janet Marlow

Kate Martin

Ehpriya Matharu

Cristian Matti

Catherine Mayo

Jenny McCabe

Douglas McCarrick

John & Sue McCoy

Graham Meadows

Guglielmo Meardi

Karolina Medwecka-Piasecka

Michal Miedzinski

Helen Miller

Tom Mitchell

John Mitchinson

Ebrahim Mohamed

Besenyei Mónika

Andrew Mullineux

Steve Munby

Linda Murgatroyd

Denis Murphy

Annie Murray

Peter Nagle

Nanja Nagorny-Koring

Mica Nava

Carlo Navato

Timea Nochta

Bill Norris

Rachel Oldroyd

Carey Oppenheim

Michelle Pace

Kishor Pala

Emily Palmer

Conrad Parke

David Parker

Margaret Patrizio

Andrea Pattison

Nicola Peterson

Deenan Pillay

Ian Plenderleith

Justin Pollard

David Prior

Michael Prior

Martin Pumphrey

Abdul Qadir

Azzam Qasrawi

John Raine

Peter Ramsden

Paul Richards

Lisa Richey

Bill Riley

Ruth Ringer

Christopher Rivers

Stuart Robert

Jill Robinson

Xavier Rodde

Christine Rogers

Philip Rose

John Rouse

Sigrid Ruschmeier

Adnan Saif

Robert Sanderson

Thorsten Schnier

Leon Sealey-Huggins

Patricia Seguin

Roger Seifert

Joseph Seliga

Roger Shannon

Lorna Shaw

Catherine Shelley

Jeevan Shoker

Ian Short

Bren Simson

Chris Skelcher

Rachel Slowey

Andrew Smith

Max Smith

Miriam Smith

Naomi Smith

Rachelle Smith

Tony Smith

Claire Spencer

Gerhard Stahl

Fred Steward

John and Theresa Stewart

Bryan Stoten

Martin Straker Welds

Mamta Suresh

Diane Sutherland

Dave Sutton

David Taylor

Sandy Taylor

Mick Terry & Sue Wright

Aled Thomas

Sue Thompson

Tom Tierney

Cllr Paul Tilsley CBE

Ged Tinley

Julian Todd

Naomi Todd

Martin Tolman

Kevin Tongue

Nancy Traquair

Xenia Tsitiridou

Edward Turner

Jonnie Turpie

Mary Tyler & Clive Attard

Nazir Ul Haq

Ron and Sue Vannelli

David Vaughan

Sarah Vernon

Tara Verrell

Pam Waddell

Ben Waddington

Karen Walford

David Walker

Steve Walker

Anne Walshe

Denis Walshe

Jonathan Watkins

Danny Webster

Andy Welch

Sue Wheeler

Gordon Will

Maya Willcocks

Patrick Willcocks

Dorothy Williams

Stuart Williams

Martin Willis

John Wilson

Robin Wilson

Carole Woddis

Jane Woddis

Joanna Woddis

Geoff Wolmark

Jenny Wolmark

## Supporters

Phil Wood

Mike Woollacott

Peter Wright

Salma Yaqoob

Szilvia Zsargo

# *A Note on the Author*

Jon Bloomfield is a historian and an urban policy specialist. He is currently an advisor to the EU's largest climate change initiative, Climate KIC, and for over a decade has been an Honorary Research Fellow at the University of Birmingham, having previously worked for Coventry and Birmingham City Councils. He lives in Birmingham.

.